PETERSON'S

MATH REVIEW

for the

GRE,* GMAT, and MCAT

Peterson's
Thomson Learning

Australia • Canada • Denmark • Japan • Mexico • New Zealand • Philippines
Puerto Rico • Singapore • Spain • United Kingdom • United States

About Peterson's

Peterson's is the country's largest educational information/communications company, providing the academic, consumer, and professional communities with books, software, and online services in support of lifelong education access and career choice. Well-known references include Peterson's annual guides to private schools, summer programs, colleges and universities, graduate and professional programs, financial aid, international study, adult learning, and career guidance. Peterson's Web site at petersons.com is the only comprehensive—and most heavily traveled—education resource on the Internet. The site carries all of Peterson's fully searchable major databases and includes financial aid sources, test-prep help, job postings, direct inquiry and application features, and specially created Virtual Campuses for every accredited academic institution and summer program in the U.S. and Canada that offers in-depth narratives, announcements, and multimedia features.

Editorial Development: American BookWorks Corporation

Editorial Review: Joan Marie Rosebush

Visit Peterson's Education Center on the Internet (World Wide Web) at
www.petersons.com

ISBN 1-7689-0232-0

Printed in the United States of America

10 9 8 7 6 5 4 3 2 1

CONTENTS

INTRODUCTION

If you are planning to take the Graduate Record Examination (GRE), the Graduate Management Admission Test (GMAT), or the Medical College Admission Test (MCAT), you will need to brush up on your knowledge and application of mathematics. This book will help you to focus on and improve specific mathematics skills that will be tested on these three exams. While the MCAT does not have a specific mathematics test section, you will be required to understand the math concepts in this book in order to handle many of the math-oriented problems you will find on the test.

THE FORMAT

The book is divided into several sections to make studying easier. Because there is an overlap of question types that appear on the different exams, we have combined everything into logical sections. The first part of the book features a sample Diagnostic Test. It is based on the four types of questions that you will encounter on these tests: Problem Solving, Quantitative Comparisons, Data Sufficiency, and Data Interpretation. The second part features our Red Alert sections. Within these sections, we present a complete analysis of the four question types and sample questions to help you more clearly understand the material as well as to improve your skills in answering these types of questions.

The third section of the book features an in-depth review of mathematics. We have covered all of the bases here—everything from basic number systems through more sophisticated material that will appear on the MCAT exam. Finally, Part IV features three full-length generic tests, followed by in-depth solutions so you can check your work and review any material that you don't understand. By taking these tests in a simulated test situation, you will gain an understanding of what you know and what needs further study. As you work through the tests in the book, you should be able to see a marked improvement from test to test.

THE QUESTIONS

As we said earlier, there are four question types that you will encounter on one or more of these examinations. While there are no specific mathematics questions on the MCAT, you will certainly find numerous questions that require you to be aware of basic math principles. And throughout the test, many of the questions will be "Data Interpretation" type questions.

As an illustration, look at the following table and question from a typical physical science section of the MCAT.

Symbol	Atomic Number	Atomic Mass	Proton Count	Neutron Count	Electron Count	Ion or Isotope?
K	19	39.0	19	20	19	Isotope
A1	13			14	13	Isotope
Ba^{+2}	56	137.0	56			Ion
		31.0	15		15	Isotope
F^{-1}	9	24.0		10		Ion
	12			12	10	

1. In the table above, which of the following correctly completes the line describing the atomic "arrangement" for Al?

   (A) Atomic Mass = 13, Proton Count = 13
   (B) Atomic Mass = 14, Proton Count = 13
   (C) Atomic Mass = 27, Proton Count = 13
   (D) Atomic Mass = 14, Proton Count = 14

On the MCAT, you will be called upon to answer data interpretation questions like the one above, whether they are tables, graphs, charts, or illustrations, in both biological and physical science.

Following is a table that will give you an idea of the types of questions that will appear on the exams. Keep in mind that both the GRE and GMAT tests are now Computer Adaptive Tests (CAT) and you will be able to take them on the computer only.

Question-Types	Examination
Problem Solving/Quantitative Analysis	GRE, GMAT, MCAT
Quantitative Comparisons	GRE
Data Sufficiency	GMAT
Data Interpretation	GRE, MCAT

All of the mathematics problems and tests throughout this book require you to be able to apply a basic knowledge of math principles to solve the problems as well as your analytical ability. We suggest that you study ALL of the Red Alert sections so that you are familiar with the different questions, and so that you are also able to develop your skills in mathematical reasoning. Regardless of which graduate-level examination you ultimately take, this knowledge will be important to you.

Take your time working through this book. Start by taking the Diagnostic Test and then check your answers. You will get a good idea of what you know and what requires additional study. After you have checked and reviewed your answers to this test, review the Red Alert sections and then move on to the Mathematics Review. Of course, you can always skip throughout these sections if your time is limited or just focus on those sections that you feel need additional work.

One final suggestion: it is important on any test to be able to conserve time, and to use it wisely in order to answer all of the questions on an exam, and to spend a greater amount of time on questions that you don't know or can't solve immediately. One trick is to learn and memorize the directions, which may be somewhat complicated—especially in the Data Sufficiency and Quantitative Comparison tests. If you don't have to read and reread the directions, you will save valuable minutes.

Good luck!

Part I
Diagnostic Test

DIAGNOSTIC TEST

Each of the Questions 1–10 has five possible answers. For each of these questions, select the best of the answer choices given.

1. What is an equation of the line passing through the point
    $(-2,1)$ with a slope of 5?

    (A) $y - 5x = -9$
    (B) $5y - x = 7$
    (C) $y - 5x = 11$
    (D) $y - 5x = -11$
    (E) none of the above

2. $\dfrac{(x^2 - 4)(x^3 + 64)}{(x^2 - 4x + 16)(x^2 + 6x + 8)}$ can be simplified to

    (A) $\dfrac{x - 2}{x + 4}$

    (B) $x - 2$

    (C) $\dfrac{x^3 + 64}{x^2 + 6x + 8}$

    (D) $x + 4$
    (E) none of the above

3. Indicate the quadrant(s) where the terminal side of θ must lie
    in order that $\cos(\theta)$ and $\tan(\theta)$ are both negative, and $\sin(\theta)$ is
    positive.

    (A) Quadrant III
    (B) Quadrants I and III
    (C) Quadrants II and IV
    (D) Quadrant II
    (E) none of the above

4. What is the exact value of $\csc(30°)$?

    (A) $\dfrac{2}{\sqrt{3}}$

    (B) 2

    (C) $\dfrac{1}{2}$

    (D) $\dfrac{\sqrt{2}}{2}$

    (E) none of the above

5. What is the probability of getting a total of 8 on a roll of 2 standard dice?

(A) $\dfrac{5}{36}$

(B) $\dfrac{8}{36}$

(C) $\dfrac{31}{36}$

(D) 0

(E) none of the above

6. If n is a positive even integer, then which of the following must be odd?

(A) $3n + 2$
(B) $n^2 + 14$
(C) $n - 6$
(D) $n^2 - 3$
(E) none of the above

7. The average of six numbers is 12. If the average of only four of these numbers is $12\frac{1}{2}$, then what is the average of the other two numbers?

(A) 12
(B) 11
(C) 10

(D) $12\frac{1}{2}$

(E) none of the above

8. A 50-ounce solution is 25 percent alcohol. If 50 ounces of water is added to the solution, what percent of the new solution is alcohol?

(A) 12.5 percent
(B) 25 percent
(C) 50 percent
(D) 13 percent
(E) none of the above

9. A stock decreases in value by 20 percent. By what percent must the stock now increase to reach its initial value?

(A) 15 percent
(B) 20 percent
(C) 25 percent
(D) 30 percent
(E) none of the above

10. In the equation $y = mx + 1$, m is constant. If $x = 4$ when $y = 13$, then what is the value of x when $y = 7$?

(A) 4
(B) 2
(C) 7
(D) 3
(E) none of the above

Each of the Questions 11–20 consists of two quantities, one in Column A and one in Column B. You are to compare the two quantities and choose

    (A) if the quantity in Column A is greater;
    (B) if the quantity in Column B is greater;
    (C) if the two quantities are equal;
    (D) if the relationship cannot be determined from the information given.

Note: Since there are only four choices, NEVER MARK (E).

Numbers: All numbers used are real numbers.
Figures: Position of points, angles, regions, etc., can be assumed to be in the order shown, and angle measures can be assumed to be positive.
Lines shown as straight, can be assumed to be straight.
Figures can be assumed to lie in a plane unless otherwise indicated.
Figures that accompany questions are intended to provide information that is useful in answering the questions. However, unless a note states that a figure is drawn to scale, you should solve these problems NOT by estimating sizes by sight or by measurement, but by using your knowledge of mathematics.

	Column A	Column B
11.	$\cos^2(30) + \sin^2(30)$	1
12.	$|x| + 4$	$|x + 4|$
13.	$\sqrt{234} + \sqrt{100}$	$\sqrt{334}$

Questions 14 and 15 refer to the following figure.

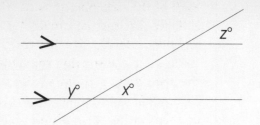

	Column A	Column B
14.	145	y

	Column A	Column B
15.	$z + x$	$2x$

16.	$(.45)^4$	$(.32)^5$

17.	The number of hours it takes a car to travel 500 miles.	The number of hours it takes a train to travel 500 miles.

For question 18, assume that $x > 0$.

	Column A	Column B
18.	$(\sqrt{x} + \sqrt{x})^2$	$(\sqrt{x})^2 + (\sqrt{x})^2$

19.	$\dfrac{1}{7} + \dfrac{1}{13}$	$\dfrac{1}{7} \times \dfrac{1}{13}$

20.	The angle sum of a pentagon.	The angle sum of a quadrilateral.

Each of the data questions 21–30 below consists of a question and two statements, labeled (1) and (2), in which certain data are given. Decide whether the data given in the statements are sufficient for answering the question. Using the data provided in the statements and knowledge of mathematics and everyday facts (such as the number of days in October or the meaning of counterclockwise), mark the following:

(A) if statement (1) ALONE is sufficient, but statement (2) alone is not sufficient to answer the question asked;

(B) if statement (2) ALONE is sufficient, but statement (1) alone is not sufficient to answer the question asked;

(C) if BOTH statement (1) and (2) TOGETHER are sufficient to answer the question, but NEITHER statement ALONE is sufficient;

(D) if EACH statement ALONE is sufficient to answer the question asked;

(E) if statements (1) and (2) TOGETHER are NOT sufficient to answer the question asked, and additional data that are specific to the problem are needed.

21. How far is it from point A to point B?

(1) Jerry drove from A to B in 3 hours.
(2) When Jerry drove from A to B, his speed averaged 45 mph.

22. What two unique numbers, x and y, have a product of 992?

(1) x and y are real numbers.
(2) x and y are consecutive integers.

23. Is x less than y?

(1) $13x + 1 < 2z$
(2) $z + 3 = 5y^2$

24.

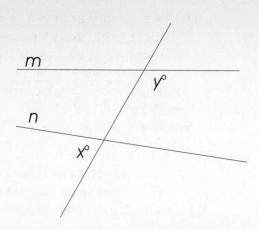

Based on the figure above, does $x + y = 180$?

   (1)   Lines *m* and *n* are parallel.

   (2) $x = 45°$

25.   If Crew A and Crew B, working together, can paint a house in 3 days, can crew A paint the same house in 5 days?

   (1)   Crew A is faster than Crew B.

   (2)   Crew B can paint the same house in 7 days.

26.   What is the average score of the bowlers in a bowling tournament?

   (1)   70 percent of the bowlers score an average of 140, and the other 30 percent score an average of 115.

   (2)   Each bowler in the tournament scored at least 85, but nobody scored over 230.

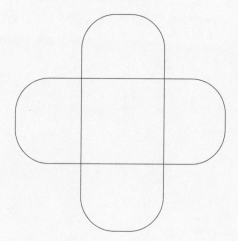

27.   What is the area of the figure above formed by a square and four semicircles?

   (1)   The perimeter of the square is 24 cm.

   (2)   The area of one of the semicircles is 3.5 cm^2.

28. A bag holds thirty red checker pieces and twenty black checker pieces. If John picks pieces from the bag, does he pick more red pieces than black pieces?

(1) John picks 41 pieces total.
(2) John picks 21 pieces total.

29. What is the distance from City A to City B?

(1) A nonstop train travels from City B to City A in two hours, traveling at a maximum speed of 70 miles per hour.
(2) A train that makes three stops in between City A and City B takes five hours to make the same run.

30. If John and Jerry can finish a job in 5 hours when they work together, what portion of the job did Jerry do?

(1) If John worked alone, he could finish the job in 8 hours.
(2) Jerry took a longer lunch break than John did.

For the following ten questions, refer to the appropriate graph, chart, etc. and answer the question accordingly.

Questions 31 and 32 refer to the following graph.

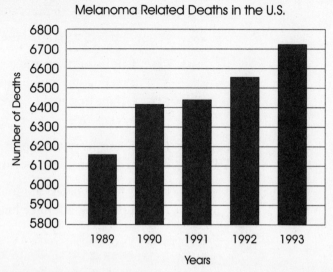

Melanoma Related Deaths in the U.S.

This graph shows the number of people in the United States who died as a result of Melanoma for various years.

31. How many more people died from Melanoma in 1992 than in 1990?

    (A) 250 people
    (B) 200 people
    (C) 180 people
    (D) 120 people
    (E) 50 people

32. What is the average rate of change in the number of deaths caused by Melanoma from 1990 to 1992?

    (A) 25 deaths per year
    (B) 60 deaths per year
    (C) 150 deaths per year
    (D) 6,570 deaths per year
    (E) 6,420 deaths per year

Questions 33 through 35 refer to the following graph.

The weight (in pounds) of a certain boy can be expressed as a function of his age. The following is a graph of this function.

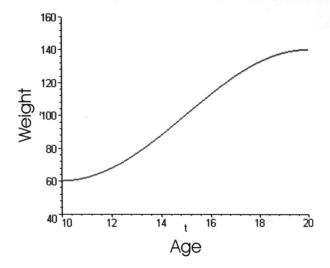

33. Over what time period is this graph concave down?

   (A) Age 10 to 15 years
   (B) Age 12 to 18 years
   (C) Age 15 to 20 years
   (D) Age 10 to 12 years
   (E) never concave down

34. At what age is the boy gaining weight most rapidly?

   (A) 15 years old
   (B) 20 years old
   (C) 10 years old
   (D) 12 years old
   (E) 18 years old

35. How much does the boy weigh when he is 14 years old?

   (A) About 90 pounds
   (B) About 100 pounds
   (C) About 40 pounds
   (D) About 140 pounds
   (E) About 120 pounds

Questions 36 through 40 refer to the following table.

This table shows the accumulated value (in dollars) of a bank account paying 6 percent interest compounded quarterly on an initial investment of *P* dollars after *t* years.

P ($)	\(t\)(years)			
	6	8	10	12
3,500	5,003.26	5,636.14	6,349.06	7,152.17
4,000	5,718.01	6,441.30	7,256.07	8,173.91
4,500	6,432.76	7,246.46	8,163.08	9,195.65
5,000	7,147.51	8,051.62	9,070.09	10,217.39
5,500	7,862.27	8,856.78	9,977.10	11,239.13
6,000	8,577.02	9,661.95	10,884.11	12,260.87
6,500	9,291.77	10,467.11	11,791.12	13,282.61

36. How much money would you make from interest if you deposited $4,000 into this type of account for 8 years?

    (A) $1,718.01
    (B) $2,441.30
    (C) $6,441.30
    (D) $5,718.01
    (E) none of the above

37. Which of the following types of investment would leave you with more money in total at the end of the specified term?

    (A) $3,500 initial investment for 12 years
    (B) $5,000 initial investment for 10 years
    (C) $4,000 initial investment for 12 years
    (D) $5,500 initial investment for 8 years
    (E) $6,000 initial investment for 6 years

38. What is the total amount you would have if you invested $5,500 for 10 years in this type of account?

    (A) $19,977.10
    (B) $11,239.13
    (C) $9,070.10
    (D) $10,884.11
    (E) none of the above

39. If you invested $4,500 into this type of account, how much money do you make from year 6 to year 10?

    (A) $1,730.32
    (B) $916.62
    (C) $1,645.67
    (D) $1,478.90
    (E) none of the above

40. In which of the following types of accounts would you see a greater return in interest alone?

    (A) $5,000 initial investment for 10 years
    (B) $4,000 initial investment for 12 years
    (C) $6,000 initial investment for 6 years
    (D) $5,500 initial investment for 8 years
    (E) $3,500 initial investment for 12 years

EXPLANATORY ANSWERS FOR THE DIAGNOSTIC TEST

1. **The correct answer is (C).** Use the point/slope form: $y - 1 = 5(x + 2)$ then reduce to $y - 5x = 11$.

2. **The correct answer is (B).** Factor the fraction into $\dfrac{(x - 2)(x + 2)(x + 4)(x^2 - 4x + 16)}{(x^2 - 4x + 16)(x + 2)(x + 4)}$ then we reduce to $x - 2$.

3. **The correct answer is (D).** Cosine is negative in quadrants II and III, tangent is negative in quadrants II and IV, and sine is positive in quadrants I and II. Only quadrant II is common to all criterions.

4. **The correct answer is (B).** $\text{Csc}(30) = \dfrac{1}{\sin(30)} = \dfrac{1}{\frac{1}{2}} = 2$.

5. **The correct answer is (A).** We can only get a total of 8 by having the combinations: (2,6), (3,5), (4,4), (5,3), (6,2). Since we can roll 36 possible outcomes, that leaves us with $\dfrac{5}{36}$ as our chances.

6. **The correct answer is (D).** An even number squared is even. Then subtract 3 and we are left with an odd number.

7. **The correct answer is (B).** If all six average to 12, then $6 \times 12 = 72$. If four average to 12.5 then $4 \times 12.5 = 50$. Now $72 - 50 = 22$ which is the sum of the last two numbers. Hence, they must average to 11.

8. **The correct answer is (A).** A 50-ounce solution at 25 percent alcohol contains $50 \times .25 = 12.5$-ounces of alcohol. If we add 50 ounces of water, we now have a total of 100 ounces of solution with 12.5 ounces of alcohol, which is a 12.5 percent solution.

9. **The correct answer is (C).** If we invest x amount and lose 20 percent we are left with $.8x$. Let the percent that the stock needs to increase by be denoted by y. We now have $(.8x)y + .8x = x$ to get back to our original amount. Divide both sides by x and simplify to get $y = .25$ or 25 percent.

10. **The correct answer is (B).** If $x = 4$ when $y = 13$, then we can see that $13 = m \times 4 + 1$, which implies that m = 3. Hence, if $y = 7$ then $7 = 3 \times x + 1$ or $x = 2$.

11. **The correct answer is (C).** $\text{Cos}^2(\theta) + \sin^2(\theta) = 1$ for any value of θ, so they are equal and we choose answer choice (C).

12. **The correct answer is (D).** We know that $|x + 4| \leq |x| + 4$ but we can't tell if it is *strictly* less than, or if they are equal. It all depends on x. We don't know if it is negative or non-negative.

13. **The correct answer is (A).** The square root of a sum is always less than the sum of the square roots, provided that we aren't trying to sum the number 0.

14. **The correct answer is (D).** We aren't given any information about actual values of the variables.

15. **The correct answer is (C).** Since the lines are parallel, then $z = x$, which implies that $z + x = 2x$.

16. **The correct answer is (A).**
$.45^4 = .04100625$ and $.32^5 = .0033554432$. Thus, $.45^4 > .32^5$.

17. **The correct answer is (D).** We don't know how fast either the car or the train travels.

18. **The correct answer is (A).**
$(\sqrt{x} + \sqrt{x})^2 = 4x > 2x = (\sqrt{x})^2 + (\sqrt{x})^2$

19. **The correct answer is (A).** $\frac{1}{7} + \frac{1}{13}$ is bigger than just $\frac{1}{7}$, while $\frac{1}{7} \times \frac{1}{13}$ is smaller than just $\frac{1}{7}$.

20. **The correct answer is (A).** The angle sum of a pentagon is 540 degrees, and the angle sum of a quadrilateral is 360 degrees.

21. **The correct answer is (C).** Time = 3 hours from (1) and speed = 45 mph from (2). Hence, distance = speed × time = 45 × 3 miles = 135 miles. So, both (1) and (2) are needed.

22. **The correct answer is (E).** We actually have two possible answers for x and y. They could be 31 and 32, or they could be -31 and -32. Even using both (1) and (2), we can't come up with a unique solution.

23. **The correct answer is (E).** From combining (1) and (2) to get an equation with only x's and y's, we see that $13x + 1 < 2(5y^2 - 3)$ or $13x < 10y^2 - 7$. We still can't tell if $x < y$, because the y is squared.

24. **The correct answer is (A).** If statement (1) is true, then x and y are alternate angles of parallel lines; hence $x + y = 180$.

25. **The correct answer is (B).** If (2) is true, then crew B can paint $\frac{1}{7}$ of the house in one day. Together, they can paint $\frac{1}{3}$ of the house in one day. Therefore, $\frac{1}{7} + \frac{1}{x} = \frac{1}{3}$ where x is the number of days that it takes crew A to paint the house. Now, we can solve for x and answer the problem without using statement (1).

26. **The correct answer is (A).** We can calculate a weighted average of 140 and 115 to reach the average score in the tournament.

27. **The correct answer is (D).** In statement (1), we can calculate the side length of the square and the radius of the semi-circle. Then, we can calculate the area. In statement (2), we can calculate the radius of the semi-circle, then the side length of the square, and then the total area. So each statement alone is enough.

28. **The correct answer is (A).** If statement (1) is true, then, at most, he can pick 20 black pieces. That leaves the other 21 pieces to be red, and $21 > 20$. If statement (2) is true, then we can't tell if he has more red than black pieces.

29. **The correct answer is (E).** Neither (1) nor (2) gives an average speed with which to calculate distance.

30. **The correct answer is (A).** Statement (2) has nothing to do with how long he took to finish. From statement (1), we can calculate John and Jerry's portion of the work.

31. **The correct answer is (D).** There were 6,570 deaths in 1992 and 6,450 deaths in 1990; therefore there were $6{,}570 - 6{,}450 = 120$ more deaths in 1992 than in 1990.

32. **The correct answer is (B).** Divide 120 by 2 years to get the average rate of change, which is 60 deaths per year.

33. **The correct answer is (C).** The graph is concave down from the inflection point to the far right side, which is the interval 15 to 20.

34. **The correct answer is (A).** The inflection point is at 15.

35. **The correct answer is (A).** Locate 14 years, go up to the graph and over to the vertical axis, and read off the weight, which is about 90 pounds.

36. **The correct answer is (B).** $4,000 for 8 years yields $6,441.30, which is an increase of $2,441.30.

37. **The correct answer is (B).** $5,000 for 10 years yields $9,070.09, which is more than the other investments.

38. **The correct answer is (E).** The answer would be $9,977.10, which is not given as a possible answer.

39. **The correct answer is (A).** $4,500 for 6 years yields $6,432.76, and $4,500 for 10 years yields $8,163.08, for a difference of $1,730.32.

40. **The correct answer is (B).** We make $4,173.91 in interest if we invest $4,000 for 12 years. This amount is larger than all the other types of investments.

Part II
Topic Reviews

RED ALERT

PROBLEM SOLVING/QUANTITATIVE ABILITY

Both the GMAT and the GRE have math sections that contain Problem Solving/Quantitative Ability problems. These questions are in the standard multiple-choice format, with five possible answers. They test your knowledge on all of the areas of mathematics that have been covered in this book (except for those that were specifically indicated to be MCAT only topics). While you have certainly seen many math problems in this format before, it is worthwhile to familiarize yourself not only with how many questions of this type will appear on your test, but also with all of the strategies and guidelines that will help you answer them. *Note that the MCAT does not contain Problem Solving/Analytic Ability questions. Instead, you will need to use the math topics discussed in this book to help answer a variety of chemistry and physics questions. Nonetheless, those taking the MCAT should read the section below. Certain strategies may come in handy when you take your test.*

As far as test format is concerned, the GMAT and GRE are now Computer Adaptive Tests (CAT), and you will have to take them on the computer. There are no longer any paper and pencil tests.

As you will probably gather from the math review in this book, the questions on the math sections of the GMAT and the GRE are based on the math that is usually covered in high school math classes—arithmetic, algebra, and geometry. There are two different types of arithmetic questions that will appear on the tests—questions that ask you to perform a computation (reduce the fractions, divide the decimals, combine the percents), and questions that ask you to solve a word problem involving fractions, decimals, percents, or ratios. Similarly, there will be algebraic computation problems (solve the equation, factor the expression, manipulate the square roots), as well as various types of algebraic word problems. As far as the geometry problems are concerned, you will only be asked to solve problems by working with the geometric properties already discussed. You will not need to create proofs or state definitions.

On the following pages, you will find some hints and strategies for Quantitative Ability questions. While the bottom line is that you need to know the math material that is used on the test, there are a number of techniques that will either save you time or help you determine the correct answers to certain questions. Carefully read the hints and strategies below, and remember what you have read when you take your test.

HINTS AND STRATEGIES FOR QUANTITATIVE ABILITY QUESTIONS

Remember that one of the five answer choices must be the correct one. Therefore, do not waste any time doing computations that are not necessary. Estimate as much as you possibly can as you try to determine which of the answers must be correct. This strategy is particularly helpful when the five multiple-choice answers are spread apart numerically. For example, if you estimate that the answer to a problem is 100, and one of the answer choices is 98, and none of the other answer choices is close to 100, then 98 must be the correct answer.

As you no doubt know, you are not permitted to use a calculator to perform your computations. This means two things: First of all, you should brush up on the rules of computation. For example, make sure you know where to put the decimal point when you divide two decimals. Second, there is another side to the calculator usage issue. Since the test-makers know that you will not have a calculator, the test problems are, in general, designed to not include messy computations. Therefore, if you ever find yourself thinking, "I need a calculator to help me with this problem," carefully reconsider the problem. There is likely an easier way to do it that you may have missed.

All fractions that appear as the answers to questions will be expressed in reduced form. If you solve a problem and obtain a fraction as the answer, this fraction must be reduced before you will find it among the multiple-choice answers. You can save some time, however, in the following way: If you solve a problem and get a fraction as the answer, look at the multiple-choice answers to see if it is there. If it is, don't waste time trying to reduce the fraction. It must be already reduced, so simply choose the appropriate answer. Otherwise, it is possible that the fraction can be reduced. Try to do this, and then look to see if the answer is there.

Similarly, all square root answers will be expressed in reduced form. As far as geometrical problems involving π are concerned, look at the answer choices to determine if you are supposed to leave the answer in terms of π, or use the approximate value of $\frac{22}{7}$.

If the answer you obtain doesn't match one of the choices given, it might still be correct. Try to write it in a different form, and then see if it matches. For example, the answer $6x + 3$ can also be written as $3(2x + 1)$. And, the answer $(x - 2)(x + 3)$ can also be written as $x^2 + x - 6$.

Make sure to answer the question that is being asked. Sometimes people get a problem wrong because, after solving an equation, they select the value of x as the answer when the problem asks for the value of y. Or, after finding the value of x, they choose that value as the answer, when the problem was actually asking for the value, for example, of $2x + 5$. In general, be sure to read every question very carefully. Is the question asking for the number of phones that are defective, or the number of phones that are *not* defective?

Be careful (especially when solving geometry problems) to give your answer in the same units of measure as the multiple-choice answers. Sometimes a problem may speak of lengths in "feet" while the answer choices are given in "inches." In such a case, you must convert your answer to the appropriate units.

If you are stuck on a particular problem, try looking at the multiple-choice *answers*. Since one of them has to be right, the answers may give you some idea of how to proceed, or at least a notion of what the question is asking.

Of course, when you read a math question on your test, the best situation is to be able to solve it directly. However, if you are not sure how to solve the problem, it does not necessarily mean that you can't figure out the answer. Following are a few alternate strategies that *may* help you determine the correct answer to a question that you are not initially sure how to approach.

STRATEGY ONE: SUBSTITUTE

Problems that involve letters instead of numbers can be confusing. If you are unsure of how to proceed with such a problem, try changing the letters to simple numbers and doing the problem with them. Then, once you see what to do, go back and do the same thing with the original letters. Alternatively, consider a problem that gives you a confusing algebraic expression and asks you which of a series of other expressions is equivalent to it. One way to approach this is to substitute simple numbers for all of the letters in the original expression and evaluate it. Then, substitute the same numbers for the letters in the answer choices. Whichever one gives you the same value that you got when you evaluated the expression in the problem statement will be the one that is equivalent.

Example

$$a - 12[\ 5 - (\ 6 - a)] =$$

(A) $13a - 11$
(B) $13a + 12$
(C) $11a + 12$
(D) $11a - 12$
(E) $2 - 11a$

Solution

While this problem can certainly be solved algebraically, let's try to solve it by substituting. If a, for example, is equal to 1, the expression becomes $1 - 12[\ 5 - (6 - 1)] = 1 - 12[\ 5 - 5] = 1 - 12[0] = 1$. Now, if we substitute 1 into each of the answer choices, we see that only choice (E) yields the value of 1. Thus, the answer must be (E). Note that if two choices had yielded the value of 1, it would be necessary to select a different value for a to determine which choice is correct.

STRATEGY TWO: WORK BACKWARDS

Frequently, if you cannot solve a problem directly, you can solve it by taking the multiple-choice answers and testing each one until you determine which is correct. This often works well with algebra problems.

Example

If $\frac{7}{8}x = 21$, then $\frac{1}{4}$ of x is

(A) 4
(B) 6
(C) 12
(D) 21
(E) 24

Solution

If you are unsure how to solve this problem directly, simply test the answers. For example, if (A) is correct, then x must be 16, but $\frac{7}{8}$ of 16 is not 21. If (B) is correct, $x = 24$, and $\frac{7}{8}$ of 24 *is* 21. The correct answer is (B).

STRATEGY THREE: ESTIMATE

Particularly in problems where the multiple-choice answers vary from each other by quite a bit, it may be possible to determine which answer is correct by simply estimating.

Example

Which of the following is the closest to $\frac{4926 \times 672}{2980}$?

(A) 1
(B) 10
(C) 100
(D) 1,000
(E) 10,000

Solution

4926 is almost 5000. Approximate 672 with 700, and 2980 with 3000. Then, the fraction becomes $\frac{5000 \times 700}{3000} = \frac{3500}{3}$, which is between 1,100 and 1,200. Thus, the correct answer is (D).

STRATEGY FOUR: LOOK FOR SHORTCUTS

If a problem ever seems to involve a series of computations that seem too complicated to do by hand, look for a shortcut. Rarely do problems on these tests involve long, cumbersome computations. Sometimes shortcuts can even help you solve problems that are not that difficult to solve directly.

Example

What is the value of $\dfrac{9^{99} - 9^{97}}{9^{98}}$?

(A) $\dfrac{8}{9}$

(B) 8

(C) 9

(D) $\dfrac{80}{9}$

(E) 81

Solution

Certainly, you are not expected to evaluate this expression straight out. Instead, notice that the numerator can be factored:

$$\frac{9^{99} - 9^{97}}{9^{98}} = \frac{9^{97}(9^2 - 1)}{9^{98}} = \frac{9^2 - 1}{9} = \frac{81 - 1}{9} = \frac{80}{9}.$$

Therefore, the correct answer is (D).

Now, for you to practice, here are some additional Problem Solving questions. Try to see if you can use any of the strategies above to help you as you solve them.

PRACTICE PROBLEMS

1. 843 is 84.3% of what number?

(A) 10
(B) 84.3
(C) 100
(D) 843
(E) 1,000

2. The sum of a group of numbers is 4,290. If the average of these numbers is 330, how many numbers are in the group?

(A) 10
(B) 12
(C) 13
(D) 14
(E) 330

3. If $3x + 13 = 10$, then $9x + 39 =$

(A) 30
(B) 40
(C) 42
(D) 46
(E) 48

4. The diagram below shows three square rooms that form the bottom floor of a house. If the area of the kitchen is 36 square feet, and the area of the den is 64 square feet, what percent of the total floor space does the living room occupy (to the nearest whole number percent)?

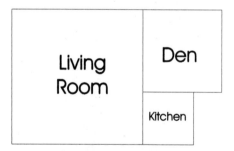

(A) 51 percent
(B) 62 percent
(C) 66 percent
(D) 68 percent
(E) 72 percent

5. If *a, b,* and *c* are integers, and $a = 5b = 11c$, which of the following is not necessarily an integer?

(A) $\dfrac{a}{5}$

(B) $\dfrac{a}{11}$

(C) $\dfrac{a}{55}$

(D) $\dfrac{a}{b}$

(E) $\dfrac{b}{a}$

6. How many numbers satisfy both the inequality $5y - 15 < 0$ and the inequality $5 - 3y < 11$?

(A) 0
(B) 1
(C) 2
(D) 3
(E) Infinitely many

7. If, $\dfrac{2x + 2y}{x + 2y} = 1$, then what is the value of *xy*?

(A) −2
(B) −1
(C) 0
(D) 1
(E) 2

8. A business budgets 30 percent of its net revenue to pay salaries. If $36,000 is budgeted for salaries, what is its net revenue?

(A) $84,000
(B) $96,000
(C) $108,000
(D) $120,000
(E) $125,000

9.

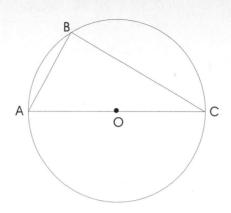

O is the center of the circle in the figure above. If AC = 8, and BC is three times as long as AB, what is the area of triangle ABC?

(A) 1.5
(B) 4
(C) 9.6
(D) 16
(E) 24

10. If the sum of x and its square is 30, what is the value of x?

(A) −6
(B) 4
(C) 5
(D) 8
(E) It can not be uniquely determined from the information given.

SOLUTIONS

1. **The correct answer is (E).** $P = R \times B$, where the Part, P, is 843, and the Rate, R, is 84.3%. Thus, $B = \dfrac{P}{R} = \dfrac{843}{.843} = 1000$.

2. **The correct answer is (C).** The definition of the average of a group of numbers is Average $= \dfrac{\text{Sum of Numbers}}{\text{Number of Numbers}}$. This formula can be reworked to give the Number of Numbers $= \dfrac{\text{Sum of Numbers}}{\text{Average}} = \dfrac{4{,}290}{333} = 13$.

3. **The correct answer is (A).** This problem can be solved very quickly. Simply note that you are given the value for $3x + 13$ and asked to find the value of $9x + 39$. Since $9x + 39 = 3(x + 13)$, we have $9x + 39 = 3(10) = 30$.

4. **The correct answer is (C).** If the area of the kitchen is 36 sq. ft., then each side of the kitchen is 6 feet. If the area of the den is 64 sq. ft., then each side of the den is 8 feet. Thus, the side of the living room is 14 feet and its area is $14 \times 14 = 196$ sq. ft. The living room is thus 196 sq. ft. out of a total of $196 + 64 + 36 = 296$ sq. ft. This means that it is about
$\dfrac{196}{296} \times 100\% \approx .66 \times 100\% = 66\%$.

5. **The correct answer is (E).** Let's consider the possible answer choices one at a time. First of all, since $a = 5b$, we have $b = \dfrac{a}{5}$. Since b is an integer, $\dfrac{a}{5}$ is an integer. Secondly, since $c = \dfrac{a}{11}$, and c is an integer, we see that $\dfrac{a}{11}$ is an integer. Now, we have seen that $\dfrac{a}{5}$ is an integer, and this tells us that is divisible by 5; we have also seen that $\dfrac{a}{11}$ is an integer, and this tells us that a is divisible by 11. Since a is divisible by both 5 and 11, a must also be divisible by $5 \times 11 = 55$. Thus, $\dfrac{a}{55}$ is an integer. Next, based on the fact that $a = 5b$, we see that $\dfrac{a}{b} = 5$, an integer. Finally, however, $\dfrac{b}{a} = \dfrac{1}{5}$, so this is not an integer.

6. **The correct answer is (E).** The solution to $5y - 15 < 0$ is $y < 3$. The solution to $5 - 3y < 11$ is $y > -2$. Since there are infinitely many numbers between -2 and 3, there are infinitely many answers.

7. **The correct answer is (C).** Multiplying both sides of the given equation by $x + 2y$ yields $2x + 2y = x + 2y$. This reduces to $2x = x$, or $x = 0$. If $x = 0$, then $xy = 0$, also.

8. **The correct answer is (D).** $P = R \times B$, where the Part P is $36,000 and the Rate R is 30%. Thus, $B = \dfrac{P}{R} = \dfrac{36{,}000}{.3} = 120{,}000$.

9. **The correct answer is (C).** First of all, you must recognize that angle B must be a right angle, as it is inscribed in a semi-circle. If AB = x, then CB = $3x$, and we can use the Pythagorean Theorem to determine x:

    $$x^2 + (3x)^2 = 8^2$$
    $$x^2 + 9x^2 = 64$$
    $$10x^2 = 64$$
    $$x^2 = 6.4 \text{ or } x = \sqrt{6.4}$$

    Now, to find the area of the triangle, use AB as the base, and CB as the height. The area is: $A = \frac{1}{2} bh = \frac{1}{2} (\sqrt{6.4})(3\sqrt{6.4}) =$

    $\frac{1}{2} (6.4)(3) = (3.2)(3) = 9.6$.

10. **The correct answer is (E).** The problem statement leads to the equation $x^2 + x = 30$. This equation can be factored and solved:

    $$x^2 + x - 30 = 0$$
    $$(x - 5)(x + 6) = 0$$
    $$x = 5, -6$$

    Therefore, the problem statement only informs us that x is either 5 or -6, so the correct answer is (E).

RED ALERT

QUANTITATIVE COMPARISON

In addition to the customary multiple choice questions which make up the majority of most standardized tests, certain tests feature what can best be termed "special format questions." Such questions typically have their own logical structure and a unique answer scheme. It is extremely important to be very familiar with any special format questions that are a part of the test you will be taking. Not only must you understand the question format so that you do not waste any time reading directions while taking the exam, but you must also be aware of the techniques and special strategies for solving such questions.

The math sections of the GRE contain a special format question known as "Quantitative Comparison." *Note that there are no Quantitative Comparison questions on the GMAT or on the MCAT, so if you are taking either of those tests, you may skip this section of the book, and move on to the next one.*

When you first look at a series of Quantitative Comparison questions, they may appear a bit unusual. First of all, there are no answer choices given. Instead, each problem contains two columns, Column A and Column B. In each of these columns, there is some sort of numerical or mathematical entry. In order to answer each question, you must determine which of the two entries (the one in Column A or the one in Column B) is the larger.

The "code" for answering each Quantitative Comparison question is always the same, and you should have it memorized before you take the GRE. If, after analyzing the entries in Column A and Column B, you decide that the entry in column A is larger, then the answer to the question is (A). If, on the other hand, you decide that the entry in Column B is larger, then the correct answer is (B). In the case where the two entries are the same size, the correct answer would be (C). Finally, if it is not possible to determine which of the two is larger (because there is not enough information), or if one of the entries is sometimes larger and sometimes smaller than the other, the correct answer is (D).

Note that, unlike the other questions on the GRE, answer choice (E) is not an option for Quantitative Comparison questions. Thus, the answer to each Quantitative Comparison question is either (A),(B),(C), or (D).

One other structural item to note about Quantitative Comparison questions is this: Occasionally you will be given some additional information to help you determine which of the two entries is the larger. Such information will be centered between Column A and Column B, just above the entries.

While the structure of a Quantitative Comparison question may initially appear confusing, once it is understood, Quantitative Comparison questions are typically easier and faster to answer than multiple choice math questions. In order to help familiarize you with the way these questions work and to help you gain a better understanding of the four answer choices, we begin with four sample questions. Note that these questions have been arranged so that the answer to the first one is (A), the answer to the second one is (B), followed by (C) and (D).

Each of the following questions consists of two quantities, one in Column A and one in Column B. You are to compare the two quantities and choose

(A) if the quantity in Column A is greater;
(B) if the quantity in Column B is greater;
(C) if the two quantities are equal;
(D) if the relationship cannot be determined from the information given.

Note: Since there are only four choices, NEVER MARK (E).

Column A	**Column B**
	$x > y > 0$
1. 0	$y - x$

Solution

This question asks us to determine if 0 or $y - x$ is larger. We are given the fact that $x > y > 0$ to help us determine the size relationship. This given information tells us that both x and y are positive and that x is larger than y. If this is the case, then $y - x$ must be negative, and therefore smaller than 0. Thus the correct answer is (A). Note that, while we have no knowledge of the actual value of $y - x$, we know that it must be negative, and that is enough to enable us to answer the question.

	Column A	Column B
2.	$2^3 \times 3 \times 5^9 \times 7^{11}$	$3^3 \times 5^9 \times 7^{11}$

Solution

It is by no means necessary to evaluate all of the exponents and do all of the multiplications to determine which column has the larger value. Simply note that both entries have factors of 5^9 and 7^{11}. Thus, the answer to the question hinges on whether $2^3 \times 3$ is larger than 3^3 or not. Since $2^3 \times 3 = 8 \times 3 = 24$ and $3^3 = 27$, the entry is Column B must be larger. Note that we have not computed the actual value of either column, but we have still determined that the answer is (B).

	Column A	Column B
	$x = 2, y = 3$	
3.	$x + 2y$	x^y

Solution

This question asks us to determine which is larger: $x + 2y$ or x^y. We are given as common information the fact that $x = 2$ and $y = 3$. This information enables us to compute that $x + 2y = 2 + 2(3) = 8$ and $x^y = 2^3 = 8$. Thus, the entries are the same size, and the answer is (C).

	Column A	Column B
4.	The cost per gram of peas if 6 cans of peas cost $1.80	The cost per gram of corn if 10 cans of corn cost $3.00

Solution

This problem does give us enough information to conclude that a can of peas costs the same as a can of corn, but since we are not told how many grams are contained in each can, we cannot determine the cost per gram. Thus, the correct answer is (D).

Now, before we examine some strategies for solving Quantitative Comparison questions, let's look at the directions the way they appear on an actual GRE.

Each of the following questions consists of two quantities, one in Column A and one in Column B. You are to compare the two quantities and choose

(A) if the quantity in Column A is greater;
(B) if the quantity in Column B is greater;
(C) if the two quantities are equal;
(D) if the relationship cannot be determined from the information given.

Note: Since there are only four choices, NEVER MARK (E).

<u>Numbers</u>: All numbers used are real numbers.

<u>Figures</u>: Position of points, angles, regions, etc., can be assumed to be in the order shown, and angle measures can be assumed to be positive.

<u>Lines</u> shown as straight can be assumed to be straight.

<u>Figures</u> can be assumed to lie in a plane unless otherwise indicated.

<u>Figures</u> that accompany questions are intended to provide information useful in answering the questions. However, unless a note states that a figure is drawn to scale, you should solve these problems NOT by estimating sizes by sight or by measurement, but by using your knowledge of mathematics.

Note that these are the directions as they will actually appear on the GRE. Read them carefully and be sure to understand them now, so that you do not waste time reading them on the actual test.

QUANTITATIVE COMPARISON GENERAL TECHNIQUES AND STRATEGIES

In this section we will examine some techniques that will help you answer Quantitative Comparison questions. The initial strategies relate to the question format in general; these strategies are followed by specific mathematical strategies.

Be very clear about the meanings of the answer choices. You should only answer (A) if the quantity in Column A is *always*, not just sometimes, larger than the quantity in Column B. If A is sometimes, but not always, larger, the answer is (D). Similarly, (C) is the answer only if the quantities are *always* equal. If they are equal sometimes, but sometimes unequal, the answer, again, is (D).

One of your goals should be to perform as few computations as necessary to answer each question. As we saw in the practice problems above, you often don't need to determine the actual size of the quantities in Columns A and B to know which one is larger. As another example, if you have enough information to determine that the quantity in Column A is positive and the quantity in Column B is negative, then the quantity in Column A is larger regardless of its actual value.

There are approximately 14–15 Quantitative Comparison questions on the math section. A good guideline is to try to average about 30 seconds for each Quantitative Comparison question, which will allow you to average about a minute and half for the more time-consuming problem solving and data interpretation questions.

You can often tell which quantity is larger by making a few quick estimates. Therefore, estimate and approximate as much as possible. You can often answer a question correctly without doing very much math.

Keep in mind that Quantitative Comparison questions have only four possible answer choices.

Whenever the entry in Column A and the entry in Column B are both purely numerical (that is, they contain only numbers, no letters), then both quantities have a definite size, and there is always a way to tell which one is larger. In these cases, the answer cannot be (D). If you are not sure how to answer a problem with two purely numerical entries, and decide to guess, guess either (A), (B), or (C).

QUANTITATIVE COMPARISON MATHEMATICAL TECHNIQUES AND STRATEGIES

Whenever you can, eliminate common factors and terms from Column A and Column B. Then, simply compare the remaining quantities. Oftentimes, sums and products can be compared term by term or factor by factor.

Example

Column A	Column B
$7^{35} - 7^{34}$	$7^{34}(6)$

Solution

Certainly you could not be expected to evaluate the expressions in the two columns without a calculator. However, it is easy to compare them for size. Simply factor the quantity 7^{34} out of both terms in Column A. We see that $7^{35} - 7^{34} = 7^{34}(7 - 1) = 7^{34}(6)$. Thus, the entries in both columns are equal, and the correct answer is (C).

Example

Column A	Column B
$(103)^4 - (102)^4$	$204(103^2 + 102^2)$

Solution

The quantity in Column A can be factored into
$$(103^2 - 102^2)(103^2 + 102^2) =$$
$$(103 - 102)(103 + 102)(103^2 + 102^2) =$$
$$(1)(205)(103^2 + 102^2) = 205(103^2 + 102^2).$$

Dividing out the common factor of $(103^2 + 102^2)$ from both sides leaves 205 in Column A and 204 in Column B. The correct answer is (A).

Example

Column A	Column B
	$xy > 0$
$(5 - x)(3 + y)$	$15 + 5y - 3x$

Solution

Doing the multiplication in Column A gives us
$15 + 5y - 3x - xy$. Crossing out the common terms in the two columns leaves us with $-xy$ in Column A and 0 in Column B. Since the common information tells us that $xy > 0$, $-xy$ must be negative. The correct answer is (B).

Remember that you can often determine which quantity is larger by simply estimating their sizes.

Example

Column A	Column B
$\dfrac{665}{999}$	$\dfrac{67}{99}$

Solution

To solve this problem, simply note that the number in Column A is less than $\dfrac{2}{3}$ (since $\dfrac{666}{999} = \dfrac{2}{3}$), while the quantity in Column B is greater than $\dfrac{2}{3}$ (since $\dfrac{66}{99} = \dfrac{2}{3}$). The correct answer is (B).

A Quantitative Comparison question can be treated as if it were an algebraic inequality, with your job being to position the correct inequality sign (=, <, >) between them. As such, you may perform any operation to both columns of a Quantitative Comparison question that you can perform on both sides of an inequality. This means, whenever you wish, you can add or subtract the same number to Column A and Column B, multiply or divide both columns by the same positive number, or square both columns (if both entries are positive). This strategy can be used to change the operations of subtraction and division to the relatively less confusing operations of addition and multiplication.

Example

Column A	Column B
$\dfrac{x}{0.25}$	$4x$

Solution

Begin by clearing the fraction in Column A by multiplying both columns by 0.25. Then, Column A becomes x and Column B becomes $0.25(4x) = x$. The correct answer is (C).

Example

Column A	Column B
$\sqrt{3}$	$\dfrac{3}{2}$

Solution

If you begin by squaring both entries, the entry in Column A becomes 3, and the entry in Column B becomes $\dfrac{9}{4} = 2\dfrac{1}{4}$. Thus, the entry in Column A is larger.

Whenever you are comparing quantities containing variables, remember to consider both positive and negative values of the variables. Similarly, remember that variables can have fractional values.

Example

Column A	Column B
	$10 < a < 12$
	$11 < b < 13$
a	b

Solution

At first it might appear as if the quantity in column B is larger than that in A. However, remember that both a and b could be fractional. If, for example, $a = 11.5$ and $b = 11.2$, the quantity in Column A is larger. The correct answer is (D).

Example

Column A	Column B
x^3	x^2

Solution

Again, at first glance, it may appear as if x^3 is larger than x^2. However, if, for example, x is negative, then x^2 would be larger than x^3. The correct answer is (D).

If the column entries contain algebraic operations, it frequently helps to begin by performing these operations.

Example

Column A	Column B
$(x + 2)^2$	$(x - 2)^2$

Solution

Performing the indicated squarings, the entry in Column A becomes $x^2 + 4x + 4$. The entry in Column B becomes $x^2 - 4x + 4$. Crossing out the common terms, the value in Column A becomes $4x$, and that in Column B becomes $-4x$. Since we have no idea what the value of x is, the value in either column could be larger. The correct answer is (D).

Example

Column A	Column B

$$n > 0$$

$$\frac{n^2 + 2}{n} \qquad\qquad n + \frac{1}{n}$$

Solution

Rewriting the entry in Column A, we obtain $\dfrac{n^2 + 2}{n} = n + \dfrac{2}{n}$.

Thus, the problem boils down to a comparison between $\dfrac{2}{n}$ in

Column A and $\dfrac{1}{n}$ in Column B. Since $n > 0$, the entry in Column A is larger. The correct answer is (A).

See if the common information can be manipulated to a form that is similar in appearance to the entry in one or both of the columns.

Example

Column A	Column B

$$24x = 18y$$

$$4x \qquad\qquad 3y$$

Solution

Dividing both sides of the given information by 6 gives us $4x = 3y$. Therefore, very quickly, we can see the answer to the problem is (C).

Example

Column A	Column B
	$5x + y = 12$
$10x + 2y$	25

Solution

If we double both sides of the equation in the given information, we obtain $10x + 2y = 24$. Thus, the value of the quantity in Column A is 24, and the correct answer is (B).

When either or both of the column entries contain variables, it is often very helpful to substitute numerical values for these variables and observe what happens. Any substitution you make will enable you to eliminate two of the possible answer choices. Suppose, for example, that you plug a value into the quantities, and, for this particular value, the quantity in Column A turns out to be larger. This means that the correct answer cannot be (B) or (C). Either A is always larger (A), or sometimes larger (D).

To try to determine which of the two remaining choices is correct, select several other values for the unknowns. Be sure to choose different types of numbers: negatives, fractions, big numbers, small numbers. One and zero are also good values to try. If, for any of these values, Column A is *not* larger than Column B, then the answer is (D). If (A) is larger for all sets of values you try, you can be fairly certain that the correct answer is (A).

Example

Column A	Column B
	$x > 0$
$\dfrac{1}{2}$	$\dfrac{1}{1 + \dfrac{1}{x}}$

Solution

If, for example, $x = 1$, the quantity in Column B is equal to $\dfrac{1}{2}$, and the quantity in Column A is the same size as that in Column B. If, on the other hand, $x = 2$, the quantity in Column B is equal to $\dfrac{2}{3}$, and the entry in Column B is larger. Clearly, then, there is no way to determine the size relationship between the two columns. The correct answer is (D).

Remember that powers of, roots of, and divisions by numbers between 0 and 1 behave differently than those greater than 1. For example, if you square a number larger than 1, the resulting number is larger than the original; yet, if you square a number less than 1, the resulting number is smaller than the original. Also remember that powers of even and odd numbers behave differently. The examples below illustrate some of these variations.

Example

Column A	Column B
y^2	y^3

$$y > 0$$

Solution

Common sense would indicate that the entry in Column B is larger, but if $0 < y < 1$, this is not true. Say, for example, $y = \dfrac{1}{2}$. Then, $y^2 = \dfrac{1}{4}$, and $y^3 = \dfrac{1}{8}$. Further, if $y = 1$, both entries are the same size. The correct answer is (D).

Example

Column A	Column B
y^2	y^3

$$y > 1$$

Solution

If we know, however, that $y > 1$, then we *can* conclude that $y^3 > y^2$. The correct answer is (B).

Example

Column A	Column B
$\sqrt{0.4}$	0.4

Solution

When you take the square root of a decimal number between 0 and 1, it actually gets larger. The correct answer is (A).

Now, here are some additional Quantitative Comparison problems for you to practice with.

QUANTITATIVE COMPARISON PRACTICE PROBLEMS

Each of the following questions consists of two quantities, one in Column A and one in Column B. You are to compare the two quantities and choose

(A) if the quantity in Column A is greater;
(B) if the quantity in Column B is greater;
(C) if the two quantities are equal;
(D) if the relationship cannot be determined from the information given.

Note: Since there are only four choices, NEVER MARK (E).

Numbers: All numbers used are real numbers.

Figures: Position of points, angles, regions, etc., can be assumed to be in the order shown, and angle measures can be assumed to be positive.

Lines shown as straight can be assumed to be straight.

Figures can be assumed to lie in a plane unless otherwise indicated.

Figures that accompany questions are intended to provide information useful in answering the questions. However, unless a note states that a figure is drawn to scale, you should solve these problems NOT by estimating sizes by sight or by measurement, but by using your knowledge of mathematics.

	Column A	**Column B**
1.	$\dfrac{10}{\frac{1}{2}}$	$\dfrac{1}{2}(10)$

2.

n is an even number

0	$(-1)^{n-1}$

3.

$$ab = 12$$
$$(a + b)^2 = 64$$

24	$a^2 + b^2$

	Column A	**Column B**

4. In triangle PQR, the length of side
PQ is 10 and the length of side QR is 8

The length of side PR 16

---

5. $x > 0$

18 percent of x 9 percent of $2x$

---

6. $x^2 + 3x - 10 = 0$

x 2

---

7. $7(a - b) = 28$

$3(a - b)$ 10

8.
$$a = \left(\frac{7}{8}\right)c$$
$$b = \left(\frac{8}{7}\right)c$$

$$\frac{b}{\left(\frac{1}{a}\right)} \qquad\qquad c^2$$

---

9. The average (arithmetic mean)
of a, b, and c is a $0 > 0$, $b > 0$

a c

---

10. $(0.753)^2$ $\sqrt{0.753}$

Solutions

1. **The correct answer is (A).** As far as Column A is concerned, $\dfrac{10}{\frac{1}{2}} = 10 \times \dfrac{2}{1}$. In Column B, we have $\dfrac{1}{2}(10) = 5$.

2. **The correct answer is (A).** If n is even, then $n-1$ is odd, and $(-1)^{n-1} = -1$, which is less than 0.

3. **The correct answer is (B).** Begin by working with the given information. Since $(a + b)^2 = 64$, we have $a^2 + 2ab + b^2 = 64$. Further, since $ab = 12$, $2ab = 24$. Thus, $a^2 + 24 + b^2 = 64$, or $a^2 + b^2 = 40$. Clearly, then, Column B is larger than Column A.

4. **The correct answer is (D).** This is a tricky question. If we assume that triangle PQR is a right triangle, with an hypotenuse of 10, then we could compute PR to be 6. But we do not know that the triangle is right, and even if we did, we don't know which side is the hypotenuse. In fact, all we can conclude is that PR is somewhere between $10 - 8 = 2$ and $10 + 8 = 18$. So, PR could be either smaller or bigger than 16.

5. **The correct answer is (C).** 18% of x = 18% $\times x = \dfrac{18x}{100}$.

   Similarly, 9% of $2x$ = 9% $\times 2x = \dfrac{9}{100} \times 2x = \dfrac{9 \times 2x}{100} = \dfrac{18x}{100}$.

6. **The correct answer is (D).** Begin by solving the equation in the common information:
   $$x^2 + 3x - 10 = 0$$
   $$(x + 5)(x - 2) = 0$$
   $$x = -5, +2$$

   Thus, x is either less than the entry in Column B, or equal to it.

7. **The correct answer is (A).** Given that $7(a - b) = 28$, we see that $(a - b) = 4$. Thus, $3(a - b) = 3 \times 4 = 12$.

8. **The correct answer is (C).** First note that $\dfrac{b}{\left(\frac{1}{a}\right)} = b \times a = ab$.

   Now, take the two equations in the common information and multiply them together, the left side to the left side, and the right to the right. We then get $ab = \left(\dfrac{7}{8}\right)c \times \left(\dfrac{8}{7}\right)c = c^2$.

9. **The correct answer is (A).** If the average of a, b, and c is 0, and a and b are positive, then c must be negative. If c is negative, it is smaller than a.

10. **The correct answer is (B).** Remember that when you square a number between 0 and 1 it gets smaller, whereas, when you take the square root of a number between 0 and 1 it gets larger.

DATA SUFFICIENCY QUESTIONS

The GMAT contains a type of special format question called "Data Sufficiency." As with the Quantitative Comparison questions on the GRE, Data Sufficiency questions adhere to their own logical format that may initially seem rather confusing but actually is quite easy to understand once studied. Each GMAT CAT test contains approximately fifteen Data Sufficiency questions. *Note that Data Sufficiency questions appear only on the GMAT. If you are taking the MCAT or the GRE, you can skip this section.*

A Data Sufficiency problem always begins with an open–ended question that cannot possibly be answered. Some sample questions of this type are "Is x bigger than y?," "Is rectangle ABCD a square?," and "Does an apple cost more than an orange?" After the question is posed, the problem then gives you two additional statements, numbered (1) and (2), that contain information that relates to the question. In order to solve the problem, you need to determine whether either or both of the two additional statements give you enough information to answer the question posed.

Such a problem is a bit unusual in that you do not actually need to find the answer to the question being asked; you just need to determine if there is sufficient information for you to answer the question. However, the answer scheme seems a bit confusing at first. An answer of (A) indicates that it is possible to answer the question using just given information (1), but it is not possible to answer the question using just given information (2). An answer of (B) indicates the reverse: given information (2) is sufficient to answer the question, but given information (1) is not. If both pieces of given information can be used separately to answer the question, then the answer is (D). If neither piece of information is sufficient to answer the question, then you must take them together and see if you can answer the question. If both pieces of information taken together enable you to answer the question, then the correct answer is (C). If, however, even using both pieces of information, you still cannot answer the question, then the correct answer is (E).

Clearly, in order to answer a Data Sufficiency question, you must have an organized method of attack. The following procedure is the most effective one to use:

Begin by reading the question and given information (1) only. Then, determine if you can answer the question based on given information (1). If you can answer the question, write the letter "S" (which stands for *sufficient*) next to the (1). On the other hand, if given information (1) is not enough to enable you to answer the question, then put an I (which stands for *insufficient*) next to the (1).

Now, *completely forget* the information contained in (1), and read given information (2). As above, mark the (2) with an S if given information (2) *by itself* is enough to enable you to answer the question. Mark the (2) with an I if it is insufficient.

If you have followed the two steps above then your paper will look like one of the four possibilities below:

S (1)	I (1)	I (1)	S (1)
I (2)	S (2)	I (2)	S (2)

In the first case, the answer to the problem will be (A) (first statement sufficient, second statement insufficient). In the second case, the answer to the problem will be (B) (first statement insufficient, second statement sufficient). In the *fourth* case, the answer to the problem will be (D) (both statements are sufficient by themselves).

In case number three (both statements by themselves are insufficient), you have one more step to go. For the first time, you must consider the two statements together and determine whether you can answer the question if you know both statements. If both statements together enable you to answer the question, then the answer is (C). Otherwise, the answer is (E).

$$S \begin{cases} I \ (1) \\ I \ (2) \end{cases} \qquad I \begin{cases} I \ (1) \\ I \ (2) \end{cases}$$

Answer: C   Answer: E

In order to help you understand the data sufficiency answering scheme, five solved problems are given below. Note that these problems have been arranged so that the correct answer to the first one is (A), the correct answer to the second one is (B), and so on.

1. The total weight of three boxes is 32 pounds. How much does the heaviest package weigh?

   (1) One of the boxes weighs 18 pounds.
   (2) One of the boxes weighs 7 pounds.

   The correct answer is (A). Statement 1 gives us enough information to answer the question, since if one box weighs 18 pounds, the combined weight of the other two packages must be $32 - 18 = 14$ pounds. Therefore, the heaviest box is, in fact, 18 pounds. As far as statement (2) is concerned, knowing that one of the boxes weighs 7 pounds certainly does not tell us how much the heaviest box weighs.

2. Given that n is an integer, is n even?

   (1) $2n$ is even
   (2) n^3 is even

   The correct answer is (B). Statement (1) is insufficient since $2n$ is even (divisible by 2) regardless of the value of n. However, the only way n^3 can be even (divisible by 2) is if n were even to begin with.

3. A cabinet is designed to hold, at most, 24 compact discs. How many discs are in the cabinet?

   (1) The number of disks in the cabinet is divisible by 3.
   (2) The number of disks in the cabinet is divisible by 5.

   The correct answer is (C). Statement 1 does not give us enough information to answer the question, since the number of discs in the cabinet could be 3, 6, 9, 12, and so on. Statement 2 does not give us enough information to answer the question, since the number of discs in the cabinet could be 5, 10, 15, or 20. However, if we take both statements together, we know that the number of discs in the cabinet must be 15, since this is the only number less than 24 that is divisible by both 3 and 5.

4. During a sale, the price of a shirt is marked down by 10 percent. How much is the sale price of the shirt?

   (1) The price was reduced by $7.
   (2) The original price was $70.

   The correct answer is (D). Statement (1) tells us that 10 percent of the price of the shirt is $7. This means the original price of the shirt was $70, and the sale price was $63. Statement (2) tells us that the original price of the shirt was $70; with a 10 percent discount, the sale price would be $63.

5. What number is Gus thinking of?

   (1) The number he is thinking of is less than 7.
   (2) The number he is thinking of is more than 5.

   The correct answer is (E). Be very careful with this question. While statements (1) and (2) together may make it appear as if the number is 6, nowhere does it says that the number Gus is thinking of is an integer. Perhaps he is thinking of $5\frac{1}{2}$ or $6\frac{1}{4}$. There is no way to tell what number he is thinking of.

Now that we have gotten a feel for the five different answer choices, let's take at look at the instructions the way they will appear on the GMAT.

Directions: Each of the data sufficiency problems below consists of a question and two statements, labeled (1) and (2), in which certain data are given. You have to decide whether the data given in the statements are *sufficient* for answering the question. Using the data given in the statements *plus* your knowledge of mathematics and everyday facts (such as the number of days in July or the meaning of counterclockwise), you must indicate whether

- statement (1) ALONE is sufficient, but statement (2) alone is not sufficient to answer the question asked;
- statement (2) ALONE is sufficient, but statement (1) alone is not sufficient to answer the question asked;
- BOTH statements (1) and (2) TOGETHER are sufficient to answer the question asked, but NEITHER statement ALONE is sufficient;
- EACH statement ALONE is sufficient to answer the question asked;
- statements (1) and (2) TOGETHER are NOT sufficient to answer the question asked, and additional data specific to the problem are *needed.*

Numbers: All numbers are real numbers.

Figures: A figure accompanying a data sufficiency problem will conform to the information given in the question, but will not necessarily conform to the additional information given in statements (1) and (2).

Lines shown as straight can be assumed to be straight and lines that appear jagged can also be assumed to be straight.

You may assume that the position of points, angles, regions, etc., exists in the order shown and that angle measures are greater than zero.

All figures lie in a plane unless otherwise indicated.

Note: In data sufficiency problems that ask for the value of a quantity, the data given in the statements are sufficient only when it is possible to determine exactly one numerical value for the quantity.

Here are some things to keep in mind as you answer Data Sufficiency questions.

1. Remember that your goal is just to determine whether you actually have enough information to answer the question. You do not actually have to answer it. Never waste your time trying to find the numerical answer. Stop once you have determined whether it is possible to find it or not. (Note that in the sample problems that follow, the solutions do show how to find the answers to the questions. This is just for illustration. It is perfectly fine for you to stop working as soon as you determine that it is or isn't possible to find the answer.)

2. Remember that both statements (1) and (2) must be examined separately before you consider them together. When analyzing statement (1), be sure not to read statement (2). Similarly, when analyzing statement (2), be sure to ignore the information in statement (1). Only consider the statements together after you have determined that they are both insufficient.

3. Many of the Data Sufficiency questions on the GMAT ask if you can determine the *value* of a certain quantity. Remember that for this type of question, a statement (or combination of statements) is sufficient only if it enables you to determine a *single* unique numerical value. Statements that determine two values or a range of values are not sufficient.

Example 1

What is the value of x?

(1) $8x = 24$
(2) $4x < 24$

The correct answer is (A). Statement (1) is sufficient since it tells us that x is 3. Statement (2) is insufficient since it only tells us that x is a number less than 6.

Example 2

What is the value of x?

(1) $x = 2y$
(2) $x^2 = 25$

The correct answer is (E). Statement (1) is insufficient; it only tells us that x varies as y varies. Statement (2) is also insufficient since it tells us that x is either 5 or -5. Even together, we cannot determine the value of x.

Example 3

What is the value of x?

(1) $2x + 3y = 12$
(2) $x - y = 6$

The correct answer is (C). Statement (1) is insufficient since without knowing the value of y, it is impossible to determine a numerical value for x. Statement (2) is insufficient for the same reason. However, when you take (1) and (2) together, you obtain a system of simultaneous equations which can be solved for x.

Typically, when each statement either gives you or contains the information to write an equation with two unknowns, the answer will be (C), as above. However, look out for examples like those below.

Example 4

What is the value of x?

(1) $2x + 2y = 12$
(2) $3x + 3y = 18$

The correct answer is (E). Statement (1) is insufficient since without knowing the value of y, it is impossible to determine a numerical value for x. Statement (2) is insufficient for the same reason. When you take (1) and (2) together, you still cannot determine x since (1) and (2), in fact, contain different forms of the same equation.

Example 5

What is the value of $5x - 7y$?

(1) $x + y = 6$
(2) $10x - 14y = 22$

The correct answer is (B). Statement (1) is insufficient since without knowing the value of y, it is impossible to determine a numerical value for x. Statement (2), however, is sufficient since, if you divide both sides of the equation by 2, you obtain $5x - 7y = 11$.

4. Another common type of data sufficiency question on the GMAT asks if a certain quantity has a certain value ("Is $y = 12$?") or if a certain geometric figure has a certain shape ("Is quadrilateral ABCD a rectangle?"). Remember that in questions of this type, "Is . . . ?," means "Does it absolutely have to be?," rather than, "Could it possibly be?"

The best way to approach these questions is to read one of the statements, then reread the question. If your answer to the question is, "Yes, it has to be," then the statement is sufficient. If, one the other hand, your answer is "Maybe it is, or maybe it isn't," then the statement is insufficient.

Example 6

Is $x = 0$?

(1)   The sum of x and 9 is 9
(2)   The product of x and 0 is 0.

The correct answer is (A). Statement (1) tells us that $x + 9 = 9$. The only solution to this equation is $x = 0$, so statement (1) is sufficient. Statement (2) tells us that $x \times 0 = 0$. In this case, x could be 0, but it could also be any other number.

Example 7

Is triangle ABC a right triangle?

(1)   The measure of angle A is 25°
(2)   The measure of angle B is 65°

The correct answer is (C). Neither statement (1) by itself, nor statement (2) by itself, is sufficient since the knowledge of one of the angles of a triangle is not enough to tell us what the other angles are. If, however, we take the two statements together, we can determine if the triangle is a right triangle, since if we know two angles, we can determine the third.

5. Sometimes, when solving a data sufficiency question, you will find yourself unsure of whether one of the two given statements is sufficient or insufficient. Note that in any problem where you know the status of one of the statements but do not know the status of the other, you are, in fact, able to make an extremely educated guess that will greatly improve your chances of selecting the correct answer.

In the situations described below, you are able to eliminate all but two of the possible answers.

Situation 1: If you are certain that statement (1) is sufficient but are unsure about statement (2), then the only possible answers are (A) or (D).

    S   (1)
    ?   (2)

Guess (A) or (D)

Situation 2: If you are certain that statement (2) is sufficient but are unsure about statement (1), then the only possible answers are (B) or (D).

    ?   (1)
    S   (2)

Guess (B) or (D)

Situation 3: If you are certain that each statement alone is insufficient but are unsure about both statements together, then the only possible answers are (C) or (E).

    I   (1)
    ?
    I   (2)

Guess (C) or (E)

In the situations described below, you are able to eliminate only two of the possible answers, but it is generally still in your benefit to guess.

Situation 4: If you are certain that statement (1) is insufficient but are unsure about statement (2), then the only possible answers are (B), (C), or (E).

I   (1)

?   (2)

Guess (B), (C), or (E)

Situation 5: If you are certain that statement (2) is insufficient but are unsure about statement (1), then the only possible answers are (A), (C), or (E).

?   (1)

I   (2)

Guess (A), (C), or (E)

DATA SUFFICIENCY PRACTICE PROBLEMS

1. A piece of rope 17 feet long is cut into three pieces. What is the length of the longest piece?
   (1) One piece is 4 feet long.
   (2) One piece is 9 feet long.

2. What is the value of $x^4 + y^5$?
   (1) $x + 3y = 12$
   (2) $3x + y = 11$

3. What is the length of the edge of cube C?
   (1) The volume of the cube is 64 cubic feet.
   (2) The surface area of the cube is 96 square feet.

4. If V, W, X, Y, and Z are five consecutive positive integers, what is the value of Z?
   (1) V is prime.
   (2) V is even.

5. How long will it take Jimmy to run around a track if he runs at a constant rate of 6 minutes per mile?
   (1) The track is 3 miles long.
   (2) Bobby ran around the track for 30 minutes running at a constant rate of 10 minutes per mile.

6. If $y = 3$, what is the value of x?
   (1) $4x^2 + y^2 = -4xy$
   (2) $x < 0$

7. Four employees, A, B, C, and D, are voted bonuses by the Board of Directors. If there is $31,000 in bonus money available, who received the largest bonus?
   (1) D received a bonus of $8,000.
   (2) A received a bonus of $9,000, and D received $1,000 more than each of B and C.

8. What is the area of triangle ABC?
   (1) Angle B and angle C are complementary.
   (2) AC is twice the length of AB, and CB = 20.

9. How many nickels and dimes does Ben have on his desk?
   (1) The total value of the coins on Ben's desk is $3.25.
   (2) There are only nickels and dimes on Ben's desk.

10. If $PQRST$ represents a 5-digit integer, what is the value of T?
    (1) $PQRST$ is divisible by 5.
    (2) $PQRST$ is divisible by 2.

SOLUTIONS

1. **The correct answer is (B).** This is a tricky question. Initially, it may appear that the answer is (C) since, if we know that one piece of rope is 4 feet and one piece is 9 feet, we can find the length of the third piece and therefore determine which piece is the longest. However, consider given information (2). If we know that one of the pieces is 9 feet long, the other two pieces together must total $17 - 9 = 8$ feet. Clearly, then, the piece of rope that is 9 feet long must be the longest. Given information (1), however, simply tells us that the other two pieces must total $17 - 4 = 13$ feet, and gives us no way to determine the length of the longest piece.

2. **The correct answer is (C).** Given information (1) is insufficient, since it does not give us enough information to determine the actual values of x and y, which we would need to evaluate $x^4 + y^5$. For the same reason, (2) is insufficient. However, if we take (1) and (2) together, we have two equations in two unknowns, and we can determine the actual values of x and y. Therefore, we can compute the value of $x^4 + y^5$ if we have information (1) and (2).

3. **The correct answer is (D).** The formula for the volume of a cube is $V = e^3$, where e is the length of the edge. Since given information (1) tells us that the volume is 64, we have $64 = e^3$, which tells us that e is 4. Thus, (1) is sufficient. Similarly, if we know the surface area of a cube, we can also find the length of an edge. In this problem, we are told that the surface area is 96. Since a cube has 6 surfaces, the area of each surface must be $96 \div 6 = 16$. The surfaces of a cube are squares and so each edge must be 4. Therefore, (2) is sufficient as well.

4. **The correct answer is (C).** Given information (1) is insufficient, since V can be any prime number whatsoever, and so Z could be many different possible integers. Given information (2) is also insufficient, as V could be any even number, again allowing Z to be many different possible integers. However, if we take the two statements together, we can conclude that V must be the number 2, since 2 is the only number which is both prime and even. This would enable us to determine that Z is 6.

5. **The correct answer is (D).** Given information (1) is sufficient since if we know how long the track is and how fast Jimmy runs, we can determine how long it will take him to run around the track. In particular, at 6 minutes per mile, it will take him 18 minutes to run around the track. Given information (2) is also sufficient. If it takes Bobby 30 minutes to run around the track at a rate of 10 minutes per mile, we can conclude that the track is three miles long. As with given information (1), this is enough for us to determine the amount of time Jimmy needs to run around the track.

6. **The correct answer is (A).** Taking the fact that $y = 3$, and substituting into $4x^2 + y^2 = -4xy$ gives us $4x^2 + 9 = -12x$, or $4x^2 + 12x + 9 = 0$. The trinomial on the left factors into a perfect square: $(2x + 3)^2 = 0$. Thus, $x = -\frac{3}{2}$. Given information (2) is useless on its own.

7. **The correct answer is (B).** Given information (1) only tells us the value of D's bonus, but it does not give us enough information to determine the value of any of the other bonuses. However, if we know that A received a bonus of $9,000, we know that B, C, and D shared the remaining $22,000. We also know that B and C received the same bonus. If we call the amount of this bonus B, we know that D got a bonus of B + 1,000. We can therefore write the equation B + B + B + 1,000 = 22,000. Solving this reveals that B = $7,000, and the amount of the other bonuses follows from this.

8. **The correct answer is (C).** Given information (1) enables us to determine that angle A is a right angle. By itself, this will not tell us the area of the triangle. Information (2) also is not sufficient to answer the question; without any information about the angles of the triangle, there are many possible areas. However, if we take both pieces of given information together, we can find the area. First of all, since the triangle is right, we can use the Pythagorean theorem to help find the length of the sides. Side CB is opposite right angle A, so the hypotenuse is 20. Let the length of side AB be equal to x; then, the length of side AC is equal to $2x$. We then have

$$x^2 + (2x)^2 = 20^2$$
$$x^2 + 4x^2 = 400$$
$$5x^2 = 400$$
$$x^2 = 80$$
$$x = \sqrt{80} = 4\sqrt{5},$$

and therefore the lengths of the legs of the triangle are $4\sqrt{5}$ and $8\sqrt{5}$.

Now, since in a right triangle the legs are perpendicular to each other, we can consider one leg to be the base and the other to be the height in the area formula. Thus,

$$A = \frac{1}{2}bh = \frac{1}{2}(4\sqrt{5})(8\sqrt{5}) = 80.$$

9. **The correct answer is (E).** Taking given information (1) and (2) together, we can determine that Ben has $3.25 on his desk, and that this is entirely made up of nickels and dimes. However, this is not enough to tell us how many nickels and dimes he has. For example, he could have 32 dimes and 1 nickel, or 31 dimes and 3 nickels, and so on.

10. **The correct answer is (C).** Information (1) tells us that T is either 0 or 5. Information (2) tells us that T is either 0, 2, 4, 6, or 8. Taking the two pieces of information together, we can determine that T is 0.

DATA INTERPRETATION

The math section of the GRE contains Data Interpretation questions and they always have the same format. Prior to the questions, you will be given one (or sometimes more than one) table or graph. The questions that follow are based on the table or graph.

The math topics that you will need to know in order to answer the questions have already been discussed; in fact, the questions typically involve only arithmetic computations with decimals and percents. However, before you can begin to answer the questions, you must be able to understand and interpret the table or graph. In this section, we will discuss the types of tables and graphs that you might see on the GRE. *Note that while the MCAT and the GMAT do not specifically contain a section of questions on table or graph interpretation, it is quite possible that tables and graphs will appear somewhere on the tests. Therefore, it would be a good idea to read the following section regardless of the test you are taking.*

CIRCLE GRAPHS

The purpose of a circle graph is to take an entire quantity and break it down into its component parts, showing their relative sizes on a percentage basis. For example, a circle graph might take a company's monthly budget and break it down into its various parts—salaries, benefits, office supplies, advertising, etc. Or a circle graph might take the total revenue of a retail store and break it down into revenue by department.

In a circle graph, also known as a pie chart, the circle is used to represent the whole quantity. This whole quantity is cut into pieces, called sectors, each piece representing a certain percentage of the total. The size of the piece, of course, is proportional to the size of the percentage, and the percentages must add up to 100%.

Examples

Questions 1–3 are based on the graph below.

Action Athletics – Apparel Revenue

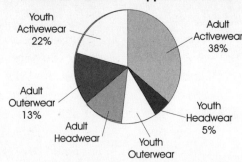

1. If Action Athletics had $320,320 in Youth Activewear revenue, what was its total apparel revenue?

2. If Action Athletics had $174,720 in Adult Headwear revenue, what percent of its apparel revenue was from Adult Headwear?

3. What was Action Athletics' revenue from Youth Outerwear?

Solutions

1. In this percent problem, we are given that the part is $320,320. From the graph, we see that the rate is 22%. We need to find the total revenue, or the base.

    $$B = \frac{P}{R} = \frac{320{,}320}{22\%} = \frac{320{,}320}{.22} = 1{,}456{,}000$$

    Therefore, the total revenue is $1,456,000

2. In this percent problem, we are given that the part is 174,720. We computed that the base was 1,456,000 in problem 1 above. Therefore,

    $$R = \frac{P}{B} = \frac{174{,}720}{1{,}456{,}000} = .12 = 12\%$$

    Therefore, the percent of the revenue received from adult headwear is 12%.

3. Notice that the percentage for youth outerwear is missing from the graph. However, we can determine it by adding up all of the percentages given (remember that we computed that the adult headwear percent is 12% in problem #2), and subtracting from 100 percent. Doing this, we determine that the youth outerwear percent is 10%. Clearly, then, the revenue from youth outerwear is

    $$1{,}456{,}000 \times 10\% = \$145{,}600$$

LINE GRAPHS

The purpose of a line graph is to show the change in the value of a certain quantity (or quantities) over a period of time. Typically, the period of time is indicated along a horizontal line called the *x*-axis, while the value of the quantity being measured is indicated along a vertical line called the *y*-axis. By drawing a line in the region between the *x*- and *y*- axes, the changes in the value of the quantity being measured can be depicted. The purpose of a line graph, is to show trends in quantities over a period of time.

It is often a bit difficult to read exact values from a line graph, since the scale is usually marked in large increments, the lines are often thick, and the point being read is often far from the scale. If you are having trouble reading a particular value, estimate its value to the nearest whole number possible. Typically, the answer choices are spread out in a wide enough range so that even when you use a quick estimate, you should be able to tell which answer choice is correct.

Examples

Questions 4–6 are based on the graph below.

Investment Banking Revenues

($ Millions)

4. By how much did Investment Banking Revenues increase from 1996 to 1999?

5. What was the ratio of Investment Banking Revenues in 1998 to Investment Banking Revenues in 1996?

6. Approximately what was the percent of increase in Investment Banking Revenues from 1998 to 1999?

Solutions

4. The revenue in 1999 is given as $2,700. The revenue from 1996 is given as $1,100. The increase in revenue, then, is $2,700 - 1,100 = \$1,600$.

5. The ratio is 2,200 to 1,100, which is the same as 2 to 1.

6. The amount of the increase from 1998 to 1999 is $2,700 - 2,200 = 500$. The percent of increase is found by taking the change divided by the original value and multiplying by 100%.

$$\text{Percent of increase} = \frac{500}{2,200} \times 100\%,$$

which is approximately 23%.

BAR GRAPHS

While bar graphs are often used to show changes over time (similar to the line graph), they can also be used to simply depict a comparison of quantities. When doing this, the bars can either be drawn horizontally or vertically. The length or height of the bar is proportional to the size of the quantity being represented.

Examples

Questions 7–10 are based on the graph below.

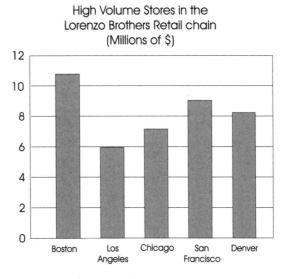

High Volume Stores in the
Lorenzo Brothers Retail chain
(Millions of $)

7. The Boston store's volume was approximately how much more than that of the Chicago store?

8. Of the stores shown, how many had a volume of more than $8 million?

9. What was the average volume of the five stores shown?

10. Approximately what was the ratio of the volume of the San Francisco store to that of the Los Angeles store?

Solutions

7. 11 million − 7 million = 4 million.

8. As the graph clearly shows, Boston, San Francisco, and Denver had volumes of more than 8 million.

9. The average volume is computed as $\dfrac{(11 + 6 + 7 + 9 + 8.5)}{5} = \dfrac{41.5}{5} = 8.3$, and is approximately $8.3 million.

10. The ratio is 9 to 6, which is the same as 3 to 2.

RED 69 **ALERT**

A special type of bar graph, called a *multiple* bar graph, can be used to compare two sets of data. The graph below, for example, shows that 86.8% of the male population 16 years and over was in the labor force in 1950. In that same year, 33.9% of the female population was in the labor force.

Percentage of Population 16 Years Old
and Over in the Labor Force

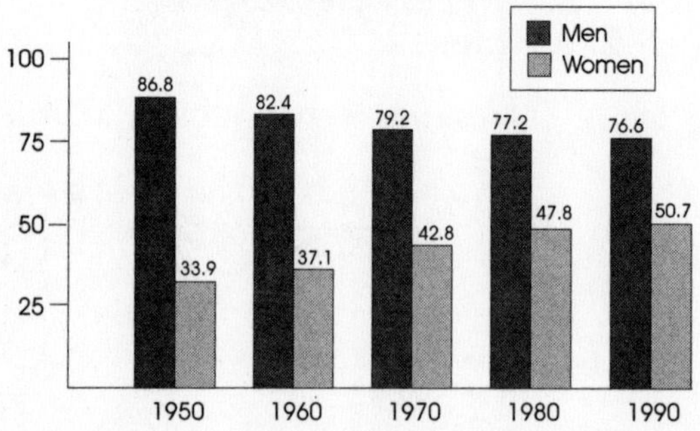

Example

If, in 1960, there were 90 million men 16 years or older, and 100 million women 16 years or older, approximately how many more men than women were in the labor force in 1960?

Solution

The number of men in the labor force in 1960 would be approximately 90 × 82.4%, which is approximately 74.2 million men. The number of women in the labor force would be approximately 100 × 37.1% = 37.1 million women. Therefore, there were 74.2 − 37.1 = 37.1 million more men than women in the workforce in 1960.

Another common type of bar graph is called a cumulative bar graph. In such a graph, each bar contains more than one kind of information and the total height is the sum of the various components. The following graph represents the percent of persons 25 years old and over who were high school (top part) and college graduates (bottom part), by region: 1970, 1980, and 1990.

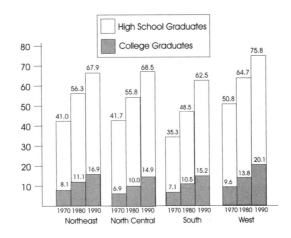

Examples

1. For each of the 3 years, which region consistently has the lowest percentage of college graduates?

2. Which region has the lowest *total* educational attainment for each of the 3 years?

3. In 1990, which region had the highest percentage of high school graduates, and what was it?

4. Which region had the greatest increase in the percentage of college graduates between 1980 and 1990?

Solutions

1. North Central

2. The South

3. For 1990, subtract the percent for college graduates from the total percent; four subtractions. The highest is the West, with 75.8% − 20.1% = 55.7%

4. The West, with 20.1% − 13.8% = 6.3%

RED 71 ALERT

TABLES

Tables present data corresponding to classifications by row and column. Tables always state the units (thousands of people, years, millions of dollars, for example) in which the numbers are expressed. Sometimes the units are percentages. Both specific and general questions can be answered by using the information in the table.

Examples

1. What language is spoken at home by almost one-half of those not speaking English at home?

2. What language has the highest percentage of its speakers in the 45- to 64-year-old age bracket?

3. How many persons between the ages of 18 and 24 speak Korean at home?

Persons 5 Years Old and Over Speaking Various Languages at Home, by Age: November 1995
(Numbers in thousands: civilian noninstitutional population)

Language spoken at home	Persons 5 years old and over	Total %	5 to 13 years	14 to 17 years	18 to 24 years	25 to 44 years	45 to 64 years	65 to 74 years	75 years and over
Total	200,812	*	30,414	15,955	27,988	59,385	43,498	15,053	8,519
Percent	*	100.0	15.1	7.9	13.9	29.6	21.7	7.5	4.2
Speaking English only	176,319	100.0	15.4	8.0	14.1	29.5	21.5	7.4	4.0
Speaking other language	17,985	100.0	14.4	6.9	12.6	30.8	21.8	7.5	6.0
Chinese	514	100.0	12.5	5.8	15.8	34.8	21.2	6.8	3.1
French	987	100.0	8.1	5.5	10.2	29.9	30.4	9.9	6.0
German	1,261	100.0	5.4	7.1	10.8	24.3	27.4	12.8	12.2
Greek	365	100.0	16.7	4.9	10.4	38.1	21.9	4.4	3.6
Italian	1,354	100.0	7.5	4.9	8.1	19.3	31.5	15.1	13.7
Japanese	265	100.0	7.9	6.8	7.9	27.2	36.6	9.4	3.8
Korean	191	100.0	16.2	5.8	17.8	35.6	19.9	3.7	1.0
Philippine languages	419	100.0	10.7	5.3	8.6	40.8	20.3	7.2	6.9
Polish	731	100.0	2.7	1.4	3.7	13.8	45.7	21.6	10.9
Portuguese	245	100.0	15.9	8.6	12.2	33.9	22.0	3.7	3.3
Spanish	8,768	100.0	20.2	8.8	15.4	34.6	15.8	3.1	2.2
Yiddish	234	100.0	8.5	0.4	3.0	15.8	20.9	29.1	21.8
Other	2,651	100.0	10.0	4.9	10.8	30.3	23.3	10.1	10.6
Not reported	6,508	100.0	11.1	8.4	13.5	26.9	25.1	9.5	5.6

(Notice that in this table the numbers are given in thousands, so that the number speaking German at home, for example, is not 1261 but 1,261,000.)

Solutions

1. Spanish; 8,768/17,985 is about 48%.

2. Polish, with 45.7%.

3. There are 191,000 of all ages speaking Korean, of which 17.8% are between 18 and 24:

   $.178 \times 191,000 = 33,998$ persons

STRATEGIES AND SUGGESTIONS FOR ANSWERING DATA INTERPRETATION QUESTIONS

Be sure to take as much time as necessary to understand exactly what information presented in the graph or table before you begin to answer the questions. Since there are typically five questions based on each graph, if you misinterpret the graph you may get all five questions wrong. Do not try to understand an entire graph at once. Instead, try to understand each component one at a time. Be sure to analyze:

- The title of the graph
- Any subtitles or legends
- The values represented along the x-axis or y-axis of a bar or line graph, or by the sectors of a circle graph
- Keys indicating what various symbols or shadings represent.
- Dates or other units of time
- The units of measurement used

The type of graph drawn will help you analyze the message that the graph is showing. A line graph depicts the change in a number of quantities over time. A bar graph either also depicts a change over time or compares the values of a variety of items. A circle graph is used to break down a whole into its component parts as percentages.

If a question involves more than one graph, be sure to look at the appropriate graph for the question being asked.

Remember that you can use the edge of your answer sheet like a ruler to help read data values off a line or a bar graph.

Before beginning to work on a question, take a quick look at the multiple-choice answers. Not only might they give you some idea of how to proceed, but they will also tell you the extent to which you can estimate your answer.

Sometimes the numbers used in graphs and tables can get very large. To save yourself computation time, use the units along the axes and write the number out in full only at the end. For example, if a problem involves adding the two numbers 5 and 7, and the legend says "all numbers in millions," don't write the numbers out in full and then add. Instead, add 5 and 7 to get 12, and, recognizing that this represents 12 million, write it out in full (12,000,000) at the end.

Sometimes, when working with graphs, it is possible to visualize an answer instead of actually computing it out. For example, if a problem involves a line graph and asks you for the average of the values in 1998 and 1999, simply locate the point midway between the two axes and read it off the graph.

Sometimes a data interpretation question will ask you to make an inference. For example, you might be asked, "If the trend depicted in the graph continues at the same pace, what would you predict for the value in 5 years?" Be sure that when you answer such a question, you only use information contained in the graph, and not any outside information that you may have about the quantities involved in the graph.

Sometimes data interpretation questions can be answered without doing any computations. Questions of the type, "In how many years was the total budget larger than $40,000?" can typically be answered just by looking at the graph. Always try to answer such questions before spending time on ones that require computation and therefore are more time-consuming.

Never do more computations than required. For example, if you are asked to find the ratio of two pieces of a circle graph, simply find the ratio of their percents. You do not have to compute the actual value first.

Try to consider the strategies above and the math reviewed in previous chapters as you try the problems below.

TABLES AND GRAPHS PROBLEMS

Use the circle graph below to answer questions 1-5.

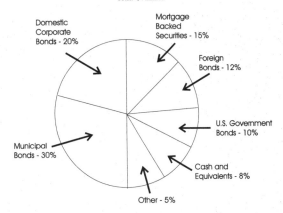

Composition of Invested Assets and Cash
December 31, 1999
Total: $4 million

1. According to the graph above, how much was invested in Mortgage Backed Securities?

2. What is the total amount invested in Domestic Corporate Bonds and Foreign Bonds?

3. How much more is invested in Municipal Bonds than in U.S. Government Bonds?

4. Next year, the amount invested in Foreign Bonds is expected to increase by 35%. How much is expected to be invested in Foreign Bonds next year?

5. Next year, Foreign Bonds are expected to make up 10% of the Total Investment in Assets and Cash. What is the projected Total Investment for next year?

Use the bar graph below to answer questions 6–10.

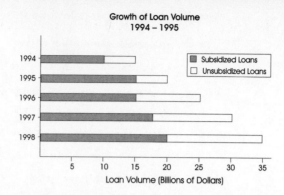

6. Approximately what was the loan volume for unsubsidized loans in 1996?

7. By how much was the volume for subsidized loans greater than the volume for unsubsidized loans in 1995?

8. Approximately what was the percent of increase in the volume for subsidized loans from 1996 to 1998?

9. Approximately what was the ratio of the loan volume for unsubsidized loans in 1996 to the loan volume for unsubsidized loans in 1997?

10. Approximately what was the percent of increase in loan volume from 1996 to 1998?

Peterson's Math Review for the GRE, GMAT and MCAT

SOLUTIONS

1. Mortgage Backed Securities represent 15% of the $4 million invested.

   $4 \times 15\% = .6$ million $= \$600,000$

2. Domestic Corporate Bonds represent 20% of the total, and Foreign Bonds represent 12% of the total. Combined, then, they represent 32% of the total.

   $4 \times 32\% = 1.28$ million $= \$1,280,000$

3. Municipal Bonds represent 30% of the total, and US Government Bonds represent 10% of the total. The difference is 20% of the total.

   $4 \times 20\% = .8 = \$800,000$

4. This year, the amount invested in Foreign Bonds was $4 \times 12\% = .48$ million $= \$480,000$. If this goes up by 35%, it will go up by

   $480,000 \times 35\% = 168,000.$

   Therefore, the projected value for next year will be $480,000 + 168,000 = \$648,000$.

5. As we saw in question 4, next year, the investment in Foreign Bonds is projected to be $648,000. If this is 10% of the total investment, then the total investment will be $6,480,000.

6. In 1996, the total loan volume appears to be about $25 billion. Since $15 million of this volume is subsidized, it must mean that $10 billion is unsubsidized.

7. In 1995, subsidized loans accounted for $15 billion, and unsubsidized loans accounted for $5 billion. Therefore, the volume for subsidized loans was greater by $10 billion.

8. Subsidized loans rose from $15 billion to $20 billion over the two-year period.

   $$\text{Percent of increase} = \left(\frac{\text{increase}}{\text{original value}}\right) \times 100\% = \frac{5}{15} \times 100\%$$
   $$= \text{approximately } 33\%$$

9. Approximately 10 to 12 = 5 to 6.

10. Loan volume went from $25 billion to $35 billion over the period indicated. The percent of increase is:

    $$\text{Percent of increase} = \frac{10}{25} \times 100\% = 40\%.$$

Part III
Mathematics Review

PROPERTIES OF NUMBERS

SYSTEMS OF NUMBERS

All of the numbers that are used in the mathematics sections of the GMAT, GRE, and MCAT are *real numbers*. In order to understand the real number system, it is the easiest to begin by looking at some familiar systems of numbers that lie within the real number system.

The numbers that are used for counting

1, 2, 3, 4, 5, ...

are called the *natural numbers,* the *counting numbers,* or, most commonly, the *positive integers*. The positive integers, together with the number 0, are called the set of *whole numbers*. Then, the positive integers, together with 0 and the *negative integers*

$-1, -2, -3, -4, -5, ...$

make up the set of *integers*. Thus, the set of integers contains the numbers

$..... -5, 4, -3, -2, -1, 0, 1, 2, 3, 4, 5, ...$

A real number is said to be a *rational number* if it can be written as the ratio of two integers, where the denominator is not 0. Thus, for example, numbers such as

$$-16, \frac{3}{4}, \frac{-5}{6}, 0, 49, 13\frac{7}{12}$$

are rational numbers. Clearly, then, all integers and fractions are rational numbers. Percents and decimal numbers are rational as well, since they can also be written as the ratio of two integers. For example, $75\% = \frac{3}{4}$, and $9.375 = \frac{3}{8}$.

Any real number that cannot be expressed as the ratio of two integers is called an *irrational number*. The most common irrational numbers that you will see on your test are square roots, such as $\sqrt{7}$ or $-\sqrt{13}$, and the number π, which represents the ratio of the circumference of a circle to its diameter.

Finally, the set of rational numbers, together with the set of irrational numbers, is called the set of *real numbers*.

Example

The number -293 is an integer. It is also rational since it can be written as $\dfrac{-293}{1}$ and is, of course, real.

The number $\dfrac{5}{8}$ is rational and real, and the number 15.0625 is also rational and real since it can be written as $15\dfrac{1}{16}$ or $\dfrac{241}{16}$.

The number $\sqrt{5}$ is irrational and real.

ROUNDING OF NUMBERS

From time to time, a test question will ask you to round an answer to a specific decimal place. The rules for the rounding of numbers are very simple. In the case of whole numbers, begin by locating the digit to which the number is being rounded. Then, if the digit just to the right is 0, 1, 2, 3, or 4, leave the located digit alone. Otherwise, increase the located digit by 1. In either case, replace all digits to the right of the one located with 0's.

When rounding decimal numbers, the rules are similar. Again, begin by locating the digit to which the number is being rounded. As before, if the digit just to the right is 0, 1, 2, 3, or 4, leave the located digit alone. Otherwise, increase the located digit by 1. Finally, drop all the digits to the right of the one located.

Example

Round the following numbers as indicated:

7,542 to the nearest 10

Begin by locating the ten's digit, which is a 4. The number to the right of the 4 is a 2. Thus, drop the 2 and replace it with a 0, yielding 7,540.

495,597 to the nearest hundred

Begin by locating the hundred's digit, which is a 5. The number to the right of the 5 is a 9. Thus, increase the hundreds digit by 1, making it a 6. Replace the ten's and unit's digits with 0's, yielding 495,600.

893.472 to the nearest tenth

The tenth's digit is 4. The digit just to the right of it is 7, so increase the tenth's digit by 1, making it a 5. Drop the two digits to the right of this. The answer is 893.5

.0679 to the nearest thousandth

Following the rules above, we obtain .068.

PROPERTIES OF NUMBERS PROBLEMS

1. Classify each of the following numbers as whole, integer, rational, irrational, and real.

    (A) -7

    (B) $\dfrac{1}{7}$

    (C) $5\dfrac{2}{3}$

    (D) 0

    (E) $\sqrt{13}$

2. Round each of the numbers below to the indicated number of decimal places.

    (A) 57,380 to the nearest hundred
    (B) 1,574,584 to the nearest hundred thousand
    (C) 847.235 to the nearest hundredth
    (D) 9.00872 to the nearest thousandth

SOLUTIONS

1. (A) -7 is real, rational, and an integer.

    (B) $\dfrac{1}{7}$ is real and rational.

    (C) $5\dfrac{2}{3}$ can be written as $\dfrac{17}{3}$ and is, thus, real and rational.

    (D) 0 is real, rational, an integer, and a whole number.

    (E) $\sqrt{13}$ is real and irrational.

2. (A) Begin by locating the hundred's digit, which is 3. The digit to the right of it is 8, so increase the hundred's digit by 1, and replace all digits to the right with 0's. The answer is 57,400.

    (B) The hundred thousandth's digit is 5. The digit to the right of it is 7, so increase the 5 by 1, and replace all digits to the right with 0's. The answer is 1,600,000.

    (C) The hundredth's digit is 3. The digit just to the right of it is 5, so increase the hundredth's digit by 1, making it a 4. Drop the digit to the right of this. The answer is 847.24.

    (D) The thousandth's digit is 8. The digit just to the right of it is 7, so increase the thousandth's digit by 1, making it a 9. Drop the digits to the right of this. The answer is 9.009.

Precision in Measurement and Computations with Approximate Numbers

Those taking the MCAT must be aware of the issue of precision in measurement and know how to compute with approximate numbers.

Any measurement made in a scientific experiment is never exact; it is always approximate. *Precision* is a measure of how close we are to the true measurement. It is determined by the smallest unit of measure used to make the measurement.

For example, consider a measurement of 16,235 kilometers. Since the unit of measure used in this example is the kilometer, we say that the measurement is precise to the nearest kilometer. The maximum possible error is always one-half of the unit that was used to make the measurement. This means that the true measure in this problem is somewhere between $16{,}235 \pm 0.5$ kilometers.

As another example, consider a measurement of 16,550 kilometers. If the unit of measurement in this example is tens of kilometers, we say that the measurement is precise to the nearest 10 kilometers. Thus, the true measurement is somewhere between $16{,}550 \pm 5$ kilometers.

Finally, consider a length measurement of $1\frac{5}{16}''$. If the unit of measurement is sixteenths of an inch, the measurement is precise to the nearest sixteenth of an inch, and the true measurement is somewhere between $1\frac{9}{32}''$ and $1\frac{11}{32}''$. Since measurement is approximate, we often need to perform computations with approximate numbers. The result of a computation with approximate numbers can never be more accurate than the least accurate number involved in the computation.

To add or subtract approximate numbers and, thus, perform the operations in the way you normally would, round the result to the unit of the least precise number involved. Similarly, to multiply or divide approximate numbers, perform the operations as you usually would, and then round the answer to the number of decimal places in the least precise number involved.

Examples

1. $1.8 + 2.586 + 4.34 = 8.726$. Since 1.8 is the least precise number, we present the answer as 8.7.

2. $5.67 \times 2.6 = 14.742$. The answer would be presented as 14.7.

WHOLE NUMBERS

As we have already seen, the set of positive integers (natural numbers, counting numbers) can be written as the set {1, 2, 3, 4, 5, ...}. The set of positive integers, together with the number 0, are called the set of *whole numbers*, and can be written as {0, 1, 2, 3, 4, ...}. (The notation { } means "set" or collection, and the three dots after the number 5 indicate that the list continues without end.)

Place Value

Whole numbers are expressed in a system of tens, called the *decimal* system. Ten *digits*—0, 1, 2, 3, 4, 5, 6, 7, 8, and 9—are used. Each digit differs not only in *face* value but also in *place* value, depending on where it stands in the number.

Example 1

237 means:

$(2 \cdot 100) + (3 \cdot 10) + (7 \cdot 1)$

The digit 2 has face value 2 but place value of 200.

Example 2

35,412 can be written as:

$(3 \cdot 10,000) + (5 \cdot 1,000) + (4 \cdot 100) + (1 \cdot 10) + (2 \cdot 1)$

The digit in the last place on the right is said to be in the units or ones place, the digit to the left of that in the tens place, the next digit to the left of that in the hundreds place, and so on.

When we take a whole number and write it out as in the two examples above, it is said to be written in *expanded form*.

Odd and Even Numbers

A whole number is *even* if it is divisible by 2; it is *odd* if it is not divisible by 2. Zero is thus an even number.

Example

2, 4, 6, 8, and 320 are even numbers; 3, 7, 9, 21, and 45 are odd numbers.

Prime Numbers

The positive integer p is said to be a prime number (or simply *a prime*) if $p = 1$ and the only positive divisors of p are itself and 1. The positive integer 1 is called a *unit*. The first ten primes are 2, 3, 5, 7, 11, 13, 17, 19, 23, and 29. All other positive integers that are neither 1 nor prime are *composite numbers*. Composite numbers can be *factored*, that is, expressed as products of their divisors or factors; for example, $56 = 7 \cdot 8 = 7 \cdot 4 \cdot 2$. In particular, composite numbers can be expressed as products of their *prime* factors in just one way (except for order).

To factor a composite number into its prime factors, proceed as follows. First, try to divide the number by the prime number 2. If this is successful, continue to divide by 2 until an odd number is obtained. Then, attempt to divide the last quotient by the prime number 3 and by 3 again, as many times as possible. Then move on to dividing by the prime number 5, and other successive primes until a prime quotient is obtained. Express the original number as a product of all its prime divisors.

Example

Find the prime factors of 210.

$$2 \overline{)210}$$
$$3 \overline{)105}$$
$$5 \overline{)\ 35}$$
$$\qquad 7$$

Therefore:

$210 = 2 \cdot 3 \cdot 5 \cdot 7$ (written in any order)
and 210 is an integer multiple of 2, of 3, of 5, and of 7.

Consecutive Whole Numbers

Numbers are consecutive if each number is the successor of the number that precedes it. In a consecutive series of whole numbers, an odd number is always followed by an even number, and an even number by an odd. If three consecutive whole numbers are given, either two of them are odd and one is even or two are even and one is odd.

Example 1

7, 8, 9, 10, and 11 are consecutive whole numbers.

Example 2

8, 10, 12, and 14 are consecutive even numbers.

Example 3

21, 23, 25, and 27 are consecutive odd numbers.

Example 4

21, 23, and 27 are *not* consecutive odd numbers because 25 is missing.

THE NUMBER LINE

A useful method of representing numbers geometrically makes it easier to understand numbers. It is called the *number line*. Draw a horizontal line, considered to extend without end in both directions. Select some point on the line and label it with the number 0. This point is called the *origin*. Choose some convenient distance as a unit of length. Take the point on the number line that lies one unit to the right of the origin and label it with the number 1. The point on the number line that is one unit to the right of 1 is labeled 2, and so on. In this way, every whole number is associated with one point on the line, but it is not true that every point on the line represents a whole number.

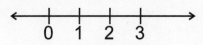

Number line

Ordering of Whole Numbers

On the number line, the point representing 8 lies to the right of the point representing 5, and we say 8 > 5 (read "8 is greater than 5"). One can also say 5 < 8 ("5 is less than 8"). For any two whole numbers a and b, there are always three possibilities:

$$a < b, \qquad a = b, \qquad \text{or} \qquad a > b.$$

If $a = b$, the points representing the numbers a and b coincide on the number line.

OPERATIONS WITH WHOLE NUMBERS

The basic operations on whole numbers are addition (+), subtraction (−), multiplication (· or ×), and division (÷). These are all *binary* operations—that is, one works with two numbers at a time in order to get a unique answer. The operations of addition and multiplication on whole numbers are said to be *closed* because the answer in each case is also a whole number. The operations of subtraction and division on whole numbers are not closed because the unique answer is not necessarily a member of the set of whole numbers.

Examples

$$3 + 4 = 7 \qquad \text{a whole number}$$
$$4 \cdot 3 = 12 \qquad \text{a whole number}$$
$$2 - 5 = -3 \qquad \text{not a whole number}$$
$$3 \div 8 = \frac{3}{8} \qquad \text{not a whole number}$$

Addition

If addition is a binary operation, how are three numbers—say, 3, 4, and 8—added? One way is to write:

$$(3 + 4) + 8 = 7 + 8 = 15$$

Another way is to write:

$$3 + (4 + 8) = 3 + 12 = 15$$

The parentheses merely group the numbers together. The fact that the same answer, 15, is obtained either way illustrates the *associative property* of addition:

$$(r + s) + t = r + (s + t)$$

The order in which whole numbers are added is immaterial—that is, $3 + 4 = 4 + 3$. This principle is called the *commutative property* of addition. Most people use this property without realizing it when they add a column of numbers from the top down and then check their results by beginning over again from the bottom. (Even though there may be a long column of numbers, only two numbers are added at a time.)

If 0 is added to any whole number, the whole number is unchanged. Zero is called the *identity element* for addition.

Subtraction

Subtraction is the inverse of addition. The order in which the numbers are written is important; there is no commutative property for subtraction.

$$4 - 3 \neq 3 - 4$$

The $\neq$ is read "does not equal."

Multiplication

Multiplication is a commutative operation:

$$43 \cdot 73 = 73 \cdot 43$$

The result or answer in a multiplication problem is called the *product*.

If a number is multiplied by 1, the number is unchanged; the *identity element* for multiplication is 1.

Zero times any number is 0:

$$42 \cdot 0 = 0$$

Multiplication can be expressed with several different symbols:

$$9 \cdot 7 \cdot 3 = 9 \times 7 \times 3 = 9(7)(3)$$

Besides being commutative, multiplication is *associative:*

$$(9 \cdot 7) \cdot 3 = 63 \cdot 3 = 189$$

and

$$9 \cdot (7 \cdot 3) = 9 \cdot 21 = 189$$

A number can be quickly multiplied by 10 by adding a zero to the right of the number. Similarly, a number can be multiplied by 100 by adding two zeros to the right:

$$38 \cdot 10 = 380$$

and

$$100 \cdot 76 = 7,600$$

Division

Division is the inverse of multiplication. It is not commutative:

$$8 \div 4 \neq 4 \div 8$$

The parts of a division example are named as follows:

$$\overset{\text{quotient}}{\text{divisor}\overline{)\text{dividend}}}$$

If a number is divided by 1, the quotient is the original number.

Division by 0 is not defined (has no meaning). Zero divided by any number other than 0 is 0:

$$0 \div 56 = 0$$

Divisors and Multiples

The whole number b *divides* the whole number a if there exists a whole number k such that $a = bk$. The whole number a is then said to be an integer *multiple* of b, and b is called a *divisor* (or *factor*) of a.

Example 1

3 divides 15 because $15 = 3 \cdot 5$. Thus, 3 is a divisor of 15 (and so is 5), and 15 is an integer multiple of 3 (and of 5).

Example 2

3 does not divide 8 because $8 \neq 3k$ for a whole number k.

Example 3

Divisors of 28 are 1, 2, 4, 7, 14, and 28.

Example 4

Multiples of 3 are 3, 6, 9, 12, 15, . . .

WHOLE NUMBERS PROBLEMS

1. What are the first seven positive multiples of 9?

2. What are the divisors of 60?

3. Find all of the factors of 47.

4. Express 176 as a product of prime numbers.

5. Find all of the common factors of 30 and 105.

6. Give an example to show that subtraction on the set of real numbers is not commutative.

7. List all of the prime numbers between 50 and 90.

8. Write the number 786,534 in expanded notation.

9. Which property is illustrated by the following statement?

    $(9 \times 7) \times 5 = 9 \times (7 \times 5)$

10. Which property is illustrated by the following statement?

    $(16 + 18) + 20 = (18 + 16) + 20$

11. Which property is illustrated by the following statement?

    $(3 + 7) + 8 = 3 + (7 + 8)$

12. In each of the statements below, replace the # with either $<$, $>$, or $=$ to make a true statement.

    (A) $-12 \# 13$

    (B) $\dfrac{1}{16} \# 0.0625$

    (C) $3\dfrac{1}{2} \# 3\dfrac{2}{5}$

SOLUTIONS

1. 9, 18, 27, 36, 45, 54, 63

2. The divisors of 60 are 1, 2, 3, 4, 5, 6, 10, 12, 15, 20, 30, and 60.

3. 1 and 47 are the only factors.

4. $176 = 2 \times 88 = 2 \times 2 \times 44 = 2 \times 2 \times 2 \times 22 = 2 \times 2 \times 2 \times 2 \times 11$

5. 30 can be factored as $2 \times 3 \times 5$. 105 can be factored as $3 \times 5 \times 7$. Thus, the common factors are 3 and 5.

6. $4 - 5 \neq 5 - 4$

7. The prime numbers between 50 and 90 are 53, 59, 61, 67, 71, 73, 79, 83, and 89.

8. $786,534 = 7(100,000) + 8(10,000) + 6(1,000) + 5(100) + 3(10) + 4$

9. The Associative Property of Multiplication

10. The Commutative Property of Addition

11. The Associative Property of Addition

12. (A) $-12 < 13$

    (B) $\dfrac{1}{16} = 0.0625$

    (C) $3\dfrac{1}{2} > 3\dfrac{2}{5}$

FRACTIONS

Definitions

If a and b are whole numbers and $b \neq 0$, the symbol $\dfrac{a}{b}$ (or a/b) is called a fraction. The upper part, a, is called the *numerator*, and the lower part, b, is called the *denominator*. The denominator indicates into how many parts something is divided, and the numerator tells how many of these parts are taken. A fraction indicates division:

$$\frac{7}{8} = 8\overline{)7}$$

If the numerator of a fraction is 0, the value of the fraction is 0. If the denominator of a fraction is 0, the fraction is not defined (has no meaning):

$$\frac{0}{17} = 0$$

$\dfrac{17}{0}$ is not defined (has no meaning)

If the denominator of a fraction is 1, the value of the fraction is the same as the numerator:

$$\frac{18}{1} = 18$$

If the numerator and denominator are the same number, the value of the fraction is 1:

$$\frac{7}{7} = 1$$

Equivalent Fractions

Fractions that represent the same number are said to be *equivalent*. If m is a counting number and $\dfrac{a}{b}$ is a fraction, then: $\dfrac{m \times a}{m \times b} = \dfrac{a}{b}$

because $\dfrac{m}{m} = 1$ and $1 \times \dfrac{a}{b} = \dfrac{a}{b}$

Example

$$\frac{2}{3} = \frac{4}{6} = \frac{6}{9} = \frac{8}{12}$$

These fractions are all equivalent.

Inequality of Fractions

If two fractions are not equivalent, one is smaller than the other. The ideas of "less than" and "greater than" were previously defined and used for whole numbers.

For the fractions $\frac{a}{b}$ and $\frac{c}{b}$:

$$\frac{a}{b} < \frac{c}{b} \text{ if } a < c \text{ and if } b > 0$$

That is, if two fractions have the same denominator, the one with the smaller numerator has the smaller value.

If two fractions have different denominators, find a common denominator by multiplying one denominator by the other. Then use the common denominator to compare numerators.

Example 1

Which is smaller, $\frac{5}{8}$ or $\frac{4}{7}$?

$8 \cdot 7 = 56 = $ common denominator

$$\frac{5}{8} \times \frac{7}{7} = \frac{35}{56} \qquad \frac{4}{7} \times \frac{8}{8} = \frac{32}{56}$$

Since $32 < 35$,

$$\frac{32}{56} < \frac{35}{56} \text{ and } \frac{4}{7} < \frac{5}{8}$$

Example 2

Which of the fractions, $\frac{2}{5}, \frac{3}{7},$ or $\frac{4}{11}$, is the largest?

We begin by comparing the first two fractions. Since $\frac{2}{5} = \frac{14}{35}$ and $\frac{3}{7} = \frac{15}{35}$, we can see that $\frac{3}{7}$ is bigger. Now, we compare $\frac{3}{7}$ to $\frac{4}{11}$. Since $\frac{3}{7} = \frac{33}{77}$ and $\frac{4}{11} = \frac{28}{77}$, we can see that $\frac{3}{7}$ is the biggest of the three fractions.

Reducing to Lowest Terms

The principle that

$$\frac{m \times a}{m \times b} = \frac{a}{b}$$

can be particularly useful in reducing fractions to lowest terms. Fractions are expressed in *lowest terms* when the numerator and denominator have no common factor except 1. To reduce a fraction to an equivalent fraction in lowest terms, express the numerator and denominator as products of their prime factors. Each time a prime appears in the numerator over the same prime in the denominator, $\frac{p}{p}$, substitute its equal value, 1.

Example 1

Reduce $\frac{30}{42}$ to an equivalent fraction in lowest terms:

$$\frac{30}{42} = \frac{2 \cdot 3 \cdot 5}{2 \cdot 3 \cdot 7} = 1 \cdot 1 \cdot \frac{5}{7} = \frac{5}{7}$$

In practice, this can be done even more quickly by dividing the numerator and the denominator by any number, prime or not, which will divide both evenly. Repeat this process until there is no prime factor remaining that is common to both the numerator and the denominator:

$$\frac{30}{42} = \frac{15}{21} = \frac{5}{7}$$

Example 2

Reduce $\frac{77}{197}$ to an equivalent fraction in lowest terms:

$$\frac{77}{197} = \frac{7 \times 11}{3 \times 5 \times 13}$$

Since the numerator and the denominator have no common factors, the fraction is already in lowest terms.

Fractions Problems

In the following problems, perform the indicated operations and reduce your answers to lowest terms.

1. $\dfrac{2}{15} + \dfrac{2}{3} =$

2. $\dfrac{4}{5} - \dfrac{2}{13} =$

3. $\dfrac{3}{8} \times \dfrac{4}{21} =$

4. $\dfrac{2}{3} \times \dfrac{12}{8} =$

5. $\dfrac{2}{3} \div \dfrac{5}{6} =$

6. $\dfrac{3}{4} \div \dfrac{7}{8} =$

7. $2\dfrac{3}{5} + 7\dfrac{3}{5} =$

8. $9\dfrac{1}{5} - 3\dfrac{1}{4} =$

9. $\dfrac{6}{7} \times \dfrac{3}{4} \times \dfrac{2}{3} =$

10. $6 \times \dfrac{2}{3} \times 2\dfrac{5}{6} =$

11. $2\dfrac{2}{3} \div 1\dfrac{7}{9} =$

12. $6\dfrac{2}{3} \times 1\dfrac{4}{5} =$

SOLUTIONS

1. $\dfrac{2}{15} + \dfrac{2}{3} = \dfrac{2}{15} + \dfrac{10}{15} = \dfrac{12}{15} = \dfrac{4}{5}$

2. $\dfrac{4}{5} - \dfrac{2}{13} = \dfrac{52}{65} - \dfrac{10}{65} = \dfrac{42}{65}$

3. $\dfrac{3}{8} \times \dfrac{4}{21} = \dfrac{3}{8} \times \dfrac{4}{21} = \dfrac{1}{2} \times \dfrac{1}{7} = \dfrac{1}{14}$

4. $\dfrac{2}{3} \times \dfrac{12}{8} = \dfrac{2}{3} \times \dfrac{12}{8} = \dfrac{1}{1} \times \dfrac{4}{4} = 1$

5. $\dfrac{2}{3} \div \dfrac{5}{6} = \dfrac{2}{3} \times \dfrac{6}{5} = \dfrac{2}{3} \times \dfrac{6}{5} = \dfrac{2}{1} \times \dfrac{2}{5} = \dfrac{4}{5}$

6. $\dfrac{3}{4} \div \dfrac{7}{8} = \dfrac{3}{4} \times \dfrac{8}{7} = \dfrac{3}{4} \times \dfrac{8}{7} = \dfrac{3}{1} \times \dfrac{2}{7} = \dfrac{6}{7}$

7. $2\dfrac{3}{5} + 7\dfrac{3}{5} = \dfrac{13}{5} + \dfrac{38}{5} = \dfrac{51}{5} = 10\dfrac{1}{5}$

8. $9\dfrac{1}{5} - 3\dfrac{1}{4} = 8\dfrac{6}{5} - 3\dfrac{1}{4} = 8\dfrac{24}{20} - 3\dfrac{5}{20} = 5\dfrac{19}{20}$

9. $\dfrac{6}{7} \times \dfrac{3}{4} \times \dfrac{2}{3} = \dfrac{6}{7} \times \dfrac{3}{4} \times \dfrac{2}{3} = \dfrac{6}{7} \times \dfrac{1}{2} \times \dfrac{1}{1} = \dfrac{3}{7} \times \dfrac{1}{1} \times \dfrac{1}{1} = \dfrac{3}{7}$

10. $6 \times \dfrac{2}{3} \times 2\dfrac{5}{6} = \dfrac{6}{1} \times \dfrac{2}{3} \times \dfrac{17}{6} = \dfrac{1}{1} \times \dfrac{2}{3} \times \dfrac{17}{1} = \dfrac{34}{3} = 11\dfrac{1}{3}$

11. $2\dfrac{2}{3} \div 1\dfrac{7}{9} = \dfrac{8}{3} \div \dfrac{16}{9} = \dfrac{8}{3} \times \dfrac{9}{16} = \dfrac{8}{3} \times \dfrac{9}{16} = \dfrac{1}{1} \times \dfrac{3}{2} = \dfrac{3}{2}$

12. $6\dfrac{2}{3} \times 1\dfrac{4}{5} = \dfrac{20}{3} \times \dfrac{9}{5} = \dfrac{20}{3} \times \dfrac{9}{5} = \dfrac{4}{1} \times \dfrac{3}{1} = 12$

DECIMALS

Earlier, we stated that whole numbers are expressed in a system of tens, or the decimal system, using the digits from 0 to 9. This system can be extended to fractions by using a period called a *decimal point*. The digits after a decimal point form a *decimal fraction*. Decimal fractions are smaller than 1—for example, .3, .37, .372, and .105. The first position to the right of the decimal point is called the *tenths' place* since the digit in that position tells how many tenths there are. The second digit to the right of the decimal point is in the *hundredths' place*. The third digit to the right of the decimal point is in the *thousandths' place*, and so on.

Example 1

.3 is a decimal fraction that means

$$3 \times \frac{1}{10} = \frac{3}{10}$$

read "three tenths."

Example 2

The decimal fraction of .37 means

$$3 \times \frac{1}{10} + 7 \times \frac{1}{100} = 3 \times \frac{10}{100} + 7 \times \frac{1}{100}$$
$$= \frac{30}{100} + \frac{7}{100} = \frac{37}{100}$$

read "thirty-seven hundredths."

Example 3

The decimal fraction .372 means

$$\frac{300}{1,000} + \frac{70}{1,000} + \frac{2}{1,000} = \frac{372}{1,000}$$

read "three hundred seventy-two thousandths."

Whole numbers have an understood (unwritten) decimal point to the right of the last digit (e.g., 4 = 4.0). Decimal fractions can be combined with whole numbers to make *decimals*—for example, 3.246, 10.85, and 4.7.

Note: Adding zeros to the right of a decimal after the last digit does not change the value of the decimal.

Rounding Off

Sometimes, a decimal is expressed with more digits than desired. As the number of digits to the right of the decimal point increases, the number increases in accuracy, but a high degree of accuracy is not always needed. Then, the number can be "rounded off" to a certain decimal place.

To round off, identify the place to be rounded off. If the digit to the right of it is 0, 1, 2, 3, or 4, the round-off place digit remains the same. If the digit to the right is 5, 6, 7, 8, or 9, add 1 to the round-off place digit.

Example 1

Round off .6384 to the nearest thousandth. The digit in the thousandths' place is 8. The digit to the right in the ten-thousandths' place is 4, so the 8 stays the same. The answer is .638

Example 2

.6386 rounded to the nearest thousandth is .639, rounded to the nearest hundredth is .64, and rounded to the nearest tenth is .6.

After a decimal fraction has been rounded off to a particular decimal place, all the digits to the right of that place will be 0.

Note: Rounding off whole numbers can be done by a similar method. It is less common but is sometimes used to get approximate answers quickly.

Example

Round 32,756 to the nearest *hundred*. This means, to find the multiple of 100 that is nearest the given number. The number in the hundreds' place is 7. The number immediately to the right is 5, so 32,756 rounds to 32,800.

DECIMALS AND FRACTIONS

Changing a Decimal to a Fraction

Place the digits to the right of the decimal point over the value of the place in which the last digit appears and reduce, if possible. The whole number remains the same.

Example

Change 2.14 to a fraction or mixed number. Observe that 4 is the last digit and is in the hundredths' place.

$$.14 = \frac{14}{100} = \frac{7}{50}$$

Therefore:

$$2.14 = 2\frac{7}{50}$$

Changing a Fraction to a Decimal

Divide the numerator of the fraction by the denominator. First, put a decimal point followed by zeros to the right of the number in the numerator. Subtract and divide until there is no remainder. The decimal point in the quotient is aligned directly above the decimal point in the dividend.

Example

Change $\frac{3}{8}$ to a decimal.

Divide

```
   .375
8)3.000
  24
  ‾‾
   60
   56
   ‾‾
    40
    40
    ‾‾
```

When the division does not terminate with a 0 remainder, two courses are possible.

First Method

Divide to three decimal places.

Example

Change $\dfrac{5}{6}$ to a decimal.

$$
\begin{array}{r}
.833 \\
6\overline{)5.000} \\
\underline{48} \\
20 \\
\underline{18} \\
20 \\
\underline{18} \\
2
\end{array}
$$

The 3 in the quotient will be repeated indefinitely. It is called an *infinite decimal* and is written .833. . . .

Second Method

Divide until there are two decimal places in the quotient and then write the remainder over the divisor.

Example

Change $\dfrac{5}{6}$ to a decimal.

$$
\begin{array}{r}
.833 \\
6\overline{)5.000} \\
\underline{48} \\
20 \\
\underline{18} \\
20
\end{array}
\;=\; .83\tfrac{1}{3}
$$

ADDITION

Addition of decimals is both commutative and associative. Decimals are simpler to add than fractions. Place the decimals in a column with the decimal points aligned under each other. Add in the usual way. The decimal point of the answer is also aligned under the other decimal points.

Example

$43 + 2.73 + .9 + 3.01 = ?$

$$
\begin{array}{r}
43. \\
2.73 \\
.9 \\
\underline{3.01} \\
49.64
\end{array}
$$

SUBTRACTION

For subtraction, the decimal points must be aligned under each other. Add zeros to the right of the decimal point if desired. Subtract as with whole numbers.

Examples

21.567	21.567	39.00
−9.4	−9.48	−17.48
12.167	12.087	21.52

MULTIPLICATION

Multiplication of decimals is commutative and associative:

$$5.39 \times .04 = .04 \times 5.39$$
$$(.7 \times .02) \times .1 = .7 \times (.02 \times .1)$$

Multiply the decimals as if they were whole numbers. The total number of decimal places in the product is the sum of the number of places (to the right of the decimal point) in all of the numbers multiplied.

Example

$8.64 \times .003 = ?$

8.64	2	places to right of decimal point
× .003	+ 3	places to right of decimal point
.02592	5	places to right of decimal point

A zero had to be added to the left of the product before writing the decimal point to ensure that there would be five decimal places in the product.

Note: To multiply a decimal by 10, simply move the decimal point one place to the right; to multiply by 100, move the decimal point two places to the right.

DIVISION

To divide one decimal (the dividend) by another (the divisor), move the decimal point in the divisor as many places as necessary to the right to make the divisor a whole number. Then move the decimal point in the dividend (expressed or understood) a corresponding number of places, adding zeros if necessary. Then divide as with whole numbers. The decimal point in the quotient is placed above the decimal point in the dividend after the decimal point has been moved.

Example

Divide 7.6 by .32.

$$.32\overline{)7.60} = 32\overline{)760.00} \quad (23.75)$$

$$
\begin{array}{r}
23.75 \\
32\overline{)760.00} \\
\underline{64} \\
120 \\
\underline{96} \\
240 \\
\underline{224} \\
160 \\
\underline{160}
\end{array}
$$

Note: "Divide 7.6 by .32" can be written as $\dfrac{7.6}{.32}$. If this fraction is multiplied by $\dfrac{100}{100}$, an equivalent fraction is obtained with a whole number in the denominator:

$$\frac{7.6}{.32} \times \frac{100}{100} = \frac{760}{32}$$

Moving the decimal point two places to the right in both the divisor and dividend is equivalent to multiplying each number by 100.

Special Cases

If the dividend has a decimal point and the divisor does not, divide as with whole numbers and place the decimal point of the quotient above the decimal point in the divisor.

If both dividend and divisor are whole numbers but the quotient is a decimal, place a decimal point after the last digit of the dividend and add zeros as necessary to get the required degree of accuracy. (See *Changing a Fraction to a Decimal,* page 99).

Note: To divide any number by 10, simply move its decimal point (understood to be after the last digit for a whole number) one place to the left; to divide by 100, move the decimal point two places to the left; and so on.

DECIMAL PROBLEMS

1. Change the following fractions into decimals.

    (A) $\dfrac{5}{8}$

    (B) $\dfrac{1}{6}$

2. Change the following decimals into fractions and reduce.

    (A) 2.08
    (B) 13.24

3. Change the following decimals into fractions and reduce.

    (A) 17.56
    (B) 21.002

In the following problems, perform the indicated operations.

4. 31.32 + 3.829

5. 5.746 + 354.34

6. 2.567 − 0.021

7. 3.261 − 2.59

8. 73 − .46

9. 0.7 × 3.1

10. 9.2 × 0.03

11. 5.43 + .154 + 17

12. 0.064 ÷ 0.04

13. 0.033 ÷ 0.11

14. Which of the three decimals .09, .769, .8 is the smallest?

SOLUTIONS

1. (A)
$$
\begin{array}{r}
0.625 \\
8\overline{)5.000} \\
48 \\
\overline{20} \\
-16 \\
\overline{40}
\end{array}
$$

(B)
$$
\begin{array}{r}
0.166... \\
6\overline{)1.0000} \\
6 \\
\overline{40} \\
-36 \\
\overline{40}
\end{array}
$$

2. (A) $2.08 = 2\dfrac{8}{100} = 2\dfrac{2}{25}$

(B) $13.24 = 13\dfrac{24}{100} = 13\dfrac{6}{25}$

3. (A) $17.56 = 17\dfrac{56}{100} = 17\dfrac{28}{50} = 17\dfrac{14}{25}$

(B) $21.002 = 21\dfrac{2}{1,000} = 21\dfrac{1}{500}$

4.
$$
\begin{array}{r}
31.32 \\
+\ 3.829 \\
\hline
35.149
\end{array}
$$

5.
$$
\begin{array}{r}
5.746 \\
+\ 354.34 \\
\hline
360.086
\end{array}
$$

6.
$$
\begin{array}{r}
2.567 \\
-\ 0.021 \\
\hline
2.546
\end{array}
$$

7.
$$
\begin{array}{r}
3.261 \\
-\ 2.59 \\
\hline
0.671
\end{array}
$$

8.
$$
\begin{array}{r}
73.00 \\
-\ .46 \\
\hline
72.54
\end{array}
$$

9.
$$
\begin{array}{r}
3.1 \\
\times\ 0.7 \\
\hline
2.17
\end{array}
$$

10. $\begin{array}{r} 9.2 \\ \times\ .003 \\ \hline .0276 \end{array}$ (One digit to the right of the decimal point)
       (Three digits to the right of the decimal point)
       (Four digits to the right of the decimal point)

11. $\begin{array}{r} 5.43 \\ .154 \\ +\ 17.000 \\ \hline 22.584 \end{array}$

12. $.04\overline{)0.064}$ with quotient 1.6

13. $.11\overline{)\!.033}$ with quotient 0.3

14.   The easiest way to determine the smallest decimal number is to append 0s to the end of each of the numbers until they all have the same number of digits. Then, ignore the decimal points and see which number is the smallest. Thus, .09 = .090, .769 = .769, .8 = .800. Clearly, the smallest number is .09.

PERCENTS

Percents, like fractions and decimals, are ways of expressing parts of whole numbers, as 93 percent, 50 percent, and 22.4 percent. Percents are expressions of hundredths—that is, of fractions whose denominator is 100. The symbol for percent is %.

Example

$$25\% = \text{twenty-five hundredths} = \frac{25}{100} = \frac{1}{4}$$

The word *percent* means *per hundred*. Its main use is in comparing fractions with equal denominators of 100.

Relationship with Fractions and Decimals

Changing Percent into Decimal

Divide the percent by 100 and drop the symbol for percent. Add zeros to the left when necessary:

30% = .30   1% = .01

Remember that the short method of dividing by 100 is to move the decimal point two places to the left.

PERCENT PROBLEMS

1. Change the following decimals into percents:

   (A) 0.374
   (B) 13.02

2. Change the following percents into decimals:

   (A) 62.9%
   (B) 0.002%

3. Change the following fractions into percents:

   (A) $\dfrac{5}{8}$
   (B) $\dfrac{44}{400}$

4. Change the following percents into fractions:

   (A) 37.5%
   (B) 0.04%

5. Change $12\frac{1}{4}\%$ to a decimal.

6. Write .07% as both a decimal and a fraction.

7. Write $\dfrac{11}{16}$ as both a decimal and a percent.

8. Write 1.25 as both a percent and a fraction.

9. Which of the following is the largest: $\dfrac{5}{8}$, 62%, .628?

SOLUTIONS

1. (A) $0.374 = 37.4\%$
   (B) $13.02 = 1,302\%$

2. (A) $62.9\% = 0.629$
   (B) $00.002\% = 0.00002$

3. (A) $\dfrac{5}{8} = 8\overline{)5.000}^{\,0.625} = 62.5\%$

   (B) $\dfrac{44}{400} = 400\overline{)44.00}^{\,0.11} = 11\%$

4. (A) $37.5\% = 0.375 = \dfrac{375}{1,000} = \dfrac{3}{8}$
   (B) $00.04\% = 0.0004 = \dfrac{4}{10,000} = \dfrac{1}{2,500}$

5. $12\frac{1}{4}\% = 12.25\% = 0.1225$

6. $.07\% = 0.0007 = \dfrac{7}{10,000}$

7. $\dfrac{11}{16} = \overline{)11.0000}^{\,.6875} = 68.75\%$

8. $1.25 = 125\% = \dfrac{125}{100} = \dfrac{5}{4} = 1\dfrac{1}{4}$

9. In order to determine the largest number, we must write them all in the same form. Writing $\dfrac{5}{8}$ as a decimal, we obtain .625. If we write 62% as a decimal, we get .62. Thus, .628 is the largest of the three numbers.

Solving Percent Problems

There are several different types of word problems involving percents that might appear on your test. In addition to generic percent problems, other applications you might be asked to solve involve taxation, commission, profit and loss, discount, and interest. All of these problems are solved in essentially the same way, as the examples that follow illustrate.

Note that when solving percent problems, it is often easier to change the percent to a decimal or a fraction before computing. When we take a percent of a certain number, that number is called the *base*, the percent we take is called the *rate*, and the result is called the part. If we let B represent the base, R represent the rate, and P represent the part, the relationship between these three quantities can be expressed by the following formula:

$$P = R \times B$$

All percent problems can be solved with the help of this formula.

The first four examples below show how to solve all types of generic percent problems. The remaining examples involve specific financial applications.

Example 1

In a class of 24 students, 25% received an A. How many students received an A?

The number of students (24) is the base, and 25% is the rate. Change the rate to a fraction for ease of handling and apply the formula.

$$25\% = \frac{25}{100} = \frac{1}{4}$$

$$P = R \times B$$

$$= \frac{1}{\cancel{4}} \times \frac{\cancel{24}^{\,6}}{1}$$

$$= 6 \text{ students}$$

To choose between changing the percent (rate) to a decimal or a fraction, simply decide which would be easier to work with. In Example 1, the fraction is easier to work with because cancellation is possible. In Example 2, the situation is the same except for a different rate. This time, the decimal form is easier.

Example 2

In a class of 24 students, 29.17% received an A. How many students received an A? Changing the rate to a fraction yields

$$\frac{29.17}{100} = \frac{2917}{10,000}$$

You can quickly see that the decimal is the better choice.

$29.17\% = .2917$

$$\begin{aligned}
P &= R \times B \\
&= .2917 \times 24 \\
&= 7 \text{ students}
\end{aligned}$$

$$\begin{array}{r}
.2917 \\
\times\ \ 24 \\
\hline
1.1668 \\
5.834 \\
\hline
7.0008
\end{array}$$

Example 3

What percent of a 40-hour week is a 16-hour schedule?

40 hours is the base and 16 hours is the part. $P = R \times B$

$$16 = R \times 40$$

Divide each side of the equation by 40.

$$\frac{16}{40} = R$$

$$\frac{2}{5} = R$$

$$40\% = R$$

Example 4

A woman paid $15,000 as a down payment on a house. If this amount was 20% of the price, what did the house cost?

The part (or percentage) is $15,000, the rate is 20%, and we must find the base. Change the rate to a fraction.

$$20\% = \frac{1}{5}$$

$$P = R \times B$$

$$\$15,000 = \frac{1}{5} \times B$$

Multiply each side of the equation by 5.

$$\$75,000 = B = \text{cost of house}$$

Commission

Example 5

A salesperson sells a new car for $24,800 and receives a 5% commission. How much commission does he receive?

The cost of the car ($24,800) is the base, and the rate is 5%. We are looking for the amount of commission, which is the part.

P = 5% × $24,800 = .05 × $24,800 = $1,240

Thus, the salesperson receives a commission of $1,240.

Taxation

Example 6

Janet buys a laptop computer for $1,199 and has to pay 7% sales tax. What is the amount of sales tax she owes, and what is the total price of the computer?

The cost of the computer ($1,199) is the base, and the rate is 7%. We are looking for the amount of sales tax, which is the part.

P = 7% × $1,199 = .07 × $1,199 = $83.93

Thus, the sales tax is $83.93, and the total cost of the computer is $1,199 + $83.93 = $1,282.93.

Discount

The amount of discount is the difference between the original price and the sale, or discount, price. The rate of discount is usually given as a fraction or as a percent. Use the formula of the percent problems $P = R \times B$, but now P stands for the part or discount, R is the rate, and B, the base, is the original price.

Example 7

A table listed at $160 is marked 20% off. What is the sale price?

$P = R \times B$
  $= .20 \times \$160 = \$32$

This is the amount of discount, or how much must be subtracted from the original price. Then:

$160 − $32 = $128 sale price

Example 8

A car priced at $9,000 was sold for $7,200. What was the rate of discount?

Amount of discount = $9,000 − $7,200
$$= \$1,800$$

Discount = rate × original price

$$\$1,800 = R \times \$9,000$$

Divide each side of the equation by $9,000:

$$\frac{\overset{20}{\cancel{1,800}}}{\underset{100}{\cancel{9,000}}} = \frac{20}{100} = R = 20\%$$

Successive Discounting

When an item is discounted more than once, it is called successive discounting.

Example 9

In one store, a dress tagged at $40 was discounted 15%. When it did not sell at the lower price, it was discounted an additional 10%. What was the final selling price?

Discount = R × original price

First discount = .15 × $40 = $6

$40 − $6 = $34 selling price after first discount

Second discount = .10 × $34 = $3.40

$34 − $3.40 = $30.60 final selling price

Example 10

In another store, an identical dress was also tagged at $40. When it did not sell, it was discounted 25% all at once. Is the final selling price lower or higher than in Example 1?

Discount = R × original price

$$= .25 \times \$40$$

$$= \$10$$

$40 − $10 = $30 final selling price

This is a lower selling price than in Example 9, where two successive discounts were taken. Although the two discounts from Example 9 add up to the discount of Example 10, the final selling price is not the same.

Interest

Interest problems are similar to discount and percent problems. If money is left in the bank for a year and the interest is calculated at the end of the year, the usual formula $P = R \times B$ can be used, where P is the *interest*, R is the *rate*, and B is the *principal* (original amount of money borrowed or loaned).

Example 11

A certain bank pays interest on savings accounts at the rate of 4% per year. If a man has $6,700 on deposit, find the interest earned after 1 year.

$$P = R \times B$$

Interest = rate · principal

$$P = .04 \times \$6,700 = \$268 \text{ interest}$$

Interest problems frequently involve more or less time than 1 year. Then the formula becomes:

Interest = rate × principal × time

Example 12

If the money is left in the bank for 3 years at simple interest (the kind we are discussing), the interest is

$$3 \times \$268 = \$804$$

Example 13

Suppose $6,700 is deposited in the bank at 4% interest for 3 months. How much interest is earned?

Interest = rate × principal × time

Here, the 4% rate is for 1 year. Since 3 months is $\frac{3}{12} = \frac{1}{4}$

$$\text{Interest} = .04 \times \$6,700 \times \frac{1}{4} = \$67$$

Percent of Change Problems

The percent of change problem is a special, yet very common, type of percent problem. In such a problem, there is a quantity that has a certain starting value (usually called the "original value"). This original value changes by a certain amount (either an increase or a decrease), leading to what is called the "new value." The problem is to express this increase or decrease as a percent.

Percent of change problems are solved by using a method analogous to that used in the problems above. First, calculate the *amount* of the increase or decrease. This amount plays the role of the part P in the formula $P = R \times B$. The base, B, is the original amount, regardless of whether there was a gain or a loss.

Example 14

By what percent does Mary's salary increase if her present salary is $20,000 and she accepts a new job at a salary of $28,000?

Amount of increase is:

$28,000 − $20,000 = $8,000

$$P = R \times B$$

$$\$8{,}000 = R \times \$20{,}000$$

Divide each side of the equation by $20,000. Then:

$$\frac{\overset{40}{\cancel{8{,}000}}}{\underset{100}{\cancel{20{,}000}}} = \frac{40}{100} = R = 40\% \text{ increase}$$

Example 15

On Tuesday, the price of Alpha stock closed at $56 a share. On Wednesday, the stock closed at a price that was $14 higher than the closing price on Tuesday. What was the percent of increase in the closing price of the stock?

In this problem, we are given the amount of increase of $14. Thus,

$$P = R \times B$$

14 = R × 56. Thus,

$$R = \frac{14}{56} = \frac{1}{4} = 25\%.$$

The percent of increase in the closing price of the stock is 25%.

PERCENT WORD PROBLEMS

1. Susan purchased a new refrigerator priced at $675. She made a down payment of 15% of the price. Find the amount of the down payment.

2. After having lunch, Ian leaves a tip of $4.32. If this amount represents 18% of the lunch bill, how much was the bill?

3. Before beginning her diet, Janet weighed 125 pounds. After completing the diet, she weighed 110 pounds. What percent of her weight did she lose?

4. A self-employed individual places $5,000 in an account that earns 8% simple annual interest. How much money will be in this account after 2 years?

5. If a $12,000 car loses 10% of its value every year, what is it worth after 3 years?

6. Peter invests $5,000 at 4% simple annual interest. How much is his investment worth after 2 months?

7. Sales volume at an office supply company climbed from $18,300 last month to $56,730 this month. Find the percent of increase in sales.

8. A men's clothing retailer orders $25,400 worth of outer garments, and receives a discount of 15%, followed by an additional discount of 10%. What is the cost of the clothing after these two discounts?

9. Janet receives a 6% commission for selling boxes of greeting cards. If she sells 12 boxes for $40 each, how much does she earn?

10. A small business office bought a used copy machine for 75% of the original price. If the original price was $3,500, how much did they pay for the copy machine?

11. A lawyer who is currently earning $42,380 annually receives a 6.5% raise. What is his new annual salary?

12. An industrial plant reduces its number of employees, which was originally 3,760, by 5%. How many employees now work at the plant?

Solutions

1. Amount of down payment = $675 × 15% = $675 × .15
    = $101.25

2. Amount of bill = Amount of tip/Percent of tip = 4.32/0.18
    = $24.

3. Amount of weight lost = 125 − 110 = 15 lb.
    Percent of weight lost = Amount of weight lost/Original
    weight = 15/125 = 12%

4. Each year, the amount of interest earned is $5000 × 8%
    = $400. Thus, in two years, $800 in interest is earned, and the
    account has $5,800 in it.

5. Value of car after 1 year = 12,000 × 0.90 = $10,800
    Value of car after 2 years = 10,800 × 0.90 = $9,720
    Value of car after 3 years = 9,720 × 0.90 = $8,748

6. Value of investment = Principal × Rate × Time
    = 5,000 × 0.04 × 1/6 = $33.33

7. Amount of increase = $56,730 − $18,300 = $38,430
    Percent of increase = 38,430/18,300 = 210%

8. Price after the first markdown = $25,400 × 85% = $21,590
    Price after the second markdown = $21,590 × 90% = $19,431

9. 12 boxes for $40 each cost $480. Since Janet makes a 6%
    commission, she will receive $480 × 6% = $28.80

10. Cost = 3,500 × 75% = $2,625

11. Amount of raise = 42,380 × 6.5% = $2,754.70.
    New Salary = $42,380 + $2,754.70 = $45,134.70

12. Number of employees who lost their jobs = 3,760 × 5% = 188
    Number of employees who now work at the plant
    = 3,760 − 188 = 3,572

SYSTEMS OF MEASUREMENTS

THE ENGLISH SYSTEM

Those taking the MCAT will need to be able to compute using both the English system of measurement and the metric system. It may also be necessary to convert measurements from one system to the other, but in such cases, you will be given the appropriate conversion factors.

Make sure that you have the following relationships within the English system memorized:

Conversion Factors for Length

36 inches = 3 feet = 1 yard
12 inches = 1 foot
5,280 feet = 1,760 yards = 1 mile

Conversion Factors for Volume
2 pints = 1 quart
16 fluid ounces = 1 pint
8 pints = 4 quarts = 1 gallon

Conversion Factors for Weight
16 ounces = 1 pound
2,000 pounds = 1 ton

These conversion factors enable you to change units within the English system.

Examples

1. How many feet are in 5 miles?

   5 miles × (5,280 feet/1 mile) = 26,400 feet

   Notice how the unit of "miles" cancels out of the numerator and denominator.

2. How many ounces are in 2 tons?

   2 tons × (2,000 pounds/1 ton) × (16 ounces/1 pound) = 64,000 ounces

   Notice how the units of "tons" and "pounds" cancel out of the numerator and denominator.

THE METRIC SYSTEM

In the metric system, distance or length is measured in meters. Similarly, volume is measured in liters, and mass is measured in grams. The prefixes below are appended to the beginning of these basic units to indicate other units of measure with sizes equal to each basic unit multiplied or divided by powers of 10.

$$giga = 10^9$$
$$mega = 10^6$$
$$kilo = 10^3$$
$$hecto = 10^2$$
$$deka = 10^1$$
$$deci = 10^{-1}$$
$$centi = 10^{-2}$$
$$milli = 10^{-3}$$
$$micro = 10^{-6}$$
$$nano = 10^{-9}$$
$$pico = 10^{-12}$$

From the table above, we can see, for example, that a kilometer is 1,000 times as long as a meter, 100,000 times as long as a centimeter, and 1,000,000 times as long as a millimeter. Similarly, a centigram is 1/100 the size of a gram.

Conversions among metric units can be made quickly by moving decimal points.

Examples

1. Convert 9.43 kilometers to meters.

    Since meters are smaller than kilometers, our answer will be larger than 9.43. There are 1,000 meters in a kilometer, so we move the decimal point three places to the right. Therefore 9.43 kilometers is equal to 9,430 meters.

2. Convert 512 grams to kilograms.

    Since kilograms are more massive than grams, our answer must less than 512. There are 10^{-3} kilograms in a gram, so we move the decimal point three places to the left. Therefore 512 grams are equal to .512 kilograms.

CONVERSIONS BETWEEN THE ENGLISH AND THE METRIC SYSTEMS

Conversions between the English and metric systems are accomplished in the same way as conversions within the English system. Recall that any problem that requires you to make such a conversion will include the necessary conversion factors.

Examples

1. If 1 meter is equivalent to 1.09 yards, how many yards are in 10 meters?

   10 meters × (1.09 yards/1 meter) = 10.9 yards.

2. If 1 yard is equivalent to .914 meters, how many meters are there in 24 yards?

   24 yards × (.914 meters/1 yard) = 21.936 meters.

SYSTEMS OF MEASUREMENT PROBLEMS

1. Express 38 meters in millimeters.

2. Express 871 millimeters in centimeters.

3. Which measurement is greater, 8,000 millimeters or 7 meters?

4. Arrange the following from smallest to largest: 6,700 meters, 672,000 centimeters, and 6.6 kilometers.

5. Express 49 milligrams in centigrams.

6. Express 4.6 liters in milliliters.

7. There are 2.2 pounds in a kilogram. A package weighing 32.5 kilograms is shipped to the U.S. What is its weight in pounds?

8. There are .914 meters in a yard. A line drawn on a blueprint measures 1.5 yards. What is its length in meters?

9. There are .62 miles in a kilometer. If the distance between two exits on a highway is 40 kilometers, what is the distance in miles?

10. There are 1.06 quarts in a liter. A particular brand of bottled water is available in two different bottle sizes—a 2.25 quart bottle and a 2.1 liter bottle. Which bottle contains more water?

SOLUTIONS

1. Since meters are larger than millimeters, our answer will be larger than 38. There are 1,000 millimeters in a meter, so we move the decimal point three places over to the right. Thirty-eight meters is equal to 38,000 millimeters.

2. Since millimeters are smaller than centimeters, our answer will be smaller than 871. There are 10 millimeters in a centimeter, so we move the decimal point one place over to the left. Therefore, 871 millimeters is equal to 87.1 centimeters.

3. In order to answer this question, we must express both measures in the same units. Since, for example, 8,000 millimeters is equal to 8 meters, we can see that 8,000 millimeters is larger than 7 meters.

4. Let's start by expressing all measurements in meters.

   672,000 centimeters = 6,720 meters
   6.6 kilometers = 6,600 meters
   6,700 meters = 6,700 meters

   Thus, from smallest to largest, we have 6.6 kilometers, 6,700 meters, and 672,000 centimeters.

5. Since there are 10 milligrams in a centigram, 49 milligrams is equal to 4.9 centigrams.

6. Since there are 1,000 milliliters in a liter, there are 4,600 milliliters in 4.6 liters.

7. 32.5 kgs = 32.5 kgs $\times$ (2.2 lbs/1 kg) = 71.5 lbs.

8. 1.5 yards = 1.5 yards $\times$ (.914 meters/1 yard) = 1.371 meters.

9. 40 kilometers = 40 kilometers $\times$ (.62 miles/1 kilometer) = 24.8 miles.

10. Express 2.1 liters in quarts.

    2.1 liters = 2.1 liters $\times$ (1.06 quarts/1 liter) = 2.226 quarts. Thus, the quart bottle holds more.

SIGNED NUMBERS

Signed Numbers

In describing subtraction of whole numbers, we said that the operation was not closed—that is, $4 - 6$ will yield a number that is not a member of the set of counting numbers and zero. The set of *integers* was developed to give meaning to such expressions as $4 - 6$. The set of integers is the set of all *signed* whole numbers and zero. It is the set $\{\ldots, -4, -3, -2, -1, 0, 1, 2, 3, 4, \ldots\}$

The first three dots symbolize the fact that the negative integers go on indefinitely, just as the positive integers do. Integers preceded by a minus sign (called *negative integers*) appear to the left of 0 on a number line.

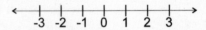

Decimals, fractions, and mixed numbers can also have negative signs. Together with positive fractions and decimals, they appear on the number line in this fashion:

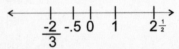

All numbers to the right of 0 are called *positive numbers*. They have the sign +, whether it is actually written or not. Business gains or losses, feet above or below sea level, and temperature above and below zero can all be expressed by means of signed numbers.

Addition

If the numbers to be added have the same sign, add the numbers (integers, fractions, decimals) as usual and use their common sign in the answer:

$$+9 + (+8) + (+2) = +19 \text{ or } 19$$
$$-4 + (-11) + (-7) + (-1) = -23$$

If the numbers to be added have different signs, add the positive numbers and then the negative numbers. Ignore the signs and subtract the smaller total from the larger total. If the larger total is positive, the answer will be positive; if the larger total is negative, the answer will be negative. The answer may be zero. Zero is neither positive nor negative and has no sign.

Example

$$+3 + (-5) + (-8) + (+2) = ?$$
$$+3 + (+2) = +5$$
$$-5 + (-8) = -13$$
$$13 - 5 = 8$$

Since the larger total (13) has a negative sign, the answer is -8.

Subtraction

The second number in a subtraction problem is called the *subtrahend*. In order to subtract, change the sign of the subtrahend and then continue as if you were *adding* signed numbers. If there is no sign in front of the subtrahend, it is assumed to be positive.

Examples

Subtract the subtrahend (bottom number) from the top number.

15	5	−35	−35	42
5	15	−42	42	35
10	−10	7	−77	7

Multiplication

If only two signed numbers are to be multiplied, multiply the numbers as you would if they were not signed. Then, if the two numbers have the *same sign,* the product is *positive.* If the two numbers have *different signs,* the product is *negative.* If more than two numbers are being multiplied, proceed two at a time in the same way as before, finding the signed product of the first two numbers, then multiplying that product by the next number, and so on. The product has a positive sign if all the factors are positive or there is an even number of negative factors. The product has a negative sign if there is an odd number of negative factors.

Example

$$-3 \cdot (+5) \cdot (-11) \cdot (-2) = -330$$

The answer is negative because there is an odd number (three) of negative factors.

The product of a signed number and zero is zero. The product of a signed number and 1 is the original number. The product of a signed number and −1 is the original number with its sign changed.

Examples

$$-5 \cdot 0 = 0$$
$$-5 \cdot 1 = -5$$
$$-5 \cdot (-1) = +5$$

Division

If the divisor and the dividend have the same sign, the answer is positive. Divide the numbers as you normally would. If the divisor and the dividend have different signs, the answer is negative. Divide the numbers as you normally would.

Examples

$$-3 \div (-2) = \frac{3}{2} = 1\frac{1}{2}$$

$$8 \div (-.2) = -40$$

If zero is divided by a signed number, the answer is zero. If a signed number is divided by zero, the answer does not exist. If a signed number is divided by 1, the number remains the same. If a signed number is divided by -1, the quotient is the original number with its sign changed.

Examples

$$0 \div (-2) = 0$$

$$-\frac{4}{3} \div 0 \qquad \text{is not defined}$$

$$\frac{2}{3} \div 1 = \frac{2}{3}$$

$$4 \div -1 = -4$$

*Peterson's Math Review for the
GRE, GMAT and MCAT*

SIGNED NUMBERS PROBLEMS

Perform the indicated operations:

1. $+12 + (-10) + (+2) + (-6) =$

2. $+7 + (-2) + (-8) + (+3) =$

3. $-3 - (-7) - (+4) + (-2) =$

4. $-(-8) - 10 - (+12) + (-4) =$

5. $-6 \times (+2) \times (-1) \times (-7) =$

6. $-2 \times (-3) \times (+4) \times (-2) =$

7. $15 \div (-0.5) =$

8. $\dfrac{(+12 \times -2)}{(-4)} =$

9. $(3)(2)(1)(0)(-1)(-2)(-3) =$

10. $\dfrac{(-8)(+3)}{(-6)(-2)(5)} =$

11. $\dfrac{6}{15} \div \left(\dfrac{-12}{5}\right) =$

12. $\dfrac{(+5) - (-13)}{(-4) + (-5)} =$

SOLUTIONS

1. $+12 + (-10) + (+2) + (-6) = +2 + (+2) + (-6)$
   $= 4 + (-6) = -2$

2. $+7 + (-2) = +7 - 2 = +5$
   $+5 + (-8) = +5 - 8 = -3$
   $-3 + (+3) = 0$

3. $-3 - (-7) = -3 + 7 = +4$
   $+4 - (+4) = +4 - 4 = 0$
   $0 + (-2) = -2$

4. $-(-8) - 10 - (+12) + (-4) = +8 - 10 - (+12) + (-4)$
   $= -2 - (+12) + (-4) = -14 + (-4) = -18$

5. $-6 \times (+2) = -12$
   $-12 \times (-1) = +12$
   $+12 \times (-7) = -84$

6. $-2 \times (-3) \times (+4) \times (-2) = +6 \times (+4) \times (-2)$
   $= 24 \times (-2) = 48$

7. $15 \div (-0.5) = -30$

8. $(+12 \times -2) = -24$
   $\dfrac{(-24)}{(-4)} = +6$

9. $(3)(2)(1)(0)(-1)(-2)(-3) = 0$, since, if 0 is a factor in any multiplication, the result is 0.

10. $\dfrac{(-8)(+3)}{(-6)(-2)(5)} = \dfrac{-24}{60} = -\dfrac{2}{5}$

11. $\dfrac{6}{15} \div \left[\dfrac{-12}{5}\right] = \dfrac{6}{15} \times \dfrac{5}{-12} = \dfrac{1}{3} \times \dfrac{1}{-2} = -\dfrac{1}{6}$

12. $\dfrac{(+5) - (-13)}{(-4) + (-5)} = \dfrac{5 + 13}{-9} = \dfrac{18}{-9} = -2$

POWERS, EXPONENTS, AND ROOTS

Exponents

The product $10 \times 10 \times 10$ can be written 10^3. We say 10 is raised to the *third power*. In general, $a \times a \times a \times \ldots \times a$ n times is written a^n. The *base a* is raised to the nth power, and n is called the *exponent*.

Examples

$3^2 = 3 \times 3$ read "3 squared"

$2^3 = 2 \times 2 \times 2$ read "2 cubed"

$5^4 = 5 \times 5 \times 5 \times 5$ read "5 to the fourth power"

If the exponent is 1, it is usually understood and not written; thus, $a^1 = a$.

Since

$$a^2 = a \times a \qquad \text{and} \qquad a^3 = a \times a \times a$$

then

$$a^2 \times a^3 = (a \times a)(a \times a \times a) = a^5$$

There are three rules for exponents. In general, if k and m are any counting numbers or zero, and a is any number,

Rule 1: $a^k \times a^m = a^{k+m}$

Rule 2: $a^m \times b^m = (ab)^m$

Rule 3: $(a^k)^n = a^{kn}$

Examples

Rule 1: $2^2 \times 2^3 = 4 \times 8 = 32$

and

$2^2 \times 2^3 = 2^5 = 32$

Rule 2: $3^2 \times 4^2 = 9 \times 16 = 144$

and

$3^2 \times 4^2 = (3 \times 4)^2 = 12^2 = 144$

Rule 3: $(3^2)^3 = 9^3 = 729$

and

$(3^2)^3 = 3^6 = 729$

Roots

The definition of roots is based on exponents. If $a^n = c$, where a is the base and n the exponent, a is called the nth *root* of c. This is written $a = \sqrt[n]{c}$. The symbol $\sqrt{\ }$ is called a *radical sign*. Since $5^4 = 625$, $\sqrt[4]{625} = 5$ and 5 is the fourth root of 625. The most frequently used roots are the second (called the square) root and the third (called the cube) root. The square root is written $\sqrt{\ }$ and the cube root is written $\sqrt[3]{\ }$.

Square Roots

If c is a positive number, there are two values, one negative and one positive, which, when multiplied together, will produce c.

Example

$+4 \times (+4) = 16$ and $-4 \times (-4) = 16$

The positive square root of a positive number c is called the *principal* square root of c (briefly, the *square root* of c) and is denoted by $\sqrt{c}$:

$\sqrt{144} = 12$

If $c = 0$, there is only one square root, 0. If c is a negative number, there is no real number that is the square root of c:

$\sqrt{-4}$ is not a real number

Cube Roots

Both positive and negative numbers have real cube roots. The cube root of 0 is 0. The cube root of a positive number is positive; that of a negative number is negative.

Example

$2 \times 2 \times 2 = 8$

Therefore $\sqrt[3]{8} = 2 - 3 \times (-3) \times (-3) = -27$

Therefore $\sqrt[3]{-27} = -3$

Each number has only one real cube root.

Expanded Form

We previously have seen how to write whole numbers in expanded form. Recall, for example, that the number 1,987 can be written as

$1{,}987 = 1(1{,}000) + 9(100) + 8(10) + 7$

Thus, 1,987 represents a number containing 7 "ones," 8 "tens," 9 "hundreds," and 1 "thousand." Using exponential notation, 1,987 can be written somewhat more compactly as

$1{,}987 = 1(10^3) + 9(10^2) + 8(10^1) + 7$

Example 1

Write the number 50,127 in expanded form using exponential notation.

$$50,127 = 5(10^4) + 0(10^3) + 1(10^2) + 2(10^1) + 7$$

Example 2

What number is represented by the expanded form $7(10^5) + 3(10^3) + 2(10^2) + 5(10^1) + 4$?

Note that there is no term corresponding to 10^4. Thus, the answer is 703,254.

Simplification of Square Roots

Certain square roots can be written in a simplified or reduced form. Just as all fractions should be simplified if possible, all square roots should also be simplified if possible. To simplify a square root means to remove any perfect square factors from under the square root sign.

The simplification of square roots is based on the *Product Rule for Square Roots:*

$$\sqrt{a \times b} = \sqrt{a} \times \sqrt{b}.$$

To illustrate the technique, let us simplify $\sqrt{12}$. Begin by writing 12 as 4×3, thus transforming the number under the square root sign into a product containing the perfect square factor 4.

$$\sqrt{12} = \sqrt{4 \times 3}$$

Then, using the Product Rule, write the square root of the product as the product of the square root.

$$\sqrt{12} = \sqrt{4 \times 3} = \sqrt{4} \times \sqrt{3}$$

Finally, compute $\sqrt{4}$ to obtain the simplified form.

$$\sqrt{12} = \sqrt{4 \times 3} = \sqrt{4} \times \sqrt{3} = 2\sqrt{3}$$

Example 1

Simplify $\sqrt{98}$.

$$\sqrt{98} = \sqrt{2 \times 49}$$
$$= \sqrt{2} \times \sqrt{49}, \quad \text{where 49 is a square number}$$
$$= \sqrt{2} \times 7$$

Therefore, $\sqrt{98} = 7\sqrt{2}$, and the process terminates because there is no whole number whose square is 2. We call $7\sqrt{2}$ a radical expression or simply a *radical.*

Example 2

Which is larger, $\left(\sqrt{96}\right)^2$ or $\sqrt{2^{14}}$?

$$\left(\sqrt{96}\right)^2 = \sqrt{96} \times \sqrt{96} = \sqrt{96 \times 96} = 96$$

$$\sqrt{2^{14}} = 2^7 = 128 \text{ because } 2^{14} = 2^7 \times 2^7 \text{ by Rule 1}$$

or because $\sqrt{2^{14}} = (2^{14})^{1/2} = 2^7$ by Rule 3

Since $128 > 96$, $\sqrt{2^{14}} > \left(\sqrt{96}\right)^2$

Example 3

Which is larger, $2\sqrt{75}$ or $6\sqrt{12}$?

These numbers can be compared if the same number appears under the radical sign. The greater number is the one with the larger number in front of the radical sign.

$$\sqrt{75} = \sqrt{25 \times 3} = \sqrt{25} \times \sqrt{3} = 5\sqrt{3}$$

Therefore:

$$2\sqrt{75} = 2(5\sqrt{3}) = 10\sqrt{3}$$

$$\sqrt{12} = \sqrt{4 \times 3} = \sqrt{4} \times \sqrt{3} = 2\sqrt{3}$$

Therefore:

$$6\sqrt{12} = 6(2\sqrt{3}) = 12\sqrt{3}$$

Since $12\sqrt{3} > 10\sqrt{3}$, $6\sqrt{12} > 2\sqrt{75}$

Radicals can be added and subtracted only if they have the same number under the radical sign. Otherwise, they must be reduced to expressions having the same number under the radical sign.

Example 4

Add $2\sqrt{18} + 4\sqrt{8} - \sqrt{2}$.

$$\sqrt{18} = \sqrt{9 \times 2} = \sqrt{9} \times \sqrt{2} = 3\sqrt{2}$$

Therefore:

$$2\sqrt{18} = 2(3\sqrt{2}) = 6\sqrt{2}$$

and

$$\sqrt{8} = \sqrt{4 \times 2} = \sqrt{4} \times \sqrt{2} = 2\sqrt{2}$$

Peterson's Math Review for the GRE, GMAT and MCAT

POWERS, EXPONENTS, AND ROOTS

Therefore:

$$4\sqrt{8} = 4(2\sqrt{2}) = 8\sqrt{2}$$

giving

$$2\sqrt{18} + 4\sqrt{8} - \sqrt{2} = 6\sqrt{2} + 8\sqrt{2} - \sqrt{2} = 13\sqrt{2}$$

Radicals are multiplied using the rule that

$$\sqrt[k]{a \times b} = \sqrt[k]{a} \times \sqrt[k]{b}$$

Example 5

$$\sqrt{2}\left(\sqrt{2} - 5\sqrt{3}\right) = \sqrt{4} - 5\sqrt{6} = 2 - 5\sqrt{6}$$

A quotient rule for radicals similar to the Product Rule is:

$$\sqrt[k]{\frac{a}{b}} = \frac{\sqrt[k]{a}}{\sqrt[k]{b}}$$

Example 6

$$\sqrt{\frac{9}{4}} = \frac{\sqrt{9}}{\sqrt{4}} = \frac{3}{2}$$

EXPONENTS, POWERS, AND ROOTS PROBLEMS

1. Simplify $\sqrt{180}$

2. Find the sum of $\sqrt{45} + \sqrt{125}$

3. Combine $2\sqrt{20} + 6\sqrt{45} - \sqrt{125}$

4. Find the difference $8\sqrt{12} - 2\sqrt{27}$

5. Simplify $(3\sqrt{32})(7\sqrt{2})$

6. Simplify $\sqrt{7}(2\sqrt{7} - \sqrt{3})$

7. Simplify $\dfrac{(20\sqrt{96})}{5\sqrt{4}}$

8. Divide and simplify $\dfrac{12\sqrt{75}}{4\sqrt{108}}$

9. Evaluate $-3^2 + (3^2)^3$

10. $3^2 \times 2^4 =$

11. Simplify $(\sqrt{15})^2$

12. Simplify $\sqrt{6}\sqrt{3}\sqrt{2}$

SOLUTIONS

1. $\sqrt{180} = \sqrt{36 \times 5} = 6\sqrt{5}$

2. $\sqrt{45} + \sqrt{125} = 3\sqrt{5} + 5\sqrt{5} = 8\sqrt{5}$

3. $2\sqrt{20} + 6\sqrt{45} - \sqrt{125}$
$= 2\sqrt{4 \times 5} + 6\sqrt{9 \times 5} - \sqrt{25 \times 5}$
$= 4\sqrt{5} + 18\sqrt{5} - 5\sqrt{5}$
$= 17\sqrt{5}$

4. $8\sqrt{12} - 2\sqrt{27} = 8\sqrt{4 \times 3} - 2\sqrt{9 \times 3} = 16\sqrt{3} = 10\sqrt{3}$

5. $(3\sqrt{32})(7\sqrt{2}) = 21(\sqrt{64}) = 21(8) = 168$

6. $\sqrt{7}(2\sqrt{7} - \sqrt{3})$
$= 2\sqrt{7}\sqrt{7} - \sqrt{7}\sqrt{3}$
$= 2\sqrt{49} - \sqrt{21}$
$= 2(7) - \sqrt{21}$
$= 14 - \sqrt{21}$

7. $\dfrac{(20\sqrt{96})}{5\sqrt{4}} = \left(\dfrac{20}{5}\right)\left(\dfrac{\sqrt{96}}{\sqrt{4}}\right) = 4\sqrt{\dfrac{96}{4}} = 4\sqrt{24} = 4\sqrt{4 \cdot 6}$
$= 8\sqrt{6}$

8. $\dfrac{12\sqrt{75}}{4\sqrt{108}} = \dfrac{12\sqrt{25 \times 3}}{4\sqrt{36 \times 3}} = \dfrac{12 \times 5\sqrt{3}}{4 \times 6\sqrt{3}} = \dfrac{60\sqrt{3}}{24\sqrt{3}} = \dfrac{60}{24} = \dfrac{5}{2}$

9. $-3^2 + (3^2)^3 = -9 + 3^6 = -9 + 729 = 720$

10. $3^2 \times 2^4 = 9 \times 16 = 144$

11. $(\sqrt{15})^2 = 15$, since squares and square roots are inverse operations

12. $\sqrt{6}\sqrt{3}\sqrt{2} = \sqrt{6 \times 3 \times 2} = \sqrt{36} = 6$

ALGEBRA

Algebra is a generalization of arithmetic. It provides methods for solving problems that cannot be done by arithmetic alone or that can be done by arithmetic only after long computations. Algebra provides a shorthand way of reducing long verbal statements to brief formulas, expressions, or equations. After the verbal statements have been reduced, the resulting algebraic expressions can be simplified. Suppose that a room is 12 feet wide and 20 feet long. Its perimeter (measurement around the outside) can be expressed as:

$$12 + 20 + 12 + 20 \text{ or } 2(12 + 20)$$

If the width of the room remains 12 feet but the letter l is used to symbolize length, the perimeter is:

$$12 + l + 12 + l \text{ or } 2(12 + l)$$

Further, if w is used for width, the perimeter of *any* rectangular room can be written as $2(w + l)$. This same room has an area of 12 feet by 20 feet, or 12×20. If l is substituted for 20, any room of width 12 has area equal to $12l$. If w is substituted for the number 12, the area of any rectangular room is given by wl or lw. Expressions such as wl and $2(w + l)$ are called *algebraic expressions*. An *equation* is a statement that two algebraic expressions are equal. A *formula* is a special type of equation.

Evaluating Formulas

If we are given an expression and numerical values to be assigned to each letter, the expression can be evaluated.

Example 1

Evaluate $2x + 3y - 7$ if $x = 2$ and $y = -4$.

Substitute given values.

$2(2) + 3(-4) - 7 = ?$

Multiply numbers using rules for signed numbers.

$4 + -12 - 7 = ?$

Collect numbers.

$4 - 19 = -15$

We have already evaluated formulas in arithmetic when solving percent, discount, and interest problems.

Example 2

Evaluate each of the following expressions if $a = 3$, $b = -2$, and $c = 0$.

    a. $-a^2$
    b. $3b - 4b^2$
    c. $ab + 4c$

a. $-a^2 = -(3)^2 = -(9) = -9$

b. $b - 4b^2 = 3(-2) - 4(-2)^2 = -6 - 4(4) = -6 - 16 = -22$

c. $ab + 4c = (3)(-2) + 4(0) = -6 + 0 = -6$

Example 3

If $x = 1$ and $y = -2$, find the value of $-x^2y^2$

$-x^2y^2 = -(1)^2(-2)^2 = -(1)(4) = -(4) = -4$

Example 4

The formula for temperature conversion is

$$F = \frac{9}{5}C + 32$$

where C stands for the temperature in degrees Celsius and F for degrees Fahrenheit. Find the Fahrenheit temperature that is equivalent to 20°C.

$$F = \frac{9}{5}(20°C) + 32 = 36 + 32 = 68°F$$

Example 5

The formula for the area of a triangle is $A = \frac{bh}{2}$. Find A if $b = 12$ and $h = 7$.

$$A = \frac{bh}{2} = \frac{12 \times 7}{2} = 42$$

ALGEBRAIC EXPRESSIONS

Formulation

A more difficult problem than evaluating an expression or formula is translating from a verbal expression to an algebraic one:

Verbal	Algebraic
Thirteen more than x	$x + 13$
Six less than twice x	$2x - 6$
The square of the sum of x and 5	$(x + 5)^2$
The sum of the square of x and the square of 5	$x^2 + 5^2$
The distance traveled by a car going 50 miles an hour for x hours	$50x$
The average of 70, 80, 85, and x	$\dfrac{70 + 80 + 85 + x}{4}$

Simplification

After algebraic expressions have been formulated, they can usually be simplified by means of the laws of exponents and the common operations of addition, subtraction, multiplication, and division. These techniques will be described in the next section. Algebraic expressions and equations frequently contain parentheses, which are removed in the process of simplifying. If an expression contains more than one set of parentheses, remove the inner set first and then the outer set. Brackets, [ ], which are often used instead of parentheses, are treated the same way. Parentheses are used to indicate multiplication. Thus, $3(x + y)$ means that 3 is to be multiplied by the sum of x and y. The *distributive law* is used to accomplish this:

$$a(b + c) = ab + ac$$

The expression in front of the parentheses is multiplied by each term inside. Rules for signed numbers apply.

Example 1

Simplify $3[4(2 - 8) - 5(4 + 2)]$.

This can be done in two ways.

Method 1: Combine the numbers inside the parentheses first:

$$3[4(2 - 8) - 5(4 + 2)] = 3[4(-6) - 5(6)]$$
$$= 3[-24 - 30]$$
$$= 3[-54] = -162$$

Method 2: Use the distributive law:

$$3[4(2 - 8) - 5(4 + 2)] = 3[8 - 32 - 20 - 10]$$
$$= 3[8 - 62]$$
$$= 3[-54] = -162$$

If there is a (+) before the parentheses, the signs of the terms inside the parentheses remain the same when the parentheses are removed. If there is a (−) before the parentheses, the sign of each term inside the parentheses changes when the parentheses are removed.

Once parentheses have been removed, the order of operations is multiplication and division, then addition and subtraction from left to right.

Example 2

$(-15 + 17) \times 3 - [(4 \times 9) \div 6] = ?$

Work inside the parentheses first: $(2) \times 3 - [36 \div 6] = ?$

Then work inside the brackets: $2 \times 3 - [6] = ?$

Multiply first, then subtract, proceeding from left to right: $6 - 6 = 0$

The placement of parentheses and brackets is important. Using the same numbers as above with the parentheses and brackets placed in different positions can give many different answers.

Example 3

$-15 + [(17 \times 3) - (4 \times 9)] \div 6 = ?$

Work inside the parentheses first:
$-15 + [(51) - (36)] \div 6 = ?$

Then work inside the brackets:

$-15 + [15] \div 6 = ?$

Since there are no more parentheses or brackets, proceed from left to right, dividing before adding:

$$-15 + 2\frac{1}{2} = -12\frac{1}{2}$$

Operations

When letter symbols and numbers are combined with [...] of arithmetic (+, −, ×, ÷) and with certain other ma[...] operations, we have an *algebraic expression.* Algeb[...] are made up of several parts connected by a plus o[...] each part is called a *term.* Terms with the same letter part a[...] *like terms.* Since algebraic expressions represent numbers, they can be added, subtracted, multiplied, and divided.

When we defined the commutative law of addition in arithmetic by writing $a + b = b + a$, we meant that a and b could represent any number. The expression $a + b = b + a$ is an *identity* because it is true for all numbers. The expression $n + 5 = 14$ is not an identity because it is not true for all numbers; it becomes true only when the number 9 is substituted for n. Letters used to represent numbers are called *variables.* If a number stands alone (the 5 or 14 in $n + 5 = 14$), it is called a *constant* because its value is constant or unchanging. If a number appears in front of a variable, it is called a *coefficient.* Because the letter x is frequently used to represent a variable, or *unknown,* the times sign ×, which can be confused with it in handwriting, is rarely used to express multiplication in algebra. Other expressions used for multiplication are a dot, parentheses, or simply writing a number and letter together:

$5 \cdot 4$ or $5(4)$ or $5a$

Of course, 54 still means fifty-four.

Addition and Subtraction

Only like terms can be combined. Add or subtract the coefficients of like terms, using the rules for signed numbers.

Example 1

Add $x + 2y - 2x + 3y$.

$x - 2x + 2y + 3y = -x + 5y$

Example 2

Perform the subtraction:

$$\begin{array}{r} -30a - 15b + 4c \\ -(-\ 5a +\ \ 3b -\ \ c + d) \end{array}$$

Change the sign of each term in the subtrahend and then add, using the rules for signed numbers:

$$\begin{array}{r} -30a - 15b + 4c \\ 5a -\ \ 3b +\ \ c - d \\ \hline -25a - 18b + 5c - d \end{array}$$

Example 3

Perform the following subtraction:

$$(b^2 + 6bk - 7k^2) - (3b^2 + 6bk - 10k^2)$$

Once again, change the sign of each term in the subtrahend and then add.

$$(b^2 + 6bk - 7k^2) - (3b^2 + 6bk - 10k^2)$$
$$= (b^2 + 6bk - 7k^2) + (3b^2 - 6bk + 10k^2)$$
$$= -2b^2 + 3k^2$$

Multiplication

Multiplication is accomplished by using the *distributive property*. If the multiplier has only one term, then
$$a(b + c) = ab + bc$$

Example

$$9x(5m + 9q) = (9x)(5m) + (9x)(9q)$$
$$= 45mx + 81qx$$

When the multiplier contains more than one term and you are multiplying two expressions, multiply each term of the first expression by each term of the second and then add like terms. Follow the rules for signed numbers and exponents at all times.

Example 1

$$(2x - 1)(x + 6)$$
$$= 2x(x + 6) - 1(x + 6)$$
$$= 2x^2 + 12x - x - 6$$
$$= 2x^2 + 11x - 6$$

Example 2

$$(3x + 8)(4x^2 + 2x + 1)$$
$$= 3x(4x^2 + 2x + 1) + 8(4x^2 + 2x + 1)$$
$$= 12x^3 + 6x^2 + 3x + 32x^2 + 16x + 8$$
$$= 12x^3 + 38x^2 + 19x + 8$$

If more than two expressions are to be multiplied, multiply the first two, then multiply the product by the third factor, and so on, until all factors have been used.

Algebraic expressions can be multiplied by themselves (squared) or raised to any power.

Example 1

$$(a + b)^2 = (a + b)(a + b)$$
$$= a(a + b) + b(a + b)$$
$$= a^2 + ab + ba + b^2$$
$$= a^2 + 2ab + b^2$$

since $ab = ba$ by the commutative law.

Example 2

$$(a + b)(a - b) = a(a - b) + b(a - b)$$
$$= a^2 - ab + ba - b^2$$
$$= a^2 - b^2$$

Factoring

When two or more algebraic expressions are multiplied, each is called a factor and the result is the *product*. The reverse process of finding the factors when given the product is called *factoring*. A product can often be factored in more than one way. Factoring is useful in multiplication, division, and solving equations.

One way to factor an expression is to remove any single-term factor that is common to each of the terms and write it outside the parentheses. It is the distributive law that permits this.

Example 1

$$3x + 12 = 3(x + 4)$$

The result can be checked by multiplication.

Example 2

$$3x^3 + 6x^2 + 9x = 3x(x^2 + 2x + 3)$$

The result can be checked by multiplication.

Expressions containing squares can sometimes be factored into expressions containing letters raised to the first power only, called *linear factors*. We have seen that

$$(a + b)(a - b) = a^2 - b^2$$

Therefore, if we have an expression in the form of a difference of two squares, it can be factored as:

$$a^2 - b^2 = (a + b)(a - b)$$

Example 1

Factor $x^2 - 16$.

$$x^2 - 16 = (x)^2 - (4)^2 = (x - 4)(x + 4)$$

Example 2

Factor $4x^2 - 9$.

$$4x^2 - 9 = (2x)^2 - (3)^2 = (2x + 3)(2x - 3)$$

Again, the result can be checked by multiplication.

A third type of expression that can be factored is one containing three terms, such as $x^2 + 5x + 6$. Since

$$(x + a)(x + b) = x(x + b) + a(x + b)$$
$$= x^2 + xb + ax + ab$$
$$= x^2 + (a + b)x + ab$$

an expression in the form $x^2 + (a + b)x + ab$ can be factored into two factors of the form $(x + a)$ and $(x + b)$. We must find two numbers whose product is the constant in the given expression and whose sum is the coefficient of the term containing x.

Example 1

Find factors of $x^2 + 5x + 6$.

First find two numbers which, when multiplied, have +6 as a product. Possibilities are 2 and 3, −2 and −3, 1 and 6, −1 and −6. From these select the one pair whose sum is 5. The pair 2 and 3 is the only possible selection, and so:

$$x^2 + 5x + 6 = (x + 2)(x + 3) \quad \text{written in either order}$$

Example 2

Factor $x^2 - 5x - 6$.

Possible factors of -6 are -1 and 6, 1 and -6, 2 and -3, -2 and 3. We must select the pair whose sum is -5. The only pair whose sum is -5 is $+1$ and -6, and so

$$x^2 - 5x - 6 = (x + 1)(x - 6)$$

In factoring expressions of this type, notice that if the last sign is plus, both a and b have the same sign and it is the same as the sign of the middle term. If the last sign is minus, the numbers have opposite signs.

Many expressions cannot be factored.

Example 3

Factor $2x^3 - 8x^2 + 8x$.

In expressions of this type, begin by factoring out the largest common monomial factor, then try to factor the resulting trinomial.

$$2x^3 - 8x^2 + 8x = 2x(x^2 - 4x + 4) = 2x(x - 2)(x - 2)$$
$$= 2x(x - 2)^2$$

Division

$$\frac{36mx^2}{9m^2x} = 4m^1x^2m^{-2}x^{-1}$$

$$= 4m^{-1}x^1 = \frac{4x}{m}$$

Method 2

Cancellation

$$\frac{36mx^2}{9m^2x} = \frac{\overset{4}{\cancel{36mxx}}}{\underset{1}{\cancel{9mxm}}} = \frac{4x}{m}$$

This is acceptable because

$$\frac{ab}{bc} = \frac{a}{b}\left(\frac{c}{c}\right) \text{ and } \frac{c}{c} = 1$$

so that $\dfrac{ac}{bc} = \dfrac{a}{b}$

Example 1

If the divisor contains only one term and the dividend is a sum, divide each term in the dividend by the divisor and simplify as you did in Method 2.

$$\frac{9x^3 + 3x^2 + 6x}{3x} = \frac{\overset{3x^2}{\cancel{9x^3}}}{\cancel{3x}} + \frac{\overset{x}{\cancel{3x^2}}}{\cancel{3x}} + \frac{\overset{2}{\cancel{6x}}}{\cancel{3x}}$$

$$= 3x^2 + x + 2$$

This method cannot be followed if there are two terms or more in the denominator since

$$\frac{a}{b+c} \neq \frac{a}{b} + \frac{a}{c}$$

In this case, write the example as a fraction. Factor the numerator and denominator if possible. Then use laws of exponents or cancel.

Example 2

Divide $x^3 - 9x$ by $x^3 + 6x^2 + 9x$.

Write as:

$$\frac{x^3 - 9x}{x^3 + 6x^2 + 9x}$$

Both numerator and denominator can be factored to give:

$$\frac{x(x^2 - 9)}{x(x^2 + 6x + 9)} = \frac{\cancel{x}\cancel{(x+3)}(x - 3)}{\cancel{x}\cancel{(x+3)}(x + 3)} = \frac{x - 3}{x + 3}$$

ALGEBRA PROBLEMS

1. Simplify: $3[4(6 - 14) - 8(-2 - 5)]$

2. Simplify: $(5x^2 - 3x + 2) - (3x^2 + 5x - 1) + (6x^2 - 2)$

3. Add: $(a - b - c) + (a - b - c) - (a - b - c)$

4. Multiply: $(x - 2)(x^2 + 3x + 7)$

5. Multiply: $(a + 1)^2 (a + 2)$

6. Multiply: $(2x + 1)(3x^2 - x + 6)$

7. Factor completely: $6x^2 - 3x - 18$

8. Factor completely: $12x^2 + 14x + 4$

9. Factor completely: $6x^4 - 150x^2$

10. Factor completely: $4a^2b + 12ab - 72b$

11. Multiply: $\dfrac{x^2 - x - 6}{x^2} \times \dfrac{x^2 + 4x + 3}{x^2 + 5x + 6}$

12. Simplify: $\dfrac{x^2 - 4x - 21}{x^2 - 9x + 14}$

SOLUTIONS

1. $3[4(6-14)-8(-2-5)] = 3[4(-8)-8(-7)]$
$$= 3[-32+56] = 3(24) = 72$$

2. $(5x^2 - 3x + 2) - (3x^2 + 5x - 1) + (6x^2 - 2)$
$= 5x^2 - 3x + 2 - 3x^2 - 5x + 1 + 6x^2 - 2 = 8x^2 - 8x + 1$

3. $(a - b - c) + (a - b - c) - (a - b - c)$
$= a - b - c + a - b - c - a + b + c = a - b - c$

4. $(x - 2)(x^2 + 3x + 7) = x(x^2 + 3x + 7) - 2(x^2 + 3x + 7)$
$= x^3 + 3x^2 + 7x - 2x^2 - 6x - 14 = x^3 + x^2 + x - 14$

5. $(a + 1)^2 (a + 2) = (a + 1)(a + 1)(a + 2)$
$$= (a^2 + 2a + 1)(a + 2)$$
$$= a^3 + 2a^2 + 2a^2 + 4a + a + 2$$
$$= a^3 + 4a^2 + 5a + 2$$

6. $(2x + 1)(3x^2 - x + 6) = 2x(3x^2 - x + 6) + 1(3x^2 - x + 6)$
$$= 6x^3 - 2x^2 + 12x + 3x^2 - x + 6$$
$$= 6x^3 + x^2 + 11x + 6$$

7. $6x^2 - 3x - 18 = 3(2x^2 - x - 6) = 3(2x + 3)(x - 2)$

8. $12x^2 + 14x + 4 = 2(6x^2 + 7x + 2) = 2(3x + 2)(2x + 1)$

9. $6x^4 - 150x^2 = 6x^2(x^2 - 25) = 6x^2(x - 5)(x + 5)$

10. $4a^2b + 12\,ab - 72b = 4b(a^2 + 3a - 18)$
$$= 4b(a + 6)(a - 3)$$

11. $\dfrac{x^2 - x - 6}{x^2 - 9} \times \dfrac{x^2 + 4x + 3}{x^2 + 5x + 6} = \dfrac{(x-3)(x+2)}{(x-3)(x+3)} \times \dfrac{(x+3)(x+1)}{(x+2)(x+3)}$

$$= \dfrac{(x-3)(x+2)}{(x-3)(x+3)} \times \dfrac{(x+3)(x+1)}{(x+2)(x+3)}$$

$$= \dfrac{x+1}{x+3}$$

12. $\dfrac{x^2 - 4x - 21}{x^2 - 9x + 14} = \dfrac{(x+3)(x-7)}{(x-7)(x-2)} = \dfrac{x+3}{x-2}$

EQUATIONS

Solving equations is one of the major objectives in algebra. If a variable x in an equation is replaced by a value or expression that makes the equation a true statement, the value or expression is called a *solution* of the equation. (Remember that an equation is a mathematical statement that one algebraic expression is equal to another.)

An equation may contain one or more variables. We begin with one variable. Certain rules apply to equations whether there are one or more variables. The following rules are applied to give equivalent equations that are simpler than the original:

Addition: If $s = t$, then $s + c = t + c$.

Subtraction: If $s + c = t + c$, then $s = t$.

Multiplication: If $s = t$, then $cs = ct$.

Division: If $cs = ct$ and $c \neq 0$, then $s = t$.

To solve for x in an equation in the form $ax = b$ with $a \neq 0$, divide each side of the equation by a:

$$\frac{ax}{a} = \frac{b}{a} \quad \text{yielding} \quad x = \frac{b}{a}$$

Then, $\frac{b}{a}$ is the solution to the equation.

Example 1

Solve $x + 5 = 12$

Subtract 5 from both sides.

$$\begin{array}{r} x + 5 = 12 \\ -5 \quad -5 \\ \hline x \quad = \quad 7 \end{array}$$

Example 2

Solve $4x = 8$.

Write $\frac{4x}{4} = \frac{8}{4}$

$x = 2$

Example 3

Solve $\frac{x}{4} = 9$.

Write $4 \times \frac{x}{4} = 9 \times 4$.

Thus, $x = 36$.

Example 4

Solve $3x + 7 = 19$.

$3x = 12$ Subtract 7 from both sides.

$x = 4$ Divide each side by 3.

Example 5

Solve $2x - (x - 4) = 5(x + 2)$ for x.

$2x - (x - 4) = 5(x + 2)$

$2x - x + 4 = 5x + 10$	Remove parentheses by distributive law.
$x + 4 = 5x + 10$	Combine like terms.
$x = 5x + 6$	Subtract 4 from each side.
$-4x = 6$	Subtract $5x$ from each side.
$x = \dfrac{6}{-4}$	Divide each side by -4.
$= -\dfrac{3}{2}$	Reduce fraction to lowest terms.
	Negative sign now applies to the entire fraction.

Check the solution for accuracy by substituting in the original equation:

$$2\left(-\frac{3}{2}\right) - \left(-\frac{3}{2} - 4\right) \overset{?}{=} 5\left(-\frac{3}{2} + 2\right)$$

$$-3 - \left(-\frac{11}{2}\right) \overset{?}{=} 5\left(\frac{1}{2}\right)$$

$$-3 + \frac{11}{2} \overset{?}{=} \frac{5}{2}$$

$$-\frac{6}{2} + \frac{11}{2} \overset{?}{=} \frac{5}{2} \quad \text{check}$$

EQUATION PROBLEMS

Solve the following equations for x:

1. $-5x + 3 = x + 2$

2. $6 + 4x = 6x - 10$

3. $x + 3(2x + 5) = -20$

4. $4(x + 2) - (2x + 1) = x + 5$

5. $3(2x + 5) = 10x + 7 + 2(x - 8)$

6. $3x - 4(3x - 2) = -x$

7. $6 + 8(8 - 2x) = 14 - 8(4x - 2)$

8. $\dfrac{2x + 3}{5} - 10 = \dfrac{4 - 3x}{2}$

9. $3(2x + 1) + 2(3x + 1) = 17$

10. $(x - 5)^2 = 4 + (x + 5)^2$

SOLUTIONS

1. $-5x + 3 = x + 2$
   $\underline{+5x +5x}$
   $3 = 6x + 2$
   $\underline{-2 -2}$
   $1 = 6x$
   $\dfrac{1}{6} = x$

2. $6 + 4x = 6x - 10$
   $6 = 2x - 10$
   $16 = 2x$
   $x = 8$

3. $x + 3(2x + 5) = -20$
   $x + 6x + 15 = -20$
   $7x + 15 = -20$
   $7x = -35$
   $x = -5$

4. $4(x + 2) - (2x + 1) = x + 5$
   $4x + 8 - 2x - 1 = x + 5$
   $2x + 7 = x + 5$
   $x = -2$

5. $3(2x + 5) = 10x + 7 + 2(x - 8)$
   $6x + 15 = 10x + 7 + 2x - 16$
   $6x + 15 = 12x - 9$
   $24 = 6x$
   $x = 4$

6. $3x - 4(3x - 2) = -x$
   $3x - 12x + 8 = -x$
   $-9x + 8 = -x$
   $8 = 8x$
   $x = 1$

7. $6 + 8(8 - 2x) = 14 - 8(4x - 2)$

$6 + 64 - 16x = 14 - 32x + 16$

$70 - 16x = 30 - 32x$

$16x = -40$

$x = -\dfrac{40}{16} = -\dfrac{5}{2}$

8. $\dfrac{2x + 3}{5} - 10 = \dfrac{4 - 3x}{2}$

$10 \times \dfrac{2x + 3}{5} - 10 \times 10 = \dfrac{4 - 3x}{2} \times 10$

$2(2x + 3) - 100 = 5(4 - 3x)$

$4x + 6 - 100 = 20 - 15x$

$4x - 94 = 20 - 15x$

$4x = 114 - 15x$

$19x = 114$

$x = 6$

9. $3(2x + 1) + 2(3x + 1) = 17$

$6x + 3 + 6x + 2 = 17$

$12x + 5 = 17$

$12x = 12$

$x = 1$

10. $(x - 5)^2 = 4 + (x + 5)^2$

$x^2 - 10x + 25 = 4 + x^2 + 10x + 25$

Subtract x^2 from both sides and combine terms

$-10x + 25 = 10x + 29$

$20x = -4$

$x = -\dfrac{1}{5}$

Word Problems Involving One Unknown

In many cases, if you read a word problem carefully, assign a letter to the quantity to be found, and understand the relationships between known and unknown quantities, you can formulate an equation with one unknown.

Number Problems and Age Problems

These two kinds of problems are similar to each other.

Example 1

One number is 3 times another, and their sum is 48. Find the two numbers.

Let x = second number. Then the first is $3x$. Since their sum is 48,

$$3x + x = 48$$
$$4x = 48$$
$$x = 12$$

Therefore, the first number is $3x = 36$.

$36 + 12 = 48$ check

Example 2

Art is now three times older than Ryan. Four years ago, Art was five times as old as Ryan was then. How old is Art now?

Let R = Ryan's age

Then $3R$ = Art's age

Four years ago, Ryan's age was $R - 4$, and Art's age was $3R - 4$.

Since at that time Art was five times as old as Ryan, we have

$$5(R - 4) = 3R - 4$$
$$5R - 20 = 3R - 4$$
$$2R = 16$$
$$R = 8, 3R = 24.$$

Art is 24 years old now.

Distance Problems

The basic concept is:

Distance = rate · time

Example 1

In a mileage test, a man drives a truck at a fixed rate of speed for 1 hour. Then he increases the speed by 20 miles per hour and drives at that rate for 2 hours. He then reduces that speed by 5 miles per hour and drives at that rate for 3 hours. If the distance traveled was 295 miles, what are the rates of speed over each part of the test?

Let x be the first speed, $x + 20$ the second, and $x + (20 - 5) = x + 15$ the third. Because distance = rate · time, multiply these rates by the time and formulate the equation by separating the two equal expressions for distance by an equals sign:

$$1x + 2(x + 20) + 3(x + 15) = 295$$
$$x + 2x + 3x + 40 + 45 = 295$$
$$6x = 210$$
$$x = 35$$

The speeds are 35, 55, and 50 miles per hour.

Example 2

Two trains leave the Newark station at the same time traveling in opposite directions. One travels at a rate of 60 mph, and the other travels at a rate of 50 mph. In how many hours will the trains be 880 miles apart?

The two trains will be 880 miles apart when the sum of the distances that they both have traveled is 880 miles.

Let r_1 = the rate of the first train; r_2 = the rate of the second train

Let t_1 = the time of the first train; t_2 = the time of the second train

Then, the distance the first train travels is $r_1 t_1$, and the distance the second train travels is $r_2 t_2$. Our equation will be $r_1 t_1 + r_2 t_2 = 880$. Since $r_1 = 60$, $r_2 = 50$, and $t_1 = t_2$, we can rewrite the equation as

$$60t + 50t = 880$$
$$110t = 880$$
$$t = 8$$

It will take 8 hours for the trains to get 880 miles apart.

Consecutive Number Problems

This type usually involves only one unknown. Two numbers are consecutive if one is the successor of the other. Three consecutive numbers are of the form x, $x + 1$, and $x + 2$. Since an even number is divisible by 2, consecutive even numbers are of the form $2x$, $2x + 2$, and $2x + 4$. An odd number is of the form $2x + 1$.

Example 1

Find three consecutive whole numbers whose sum is 75.

Let the first number be x, the second $x + 1$, and the third $x + 2$. Then:

$$x + (x + 1) + (x + 2) = 75$$
$$3x + 3 = 75$$
$$3x = 72$$
$$x = 24$$

The numbers whose sum is 75 are 24, 25, and 26. Many versions of this problem have no solution. For example, no three consecutive whole numbers have a sum of 74.

Example 2

Find three consecutive even integers whose sum is 48.

We can express three consecutive even integers as x, $x + 2$, and $x + 4$. Thus, we have

$$x + (x + 2) + (x + 4) = 48$$
$$3x + 6 = 48$$
$$3x = 42$$
$$x = 14$$

The integers are 14, 16, and 18.

Work Problems

These problems concern the speed with which work can be accomplished and the time necessary to perform a task if the size of the work force is changed.

Example 1

If Joe can type a chapter alone in 6 days and Ann can type the same chapter in 8 days, how long will it take them to type the chapter if they both work on it?

We let x = number of days required if they work together and then put our information into tabular form:

	Joe	Ann	Together
Days to type chapter	6	8	x
Part typed in 1 day	$\dfrac{1}{6}$	$\dfrac{1}{8}$	$\dfrac{1}{x}$

Since the part done by Joe in 1 day plus the part done by Ann in 1 day equals the part done by both in 1 day, we have

$$\frac{1}{6} + \frac{1}{8} = \frac{1}{x}$$

Next we multiply each member by $48x$ to clear the fractions, giving:

$$8x + 6x = 48$$
$$14x = 48$$
$$x = 3\frac{3}{7} \text{ days}$$

Example 2

Working alone, one pipe can fill a pool in 8 hours, a second pipe can fill the pool in 12 hours, and a third can fill it in 24 hours. How long would it take all three pipes, working at the same time, to fill the pool?

Using the same logic as in the previous problem, we obtain the equation

$$\frac{1}{8} + \frac{1}{12} + \frac{1}{24} = \frac{1}{x}$$

To clear the fractions, we multiply each side by $24x$, giving

$$3x + 2x + x = 24$$
$$6x = 24$$
$$x = 4$$

It would take the pipes 4 hours to fill the pool.

Word Problems Involving One Unknown—Problems

1. One integer is two more than a second integer. The first integer added to four times the second is equal to 17. Find the values of the two integers.

2. If 6 times a number is decreased by 4, the result is the same as when 3 times the number is increased by 2. What is the number?

3. The smaller of two numbers is 31 less than three times the larger. If the numbers differ by 7, what is the smaller number?

4. The sum of three consecutive even integers is 84. Find the smallest of the integers.

5. In a recent local election with two candidates, the winner received 372 more votes than the loser. If the total number of votes cast was 1,370, how many votes did the winning candidate receive?

6. Mike is three years older than Al. In nine years, the sum of their ages will be 47. How old is Mike now?

7. At the Wardlaw Hartridge School Christmas program, student tickets cost $3, and adult tickets cost twice as much. If a total of 200 tickets were sold, and $900 was collected, how many student tickets were sold?

8. Mrs. Krauser invested a part of her $6,000 inheritance at 9 percent simple annual interest and the rest at 12 percent simple annual interest. If the total interest earned in one year was $660, how much did she invest at 12 percent?

9. One pump working continuously can fill a reservoir in thirty days. A second pump can fill the reservoir in twenty days. How long would it take both pumps working together to fill the reservoir?

10. Working together, Brian, Peter, and Jared can shovel the driveway in 12 minutes. If Brian, alone, can shovel the driveway in 21 minutes, and Peter, alone, can shovel the driveway in 84 minutes, how long would it take Jared to shovel the driveway alone?

11. Jimmy is now three years older than Bobby. If seven years from now the sum of their ages is 79, how old is Jimmy now?

12. A freight train and a passenger train leave the same station at noon and travel in opposite directions. If the freight train travels 52 mph and the passenger train travels 84 mph, at what time are they 680 miles apart?

SOLUTIONS

1. Let x = the first integer

   Then, $x - 2$ = the second integer, and

   $$x + 4(x - 2) = 17$$
   $$x + 4x - 8 = 17$$
   $$5x - 8 = 17$$
   $$5x = 25$$
   $$x = 5.$$

   The second integer is $x - 2 = 5 - 2 = 3$.

   The integers are 3 and 5.

2. Let x = the number. Then,

   $6x - 4 = 3x + 2$ Thus,

   $3x = 6$ And

   $x = 2$ The number is 2.

3. Let S = the smaller number.
   Then, the larger number = S + 7, and

   $$S + 31 = 3(S + 7)$$
   $$S + 31 = 3S + 21$$
   $$2S = 10$$
   $$S = 5$$ The smaller number is 5.

4. Let x = the smallest integer. Then,

   $x + 2$ = the middle integer, and

   $x + 4$ = the largest integer

   $$x + (x + 2) + (x + 4) = 84$$
   $$3x + 6 = 84$$
   $$3x = 78$$
   $$x = 26$$

   The smallest of the three integers is 26.

5. Let W = the number of votes the winner received.
   Then, W − 372 = the number of votes the loser received.

   $$W + (W - 372) = 1,370$$
   $$2W - 372 = 1,370$$
   $$2W = 1,742$$
   $$W = 871$$

   The winner received 871 votes.

6. Let M = Mike's age now. Then, M − 3 = Al's age. In nine years, Mike will be M + 9, and Al will be M + 6. Therefore,

$$M + 9 + M + 6 = 47$$
$$2M + 15 = 47$$
$$2M = 32$$
$$M = 16$$

Thus, Mike is 16 now.

7. Let S = the number of student tickets sold. Then, 200 − S = the number of adult tickets sold.

Thus, the money from student tickets is 3S, and the money received from adult tickets is 6(200 − S). Since a total of $900 was collected,

$$3S + 6(200 − S) = 900$$
$$3S + 1200 − 6S = 900$$
$$3S = 300$$
$$S = 100$$

Therefore, 100 student tickets were sold.

8. Let x = the amount invested at 12 percent. Then, since she invested a total of $6,000, she must have invested $,6000 −$x$ at 9 percent. And, since she received $660 in interest, we have

$$12\%(x) + 9\%(6,000 − x) = 660 \quad \text{or,}$$
$$.12x + .09(6,000 − x) = 660$$
$$.12x + 540 − .09x = 660$$
$$.03x + 540 = 660$$
$$.03x = 120$$
$$x = \frac{120}{.03} = 4,000$$

She invested $4,000 at 12 percent.

9. Let x = the number of minutes *(Days)* that it would take both pumps working together to fill the reservoir. In this time, the first pump will fill $\frac{x}{30}$ of the reservoir, and the second pump will fill $\frac{x}{20}$ of the reservoir. Thus,

$$\frac{1}{30} + \frac{1}{20} = \frac{1}{x}$$

Multiply both sides by $60x$.

$$2x + 3x = 60$$
$$5x = 60$$
$$x = 12 \quad \text{(Days)}$$

It takes 12 ~~minutes~~ for both pumps to fill the reservoir together.

10. Let J = the time Jared needs to shovel the driveway alone.

In 12 minutes, Brian can shovel $\frac{12}{21}$ of the driveway

In 12 minutes, Peter can shovel $\frac{12}{84}$ of the driveway

In 12 minutes, Jared can shovel $\frac{12}{J}$ of the driveway. Therefore,

$$\frac{12}{21} + \frac{12}{84} + \frac{12}{J} = 1 \quad \text{Multiply both sides by } 84J$$

$$48J + 12J + 1{,}008 = 84J$$
$$24J = 1{,}008$$
$$J = 42.$$

Jared can shovel the driveway in 42 minutes.

11. Let B = Bobby's age. Then, $B + 3$ = Jimmy's age.

In seven years, Bobby's age will be $B + 7$, and Jimmy's will be $B + 10$.

Therefore, in 7 years, we will have

$$(B + 7) + (B + 10) = 79$$
$$2B + 17 = 79$$
$$2B = 62$$
$$B = 31$$

Bobby is 31 now. *(← except you Morons asked how old Jimmy was!! in the original question)*

★ 34 yr old.

12. Let t = the amount of time each train travels. Then, the distance the freight train travels is $52t$, and the distance the passenger train travels is $84t$. Thus,

$$52t + 84t = 680$$
$$136t = 680$$
$$t = 5$$

The trains each travel for 5 hours, so they will be 680 miles apart at 5 p.m.

LITERAL EQUATIONS

An equation may have other letters in it besides the variable (or variables). Such an equation is called a *literal equation*. An illustration is $x + b = a$, with x being the variable. The solution of such an equation will not be a specific number but will involve letter symbols. Literal equations are solved by exactly the same methods as those involving numbers, but we must know which of the letters in the equation is to be considered the variable. Then the other letters are treated as constants.

Example 1

Solve $ax - 2bc = d$ for x.

$ax = d + 2bc$

$x = \dfrac{d + 2bc}{a}$ if $a \neq 0$

Example 2

Solve $ay - by = a^2 - b^2$ for y.

$y(a - b) = a^2 - b^2$	Factor out common term.
$y(a - b) = (a + b)(a - b)$	Factor expression on right side.
$y = a + b$	Divide each side by $a - b$ if $a \neq b$.

Example 3

Solve for S the equation

$$\frac{1}{R} = \frac{1}{S} + \frac{1}{T}$$

Multiply every term by RST, the LCD:

$$ST = RT + RS$$
$$ST - RS = RT$$
$$S(T - R) = RT$$
$$S = \frac{RT}{T - R} \qquad \text{If } T \neq R$$

QUADRATIC EQUATIONS

An equation containing the square of an unknown quantity is called a *quadratic* equation. One way of solving such an equation is by factoring. If the product of two expressions is zero, at least one of the expressions must be zero.

Example 1

Solve $y^2 + 2y = 0$.

$y(y + 2) = 0$ Remove common factor.

$y = 0$ or $y + 2 = 0$ Since product is 0, at least one of the factors must be 0.

$y = 0$ or $y = -2$

Check by substituting both values in the original equation:

$$(0)^2 + 2(0) = 0$$
$$(-2)^2 + 2(-2) = 4 - 4 = 0$$

In this case there are two solutions.

Example 2

Solve $x^2 + 7x + 10 = 0$.

$x^2 + 7x + 10 = (x + 5)(x + 2) = 0$

$x + 5 = 0$ or $x + 2 = 0$

$x = -5$ or $x = -2$

Check:

$$(-5)^2 + 7(-5) + 10 = 25 - 35 + 10 = 0$$
$$(-2)^2 + 7(-2) + 10 = 4 - 14 + 10 = 0$$

Not all quadratic equations can be factored using only integers, but solutions can usually be found by means of a formula. A quadratic equation may have two solutions, one solution, or occasionally no real solutions. If the quadratic equation is in the form $Ax^2 + Bx + C = 0$, x can be found from the following formula:

$$x = \frac{-B \pm \sqrt{B^2 - 4AC}}{2A}$$

Example 3

Solve $2y^2 + 5y + 2 = 0$ by formula. Assume $A = 2$, $B = 5$, and $C = 2$.

$$x = \frac{-5 \pm \sqrt{5^2 - 4(2)(2)}}{2(2)}$$

$$= \frac{-5 \pm \sqrt{25 - 16}}{4}$$

$$= \frac{-5 \pm \sqrt{9}}{4}$$

$$= \frac{-5 \pm 3}{4}$$

This yields two solutions:

$$x = \frac{-5 + 3}{4} = \frac{-2}{4} = \frac{-1}{2} \quad \text{and}$$

$$x = \frac{-5 - 3}{4} = \frac{-8}{4} = -2$$

So far, each quadratic we have solved has had two distinct answers, but an equation may have a single answer (repeated), as in

$$x^2 + 4x + 4 = 0$$

$$(x + 2)(x + 2) = 0$$

$$x + 2 = 0 \text{ and } x + 2 = 0$$

$$x = -2 \text{ and } x = -2$$

The only solution is -2.

It is also possible for a quadratic equation to have no real solution at all.

Example

If we attempt to solve $x^2 + x + 1 = 0$ by formula, we get:

$$x = \frac{-1 \pm \sqrt{1 - 4(1)(1)}}{2} = \frac{-1 \pm \sqrt{-3}}{2} \text{ Since } \sqrt{-3} \text{ is not}$$

defined, this quadratic has no real answer.

Rewriting Equations

Certain equations written with a variable in the denominator can be rewritten as quadratics.

Example

Solve $-\dfrac{4}{x} + 5 = x$

$-4 + 5x = x^2$ Multiply both sides by $x \neq 0$.

$-x^2 + 5x - 4 = 0$ Collect terms on one side of equals and set sum equal to 0.

$x^2 - 5x + 4 = 0$ Multiply both sides by -1.

$(x - 4)(x - 1) = 0$ Factor

$x - 4 = 0$ or $x - 1 = 0$

$x = 4$ or $x = 1$

Check the result by substitution:

$$-\dfrac{4}{4} + 5 \overset{?}{=} 4 \quad \text{and} \quad -\dfrac{4}{1} + 5 \overset{?}{=} 1$$

$$-1 + 5 = 4 \qquad -4 + 5 = 1$$

Some equations containing a radical sign can also be converted into a quadratic equation. The solution of this type of problem depends on the principle that

If $A = B$ then $A^2 = B^2$

and If $A^2 = B^2$ then $A = B$ or $A = -B$

Equations Involving Square Roots

To solve equations in which the variable appears under a square root sign, begin by manipulating the equation so that the square root is alone on one side. Then square both sides of the equation. Since squares and square roots are inverses, the square root will be eliminated from the equation.

Example 1

Solve $\sqrt{12x + 4} + 2 = 6$

Rewrite the equation as $\sqrt{12x + 4} = 4$. Now square both sides.

$$(\sqrt{12x + 4})^2 = 4^2$$

$$12x + 4 = 16$$

$$12x = 12$$

$$x = 1$$

It is easy to check that 1 is a solution to the equation by plugging the 1 into the original equation. However, sometimes when we use this procedure, the solution obtained will not solve the original equation. Thus, it is crucial to check your answer to all square root equations.

Example 2

Solve $y = \sqrt{3y + 4}$

$$y = \sqrt{3y + 4}$$
$$y^2 = 3y + 4$$
$$y^2 - 3y - 4 = 0$$
$$(y - 4)(y + 1) = 0$$
$$y = 4 \text{ or } y = -1$$

Check by substituting values into the original equation:

$$4 \stackrel{?}{=} \sqrt{3(4) + 4} \text{ and}$$
$$-1 = \sqrt{3(-1) + 4}$$
$$4 \stackrel{?}{=} \sqrt{16} \qquad -1 \stackrel{?}{=} \sqrt{1}$$
$$4 = 4 \qquad -1 \neq 1$$

The single solution is y = 4; the false root y = −1 was introduced when the original equation was squared.

EQUATION SOLVING PROBLEMS

Solve the following equations for the variable indicated:

1. Solve for c: $A = \frac{1}{2}b(b + c)$

2. Solve for b_2: $2A = (b_1 + b_2)h$

3. Solve for w: $aw - b = cw + d$

4. Solve for d: $\left(\dfrac{a}{b}\right) = \left(\dfrac{c}{d}\right)$

5. Solve for x $10x^2 = 5x$

6. Solve for x: $2x^2 - x = 21$

7. Solve for x: $3x^2 - 12 = x(1 + 2x)$

8. Solve for x: $2\sqrt{x + 5} = 8$

9. Solve for x: $5x^2 = 36 + x^2$

10. Solve for x: $4\sqrt{\dfrac{2x}{3}} = 48$

11. $3x^2 - x - 4 = 0$

12. Solve $\dfrac{q}{x} + \dfrac{p}{x} = 1$ for x

13. Solve for x: $3x^2 - 5 = 0$

SOLUTIONS

1.
$$A = \frac{1}{2}b(b + c)$$
$$2A = bb + bc$$
$$2A - bb = bc$$
$$c = \left(\frac{2A - bb}{b}\right)$$

2.
$$2A = (b_1 + b_2)b$$
$$2A = b_1b + b_2b$$
$$2A - b_1b = b_2b$$
$$\frac{(2A - b_1b)}{b} = b_2$$

3.
$$aw - b = cw + d$$
$$aw - cw = b + d$$
$$w(a - c) = b + d$$
$$w = \frac{(b + d)}{(a - c)}$$

4.
$$\left(\frac{a}{b}\right) = \left(\frac{c}{d}\right) \quad \text{Cross multiply}$$
$$ad = bc$$
$$d = \frac{(bc)}{a}$$

5.
$$10x^2 = 5x$$
$$10x^2 - 5x = 0$$
$$5x(2x - 1) = 0$$
$$x = 0, \frac{1}{2}$$

6.
$$2x^2 - x = 21$$
$$2x^2 - x - 21 = 0$$
$$(2x - 7)(x + 3) = 0$$
$$x = -3, \frac{7}{2}$$

7.
$$3x^2 - 12 = x(1 + 2x)$$
$$3x^2 - 12 = x + 2x^2$$
$$x^2 - x - 12 = 0$$
$$(x - 4)(x + 3) = 0 \quad \text{Thus, } x = 4 \text{ or } -3$$

8.
$$2\sqrt{x+5} = 8$$
$$\sqrt{x+5} = 4$$
$$(\sqrt{x+5})^2 = 4^2$$
$$x+5 = 16$$
$$x = 11$$

9.
$$5x^2 = 36 + x^2$$
$$4x^2 - 36 = 0$$
$$4(x^2 - 9) = 0$$
$$4(x+3)(x-3) = 0 \quad \text{Thus, } x = -3 \text{ or } +3$$

10. Begin by dividing both sides by 4 to get $\sqrt{\dfrac{2x}{3}} = 12$. Then, square both sides:

$$\left(\sqrt{\dfrac{2x}{3}}\right)^2 = 12^2$$

$$\dfrac{2x}{3} = 144 \quad \text{Now, multiply both sides by 3.}$$

$$2x = 432$$
$$x = 216$$

11. $3x^2 - x - 4 = 0$ Here, A = 3, B = −1, and C = −4. Using the quadratic formula, we get:

$$x = \frac{-B \pm \sqrt{B^2 - 4AC}}{2A} = \frac{1 \pm \sqrt{1 - 4(3)(-4)}}{6}$$

$$= \frac{1 \pm \sqrt{1 + 48}}{6} = \frac{1 \pm \sqrt{49}}{6} = \frac{1 \pm 7}{6} = \frac{8}{6}, \frac{-6}{6}$$

Thus, $w = \dfrac{4}{3}$ or -1. Note that this equation could have been solved as well by factoring. The quadratic formula, however, can be used to solve all quadratic equations, including those that cannot be factored.

12. $\dfrac{q}{x} + \dfrac{p}{x} = 1$ Multiply both sides by x to clear the fraction, and obtain $q + p = x$

13. $3x^2 - 5 = 0$

This equation can easily be solved for x by first solving for x^2 and then taking the square root of both sides.

$$3x^2 = 5$$

$$x^2 = \frac{5}{3}$$

$$\sqrt{x^2} = \pm\sqrt{\frac{5}{3}}$$ Since $\sqrt{x^2} = x$, we have $x \pm\sqrt{\frac{5}{3}}$

LINEAR INEQUALITIES

For each of the sets of numbers we have considered, we have established an ordering of the members of the set by defining what it means to say that one number is greater than the other. Every number we have considered can be represented by a point on a number line.

An *algebraic inequality* is a statement that one algebraic expression is greater than (or less than) another algebraic expression. If all the variables in the inequality are raised to the first power, the inequality is said to be a *linear inequality*. We solve the inequality by reducing it to a simpler inequality whose solution is apparent. The answer is not unique, as it is in an equation, since a great number of values may satisfy the inequality.

There are three rules for producing equivalent inequalities:

1. The same quantity can be added or subtracted from each side of an inequality.

2. Each side of an inequality can be multiplied or divided by the same *positive* quantity.

3. If each side of an inequality is multiplied or divided by the same *negative* quantity, the sign of the inequality must be reversed so that the new inequality is equivalent to the first.

Example 1

Solve $5x - 5 > -9 + 3x$.

$5x > -4 + 3x$ Add 5 to each side.
$2x > -4$ Subtract $3x$ from each side.
$\ x > -2$ Divide by $+2$.

Any number greater than -2 is a solution to this inequality.

Example 2

Solve $2x - 12 < 5x - 3$.

$2x < 5x + 9$ Add 12 to each side.

$-3x < 9$ Subtract $5x$ from each side.

$x > -3$ Divide each side by -3, changing sign of inequality.

Any number greater than -3—for example, $-2\frac{1}{2}$, 0, 1, or 4—is a solution to this inequality.

Example 3

$$\frac{x}{3} - \frac{x}{2} > 1$$

Begin by multiplying both sides by 6 to clear the fractions. We then obtain

$2x - 3x > 6$

$-x > 6$

Now, divide both sides by -1, and reverse the inequality.

$x < -6$

LINEAR EQUATIONS IN TWO UNKNOWNS

Graphing Equations

The number line is useful in picturing the values of one variable. When two variables are involved, a coordinate system is effective. The Cartesian coordinate system is constructed by placing a vertical number line and a horizontal number line on a plane so that the lines intersect at their zero points. This meeting place is called the *origin*. The horizontal number line is called the *x* axis, and the vertical number line (with positive numbers above the *x* axis) is called the *y* axis. Points in the plane correspond to ordered pairs of real numbers.

Example

The points in this example are:

x	y
0	0
1	1
3	−1
−2	−2
−2	1

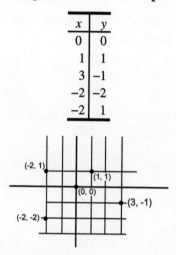

A first-degree equation in two variables is an equation that can be written in the form $ax + by = c$, where a, b, and c are constants. *First-degree* means that x and y appear to the first power. *Linear* refers to the graph of the solutions (x, y) of the equation, which is a straight line. We have already discussed linear equations of one variable.

Example

Graph the line $y = 2x - 4$.

First make a table and select small integral values of x. Find the value of each corresponding y and write it in the table:

x	y
0	–4
1	–2
2	0
3	2

If $x = 1$, for example, $y = 2(1) - 4 = -2$. Then plot the four points on a coordinate system. It is not necessary to have four points; two would do, since two points determine a line, but plotting three or more points reduces the possibility of error.

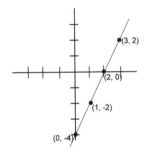

After the points have been plotted (placed on the graph), draw a line through the points and extend it in both directions. This line represents the equation $y = 2x - 4$.

Solving Simultaneous Linear Equations

Two linear equations can be solved together (simultaneously) to yield an answer (x, y) if it exists. On the coordinate system, this amounts to drawing the graphs of two lines and finding their point of intersection. If the lines are parallel and therefore never meet, no solution exists.

Simultaneous linear equations can be solved in the following manner without drawing graphs. From the first equation, find the value of one variable in terms of the other; substitute this value into the second equation. The second equation is now a linear equation in one variable and can be solved. After the numerical value of the one variable has been found, substitute that value into the first equation to find the value of the second variable. Check the results by putting both values into the second equation.

Example 1

Solve the system

$2x + y = 3$
$4x - y = 0$

From the first equation, $y = 3 - 2x$. Substitute this value of y into the second equation to get

$4x - (3 - 2x) = 0$
$4x - 3 + 2x = 0$
$6x = 3$
$x = \dfrac{1}{2}$

Substitute $x = \dfrac{1}{2}$ into the first of the original equations:

$2\left(\dfrac{1}{2}\right) + y = 3$
$1 + y = 3$
$y = 2$

Check by substituting both x and y values into the second equation:

$4\left(\dfrac{1}{2}\right) - 2 = 0$
$2 - 2 = 0$

Example 2

The sum of two numbers is 87 and their difference is 13. What are the numbers?

Let x = the larger of the two numbers and y the smaller. Then,

$x + y = 87$
$x - y = 13.$

Rewrite the second equation as $x = y + 13$ and plug it into the first equation.

$(y + 13) + y = 87$
$2y + 13 = 87$
$2y = 74$
$y = 37$

Then, $x = 13 + 37 = 50.$

The numbers are 50 and 37.

Example 3

A change-making machine contains $30 in dimes and quarters. There are 150 coins in the machine. Find the number of each type of coin.

Let x = number of dimes and y = number of quarters. Then:

$x + y = 150$

Since $.25y$ is the product of a quarter of a dollar and the number of quarters and $.10x$ is the amount of money in dimes,

$.10x + .25y = 30$

Multiply the last equation by 100 to eliminate the decimal points:

$10x + 25y = 3000$

From the first equation, $y = 150 - x$. Substitute this value into the equivalent form of the second equation.

$$10x + 25(150 - x) = 3000$$
$$-15x = -750$$
$$x = 50$$

This is the number of dimes. Substitute this value into $x + y = 150$ to find the number of quarters, $y = 100$.

Check:

$$.10(50) + .25(100) = 30$$
$$\$5 + \$25 = \$30$$

EXPONENTIAL EQUATIONS

Students taking the MCAT may also have to solve exponential equations. An exponential equation is an equation whose variable appears in a exponent. Such equations can be solved by algebraic means if it is possible to express both sides of the equation as powers of the same base.

Example 1

Solve $5^{2x-1} = 25$

Rewrite the equation as $5^{2x-1} = 5^2$. Then it must be true that $2x - 1 = 2$. This means that $x = \dfrac{3}{2}$.

Example 2

Solve $9^{x+3} = 27^{2x}$.

Rewrite the left side of the equation as $(3^2)^{x+3} = 3^{2x+6}$. Rewrite the right side of the equation as $(3^3)^{2x} = 3^{6x}$. Then, it must be true that $2x + 6 = 6x$. This means that $x = \dfrac{3}{2}$.

Exponential equations, in which the bases cannot both be changed to the same number, can be solved by using logarithms.

LINEAR INEQUALITIES AND EQUATIONS PROBLEMS

1. Solve for x: $12 - 2x > 4$

2. Solve for x: $\left(\dfrac{x}{6}\right) - \left(\dfrac{x}{2}\right) < 1$

3. Solve for x: $108x < 15(6x + 12)$

4. Solve for a: $4a - 9 > 9a - 24$

5. Solve for z: $6z + 1 \leq 3(z - 2)$

6. Find the common solution:

   $y = 3x + 1$

   $x + y = 9$

7. Find the common solution:

   $2x + y = 8$

   $x - y = 1$

8. Find the common solution:

   $3x + 2y = 11$

   $5x - 4y = 11$

9. Solve for a common solution:

   $5x + 3y = 28$

   $7x - 2y = 2$

10. The sum of two numbers is 45 and their difference is 11. What are the two numbers?

11. Three binders and four notebooks cost a total of $4.32. One binder and 5 notebooks cost $3.97. What is the cost of one notebook?

12. A printer and monitor together cost $356. The monitor cost $20 more than two times the printer. How much do the printer and monitor cost separately?

SOLUTIONS

1. $12 - 2x > 4$

   $-2x > -8$ Divide by -2, and flip inequality sign.

   $x < 4$

2. $\left(\dfrac{x}{6}\right) - \left(\dfrac{x}{2}\right) < 1$ Multiply both sides by 6.

   $x - 3x < 6$

   $-2x < 6$ Divide by -2, and flip the inequality sign.

   $x > -3$

3. $108x < 15(6x + 12)$

   $108x < 90x + 180$

   $18x < 180$

   $x < 10$

4. $4a - 9 > 9a - 24$

   $-5a > -15$ Divide by -5, and reverse the inequality sign.

   $a < 3$

5. $6z + 1 \le 3(z - 2)$

   $6z + 1 \le 3z - 6$

   $3z \le -7$

   $z \le \dfrac{-7}{3}.$

   Note that even though the answer is negative, we do not reverse the inequality sign since we never multiplied or divided by a negative number.

6. $y = 3x + 1$

   $x + y = 9$

   Begin by substituting $y = 3x + 1$ into the second equation.

   $x + (3x + 1) = 9$

   $4x + 1 = 9$

   $4x = 8$

   $x = 2.$

   If $x = 2$, $y = 3(2) + 1 = 6 + 1 = 7$.

7. $2x + y = 8$

$x - y = 1$

From the second equation, we can see $x = y + 1$. Then, substituting into the first equation:

$2(y + 1) + y = 8$

$3y + 2 = 8$

$3y = 6$

$y = 2.$

If $y = 2$, then $x = y + 1 = 2 + 1 = 3$.

8. $3x + 2y = 11$

$5x - 4y = 11$

Multiply the top equation by 2.

$2(3x + 2y) = 2(11)$

$5x - 4y = 11$

$6x + 4y = 22$

$\underline{5x - 4y = 11}$

$11x = 33$

$x = 3$

Now, substitute this value for x in the first equation.

$3(3) + 2y = 11$

$9 + 2y = 11$

$2y = 2$

$y = 1$

The common solution is $(3, 1)$.

9. $5x + 3y = 28$
$7x - 2y = 2$

Multiply the first equation by 2, and the second equation by 3.

$2(5x + 3y) = 2(28)$
$3(7x - 2y) = 3(2)$ Thus,

$$10x + 6y = 56$$
$$\underline{21x - 6y = 6} \quad \text{Add the equations together}$$
$$31x = 62$$
$$x = 2$$

Now, solve for y by plugging $x = 2$ into (say) the second equation.

$7(2) - 2y = 2$
$14 - 2y = 2$
$-2y = -12$
$y = 6$

Thus, the common solution is (2, 6).

10.   Let x = the larger of the two numbers.
Let y = the smaller of the two numbers.
Then, we have

$x + y = 45$
$x - y = 11$

Add the two equations together.
$$x + y = 45$$
$$\underline{x - y = 11}$$
$$2x = 56$$
$$x = 28$$

If x is 28, and the numbers differ by 11, the $y = 17$.

The numbers are 28 and 17.

11. Let B = the cost of a binder.
Let N = the cost of a notebook.

Then, we have

3B + 4N = 4.32
1B + 5N = 3.97

Multiply the second equation by −3:

3B + 4N = 4.32
−3(1B + 5N) = (3.97)(−3) or,

$$3B + 4N = 4.32$$
$$\underline{-3B - 15N = 11.91}$$
$$-11N = -7.59$$
$$N = 0.69$$

Thus, the cost of a notebook is $ 0.69.

12. A printer and monitor together cost $356. The monitor cost $20 more than two times the printer.

Let P = the cost of the printer.
Let M = the cost of the monitor. Then,

P + M = 356
   M = 20 + 2P.

Substituting for M in the first equation, we get

P + (20 + 2P) = 356
       3P + 20 = 356
            3P = 336
             P = 112.

Then, M = 20 + 2(112) = 244.

The printer costs $112, and the monitor costs $244.

RATIO AND PROPORTION

Many problems in arithmetic and algebra can be solved using the concept of *ratio* to compare numbers. The ratio of a to b is the fraction $\frac{a}{b}$. If the two ratios $\frac{a}{b}$ and $\frac{c}{d}$ represent the same comparison, we write:

$$\frac{a}{b} = \frac{c}{d}$$

This equation (statement of equality) is called a *proportion*. A proportion states the equivalence of two different expressions for the same ratio.

Example 1

In a class of 39 students, 17 are men. Find the ratio of men to women.

39 students − 17 men = 22 women

Ratio of men to women is 17/22, also written 17:22.

Example 2

The scale on a map is $\frac{3}{4}$ inch = 12 miles. If the distance between City A and City B on the map is $4\frac{1}{2}$ inches, how far apart are the two cities actually?

Let x = the distance between the two cities in miles.

Begin by writing a proportion that compares inches to miles.

$$\frac{Inches \rightarrow}{Miles \rightarrow}\ \frac{\frac{3}{4}}{12} = \frac{\frac{9}{2}}{x} \quad \text{Cross multiply to solve the equation.}$$

$$\left(\frac{3}{4}\right)x = 12\left(\frac{9}{2}\right)$$

$$\left(\frac{3}{4}\right)x = 54 \quad \text{Multiply by 4}$$

$$3x = 216$$

$$x = 72$$

The two cities are 72 miles apart.

Example 3

A fertilizer contains 3 parts nitrogen, 2 parts potash, and 2 parts phosphate by weight. How many pounds of fertilizer will contain 60 pounds of nitrogen?

The ratio of pounds of nitrogen to pounds of fertilizer is 3 to 3 + 2 + 2 = 3/7. Let x be the number of pounds of mixture. Then:

$$\frac{3}{7} = \frac{60}{x}$$

Multiply both sides of the equation by $7x$ to get:

$$3x = 420$$

$$x = 140 \text{ pounds}$$

Variation

Here is another topic which primarily appears on the MCAT. The terminology of variation is useful for describing a number of situations which arise in science. If x and y are variables, then *y is said to vary directly as x* if there is a non-zero constant k such that $y = kx$.

Similarly, we say that *y varies inversely as x* if $y = \frac{k}{x}$ for some non-zero constant k. To say that *y varies inversely as the square of x* means that $y = \frac{k}{x^2}$ for some non-zero constant k. Finally, to say *y varies jointly as s and t* means that $y = kst$ for some non-zero constant k.

Example

Boyle's law says that, for an enclosed gas at a constant temperature, the pressure p varies inversely as the volume v. If $v = 10$ cubic inches when $p = 8$ pounds per square inch, find v when $p = 12$ pounds per square inch.

Since p varies inversely as v, we have $p = \frac{k}{v}$, for some value of k. We know that when $p = 8$, $v = 10$, so $8 = \frac{k}{10}$. This tells us that the value of k is 80, and we have $p = \frac{80}{v}$. For $p = 12$, we have $12 = \frac{80}{v}$, or $v = \frac{80}{12} = 6.67$ cubic inches.

COMPUTING AVERAGES AND MEDIANS

Mean

Several statistical measures are used frequently. One of them is the *average* or *arithmetic mean.* To find the average of N numbers, add the numbers and divide their sum by N.

Example 1

Seven students attained test scores of 62, 80, 60, 30, 50, 90, and 20. What was the average test score for the group?

$$62 + 80 + 60 + 30 + 50 + 90 + 20 = 392$$

Since there are 7 scores, the average score is

$$\frac{392}{7} = 56$$

Example 2

Brian has scores of 88, 87, and 92 on his first three tests. What grade must he get on his next test to have an overall average of 90?

Let x = the grade that he needs to get. Then we have

$$\frac{88 + 87 + 92 + x}{4} = 90 \text{ Multiply by 4 to clear the fraction.}$$
$$88 + 87 + 92 + x = 360$$
$$267 + x = 360$$
$$x = 93$$

Brian needs to get a 93 on his next test.

Example 3

Joan allotted herself a budget of $50 a week, on the average, for expenses. One week she spent $35, the next $60, and the third $40. How much can she spend in the fourth week without exceeding her budget?

Let x be the amount spent in the fourth week. Then:

$$\frac{35 + 60 + 40 + x}{4} = 50$$
$$35 + 60 + 40 + x = 200$$
$$135 + x = 200$$
$$x = 65$$

She can spend $65 in the fourth week.

Median

If a set of numbers is arranged in order, the number in the middle is called the *median*.

Example

Find the median test score of 62, 80, 60, 30, 50, 90, and 20. Arrange the numbers in increasing (or decreasing) order

20, 30, 50, 60, 62, 80, 90

Since 60 is the number in the middle, it is the median. It is not the same as the arithmetic mean, which is 56.

If the number of scores is an even number, the median is the arithmetic mean of the middle two scores.

PLANE GEOMETRY

Plane geometry is the science of measurement. Certain assumptions are made about undefined quantities called points, lines, and planes, and then logical deductions about relationships between figures composed of lines, angles, and portions of planes are made based on these assumptions. The process of making the logical deductions is called a *proof.* In this summary, we are not making any proofs but are giving the definitions frequently used in geometry and stating relationships that are the results of proofs.

Lines and Angles

Angles

A line in geometry is always a straight line. When two straight lines meet at a point, they form an *angle.* The lines are called *sides* or *rays* of the angle, and the point is called the *vertex.* The symbol for angle is ∠. When no other angle shares the same vertex, the name of the angle is the name given to the vertex, as in angle *A:*

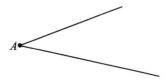

An angle may be named with three letters. In the following example, *B* is a point on one side and *C* is a point on the other. In this case, the name of the vertex must be the middle letter, and we have angle *BAC.*

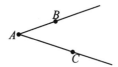

Occasionally, an angle is named by a number or small letter placed in the angle.

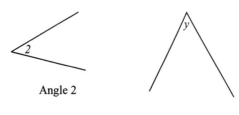

Angle 2   Angle *y*

Angles are usually measured in degrees. An angle of 30 degrees, written 30°, is an angle whose measure is 30 degrees. Degrees are divided into minutes; 60′ (read ''minutes'') = 1°. Minutes are further divided into seconds; 60″ (read ''seconds'') = 1′.

Vertical Angles

When two lines intersect, four angles are formed. The angles opposite each other are called *vertical angles* and are equal to each other.

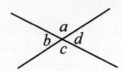

a and *c* are vertical angles.
$\angle a = \angle c$
b and *d* are vertical angles.
$\angle b = \angle d$

Straight Angle

A *straight angle* has its sides lying along a straight line. It is always equal to 180°.

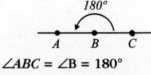

$\angle ABC = \angle B = 180°$
$\angle B$ is a straight angle.

Adjacent Angles

Two angles are *adjacent* if they share the same vertex and a common side but no angle is inside another angle. $\angle ABC$ and $\angle CBD$ are adjacent angles. Even though they share a common vertex B and a common side AB, $\angle ABD$ and $\angle ABC$ are not adjacent angles because one angle is inside the other.

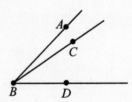

Supplementary Angles

If the sum of two angles is a straight angle (180°), the two angles are *supplementary* and each angle is the supplement of the other.

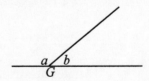

∠G is a straight angle = 180°.

∠a + ∠b = 180°

∠a and ∠b are supplementary angles.

Right Angles

If two supplementary angles are equal, they are both *right angles*. A right angle is one half a straight angle. Its measure is 90°. A right angle is symbolized by ∟.

∠G is a straight angle.

∠b + ∠a = ∠G, and ∠a = ∠b. ∠a and ∠b are right angles.

Complementary Angles

Complementary angles are two angles whose sum is a right angle (90°).

∠Y is a right angle.

∠a + ∠b = ∠Y = 90°.

∠a and ∠b are complementary angles.

Acute Angles

Acute angles are angles whose measure is less than 90°. No two acute angles can be supplementary angles. Two acute angles can be complementary angles.

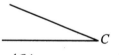

∠C is an acute angle.

Obtuse Angles

Obtuse angles are angles that are greater than 90° and less than 180°.

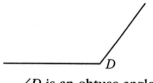

∠D is an obtuse angle.

Example 1

In the figure, what is the value of x?

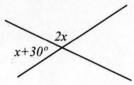

Since the two labeled angles are supplementary angles, their sum is 180°.

$$(x + 30°) + 2x = 180°$$
$$3x = 150°$$
$$x = 50°$$

Example 2

Find the value of x in the figure.

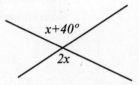

Since the two labeled angles are vertical angles, they are equal.

$$x + 40° = 2x$$
$$40° = x$$

Example 3

If angle Y is a right angle and angle b measures 30°15′, what does angle a measure?

Since angle Y is a right angle, angles a and b are complementary angles and their sum is 90°.

$$\angle a + \angle b = 90°$$
$$\angle a + 30°15' = 90°$$
$$\angle a = 59°45'$$

Example 4

In the figure below, what is the value of *x*?

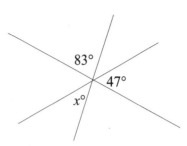

The angle that is vertical to the angle labeled *x*° also has a measure of *x*°. This angle, along with those labeled 83° and 47°, form a straight line and are thus supplementary. Therefore,

$$83 + 47 + x = 180$$
$$130 + x = 180$$
$$x = 50$$

The value of *x* is 50°.

Lines

A *line* in geometry is always assumed to be a straight line. It extends infinitely far in both directions. It can be determined if two of its points are known. It can be expressed in terms of the two points, which are written as capital letters. The following line is called *AB*.

Or a line may be given one name with a small letter. The following line is called line *k*.

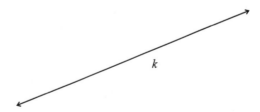

A *line segment* is a part of a line between two *endpoints*. It is named by its endpoints, for example, *A* and *B*.

AB is a line segment.
It has a definite length.

If point *P* is on the line and is the same distance from point *A* as from point *B*, then *P* is the *midpoint* of segment *AB*. When we say *AP = PB*, we mean that the two line segments have the same length.

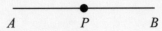

A part of a line with one endpoint is called a *ray. AC* is a ray, of which *A* is an endpoint. The ray extends infinitely in the direction away from the endpoint.

Parallel Lines

Two lines meet or intersect if there is one point that is on both lines. Two different lines may either intersect at one point or never meet, but they can never meet out more than one point.

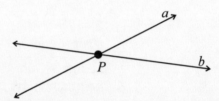

Two lines in the same plane that never meet no matter how far they are extended are said to be *parallel,* for which the symbol is ∥. In the following diagram, *a* ∥ *b*.

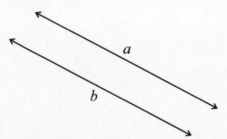

If two lines in the same plane are parallel to a third line, they are parallel to each other. Since *a* ∥ *b* and *b* ∥ *c,* we know that *a* ∥ *c.*

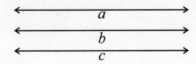

Two lines that meet each other at right angles are said to be *perpendicular,* for which the symbol is ⊥. Line *a* is perpendicular to line *b*.

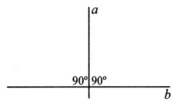

Two lines in the same plane that are perpendicular to the same line are parallel to each other.

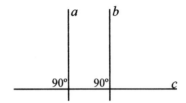

Line *a* ⊥ line *c* and line *b* ⊥ line *c*.
Therefore, *a* ∥ *b*.

A line intersecting two other lines is called a *transversal.* Line *c* is a transversal intersecting lines *a* and *b*.

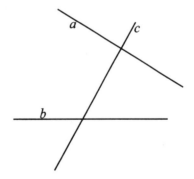

The transversal and the two given lines form eight angles. The four angles between the given lines are called *interior angles;* the four angles outside the given lines are called *exterior angles.* If two angles are on opposite sides of the transversal, they are called *alternate angles.*

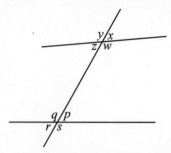

∠z, ∠w, ∠q, and ∠p are interior angles.
∠y, ∠x, ∠s, and ∠r are exterior angles.
∠z and ∠p are alternate interior angles; so are ∠w and ∠q.
∠y and ∠s are alternate exterior angles; so are ∠x and ∠r.

Pairs of *corresponding* angles are ∠y and ∠q, ∠z and ∠r, ∠x and ∠p, and, ∠w and ∠s. Corresponding angles are sometimes called exterior-interior angles.

When the two given lines cut by a transversal are parallel lines:

1. the corresponding angles are equal.
2. the alternate interior angles are equal.
3. the alternate exterior angles are equal.
4. interior angles on the same side of the transversal are supplementary.

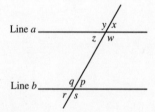

If line *a* is parallel to line *b:*

1. ∠y = ∠q, ∠z = ∠r, ∠x = ∠p, and ∠w = ∠s.
2. ∠z = ∠p and ∠w = ∠q.
3. ∠y = ∠s and ∠x = ∠r.
4. ∠z + ∠q = 180° and ∠p + ∠w = 180°.

Because vertical angles are equal, ∠p = ∠r, ∠q = ∠s, ∠y = ∠w, and ∠x = ∠z. If any one of the four conditions for equality of angles holds true, the lines are parallel; that is, if two lines are cut by a transversal and one pair of the corresponding angles is equal, the lines are parallel. If a pair of alternate interior angles or a pair of alternate exterior angles is equal, the lines are parallel. If interior angles on the same side of the transversal are supplementary, the lines are parallel.

Example 1

In the figure, two parallel lines are cut by a transversal. Find the measure of angle y.

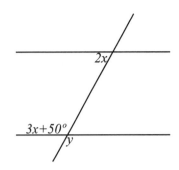

The two labeled angles are supplementary.

$$2x + (3x + 50°) = 180°$$
$$5x = 130°$$
$$x = 26°$$

Since $\angle y$ is vertical to the angle whose measure is $3x + 50°$, it has the same measure.

$$y = 3x + 50° = 3(26°) + 50° = 128°$$

Example 2

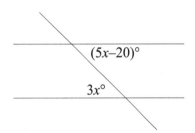

In the figure above, two parallel lines are cut by a transversal. Find the measure of angle x.

The two labeled angles are alternate interior angles and thus are congruent. Therefore,

$$5x - 20 = 3x$$
$$2x = 20$$
$$x = 10$$

The measure of angle x is 10°.

Polygons

A *polygon* is a closed plane figure composed of line segments joined together at points called *vertices* (singular, *vertex*). A polygon is usually named by giving its vertices in order.

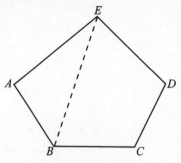

Polygon *ABCDE*

In the figure, points *A*, *B*, *C*, *D*, and *E* are the vertices, and the sides are *AB*, *BC*, *CD*, *DE*, and *EA*. *AB* and *BC* are *adjacent* sides, and *A* and *B* are adjacent vertices. A *diagonal* of a polygon is a line segment joining any two nonadjacent vertices. *EB* is a diagonal.

Polygons are named according to the number of sides or angles. A *triangle* is a polygon with three sides, a *quadrilateral* a polygon with four sides, a *pentagon* a polygon with five sides, and a *hexagon* a polygon with six sides. The number of sides is always equal to the number of angles.

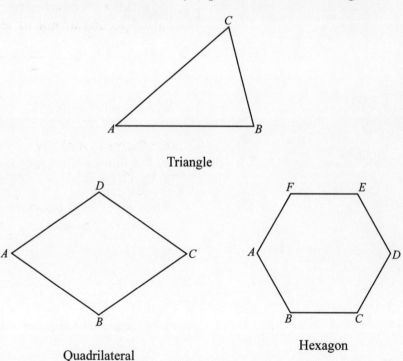

Triangle

Quadrilateral

Hexagon

The *perimeter* of a polygon is the sum of the lengths of its sides. If the polygon is regular (all sides equal and all angles equal), the perimeter is the product of the length of *one* side and the number of sides.

Congruent and Similar Polygons

If two polygons have equal corresponding angles and equal corresponding sides, they are said to be *congruent*. Congruent polygons have the same size and shape. They are the same in all respects except possibly position. The symbol for congruence is ≅.

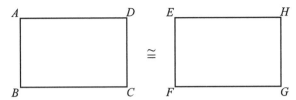

When two sides of congruent or different polygons are equal, we indicate the fact by drawing the same number of short lines through the equal sides.

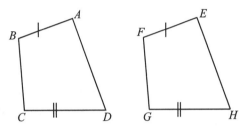

This indicates that *AB* = *EF* and *CD* = *GH*.

Two polygons with equal corresponding angles and corresponding sides in proportion are said to be *similar*. The symbol for similar is ~.

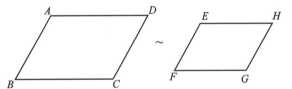

Similar figures have the same shape but not necessarily the same size.

A *regular polygon* is a polygon whose sides are equal and whose angles are equal.

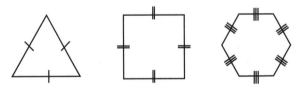

Triangles

A *triangle* is a polygon of three sides. Triangles are classified by measuring their sides and angles. The sum of the angles of a plane triangle is always 180°. The symbol for a triangle is Δ. The sum of any two sides of a triangle is always greater than the third side.

Equilateral

Equilateral triangles have equal sides and equal angles. Each angle measures 60° because $\frac{1}{3}(180°) = 60°$.

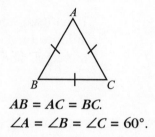

AB = AC = BC.
$\angle A = \angle B = \angle C = 60°.$

Isosceles

Isosceles triangles have two equal sides. The angles opposite the equal sides are equal. The two equal angles are sometimes called the *base* angles and the third angle is called the *vertex* angle. Note that an equilateral triangle is isosceles.

FG = FH.
$FG \neq GH.$
$\angle G = \angle H.$
$\angle F$ is the vertex angle.
$\angle G$ and $\angle H$ are base angles.

Scalene

Scalene triangles have all three sides of different length and all angles of different measure. In scalene triangles, the shortest side is opposite the angle of smallest measure, and the longest side is opposite the angle of greatest measure.

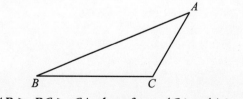

$AB > BC > CA;$ therefore $\angle C > \angle A > \angle B.$

Example 1

In triangle XYZ, $\angle Y$ is twice $\angle X$, and $\angle Z$ is 40° more than $\angle Y$. How many degrees are in the three angles?

Solve this problem just as you would an algebraic word problem, remembering that there are 180° in a triangle.

Let x = the number of degrees in $\angle X$

Then $2x$ = the number of degrees in $\angle Y$

and $2x + 40$ = the number of degrees in $\angle Z$

Thus,

$$x + 2x + (2x + 40) = 180$$
$$5x + 40 = 180$$
$$5x = 140$$
$$x = 28°$$

Therefore, the measure of $\angle X$ is 28°, the measure of $\angle Y$ is 56°, and the measure of $\angle Z$ is 96°.

Example 2

In the figure below, the two lines are parallel. What is the value of x?

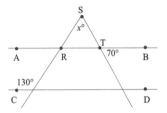

Corresponding angles are equal, so $\angle ARS$ is also 130°. $\angle SRT$ is the supplement of $\angle ARS$ and thus is 50°. By the property of vertical angles, we have $\angle STR = 70°$. Finally, since the sum of the angles in triangle SRT is 180°, we have

$$x + 50 + 70 = 180$$
$$x + 120 = 180$$
$$x = 60°.$$

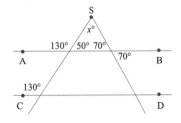

Right

Right triangles contain one right angle. Since the right angle is 90°, the other two angles are complementary. They may or may not be equal to each other. The side of a right triangle opposite the right angle is called the *hypotenuse*. The other two sides are called *legs*. The *Pythagorean theorem* states that the square of the length of the hypotenuse is equal to the sum of the squares of the lengths of the legs.

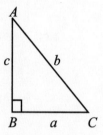

AC is the hypotenuse.
AB and BC are legs.
$\angle B = 90°$.
$\angle A + \angle C = 90°$.
$a^2 + c^2 = b^2$.

Example 1

If *ABC* is a right triangle with right angle at *B*, and if $AB = 6$ and $BC = 8$, what is the length of *AC*?

$$AB^2 + BC^2 = AC^2$$
$$6^2 + 8^2 = 36 + 64 = 100 = AC^2$$
$$AC = 10$$

If the measure of angle A is 30°, what is the measure of angle *C* ?

Since angles *A* and *C* are complementary:

$$30° + C = 90°$$
$$C = 60°$$

If the lengths of the three sides of a triangle are *a, b,* and *c* and the relation $a^2 + b^2 = c^2$ holds, the triangle is a right triangle and side *c* is the hypotenuse.

Example 2

Show that a triangle of sides 5, 12, and 13 is a right triangle. The triangle will be a right triangle if $a^2 + b^2 = c^2$.

$5^2 + 12^2 = 13^2$
$25 + 144 = 169$

Therefore, the triangle is a right triangle and 13 is the length of the hypotenuse.

Example 3

A plane takes off from the airport in Buffalo and flies 600 miles to the north and then flies 800 miles to the east to City C. What is the straight-line distance from Buffalo to City C?

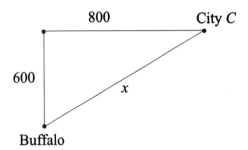

As the diagram above shows, the required distance x is the hypotenuse of the triangle. Thus,

$$(600)^2 + (800)^2 = x^2$$
$$3,600 + 6,400 = x^2$$
$$10,000 = x^2$$
$$x = \sqrt{100,000} = 1,000$$

Thus, the distance from Buffalo to City C is 1,000 miles.

Area of a Triangle

An *altitude* (or height) of a triangle is a line segment dropped as a perpendicular from any vertex to the opposite side. The area of a triangle is the product of one half the altitude and the base of the triangle. (The base is the side opposite the vertex from which the perpendicular was drawn.)

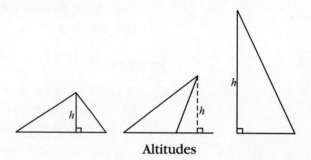

Altitudes

Example 1

What is the area of a right triangle with sides 5, 12, and 13?

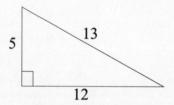

As the picture above shows, the triangle has hypotenuse 13 and legs 5 and 12. Since the legs are perpendicular to each other, we can use one as the height and one as the base of the triangle. Therefore, we have

$$A = \frac{1}{2bh}$$

$$A = \frac{1}{2}(12)(5)$$

$$A = 30$$

The area of the triangle is 30.

Example 2

Find the area A of the following isosceles triangle.

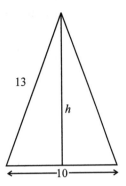

In an isosceles triangle, the altitude from the vertex angle bisects the base (cuts it in half).

The first step is to find the altitude. By the Pythagorean theorem, $a^2 + b^2 = c^2$; $c = 13$, $a = b$, and $b = \frac{1}{2}(10) = 5$.

$$b^2 + 5^2 = 13^2$$
$$b^2 + 25 = 169$$
$$b^2 = 144$$
$$b = 12$$
$$A = \frac{1}{2} \cdot \text{base} \cdot \text{height}$$
$$= \frac{1}{2} \cdot 10 \cdot 12$$
$$= 60$$

Similarity

Two triangles are *similar* if all three pairs of corresponding angles are equal. The sum of the three angles of a triangle is 180°; therefore, if two angles of triangle I equal two corresponding angles of triangle II, the third angle of triangle I must be equal to the third angle of triangle II and the triangles are similar. The lengths of the sides of similar triangles are in proportion to each other. A line drawn parallel to one side of a triangle divides the triangle into two portions, one of which is a triangle. The new triangle is similar to the original triangle.

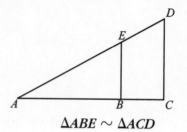

$$\triangle ABE \sim \triangle ACD$$

Example 1

In the following figure, if $AC = 28$ feet, $AB = 35$ feet, $BC = 21$ feet, and $EC = 12$ feet, find the length of DC if $DE \parallel AB$.

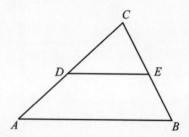

Because $DE \parallel AB$, $\triangle CDE \sim \triangle CAB$. Since the triangles are similar, their sides are in proportion:

$$\frac{DC}{AC} = \frac{EC}{BC}$$

$$\frac{DC}{28} = \frac{12}{21}$$

$$DC = \frac{12 \cdot 28}{21} = 16 \text{ feet}$$

Example 2

A pole that is sticking out of the ground vertically is 10 feet tall and casts a shadow of 6 feet. At the same time, a tree next to the pole casts a shadow of 24 feet. How tall is the tree?

Below is a diagram of the tree and the pole. At the same time of the day, nearby objects and their shadows form similar triangles.

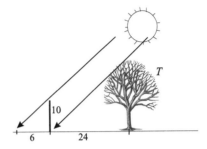

Call the height of the tree T. Then we can write a proportion between the corresponding sides of the triangles.

$$\frac{10}{T} = \frac{6}{24}$$

To solve this proportion, multiply by $24T$.

$$24 \times 10 = 6T$$
$$240 = 6T$$
$$T = 40$$

The tree is 40 feet tall.

Quadrilaterals

A quadrilateral is a polygon of four sides. The sum of the angles of a quadrilateral is 360°. If the opposite sides of a quadrilateral are parallel, the quadrilateral is a *parallelogram*. Opposite sides of a parallelogram are equal and so are opposite angles. Any two consecutive angles of a parallelogram are supplementary. A diagonal of a parallelogram divides the parallelogram into congruent triangles. The diagonals of a parallelogram bisect each other.

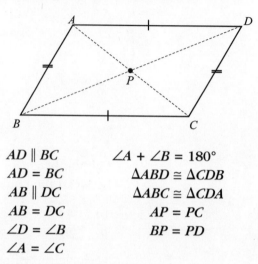

$$AD \parallel BC \qquad \angle A + \angle B = 180°$$
$$AD = BC \qquad \triangle ABD \cong \triangle CDB$$
$$AB \parallel DC \qquad \triangle ABC \cong \triangle CDA$$
$$AB = DC \qquad AP = PC$$
$$\angle D = \angle B \qquad BP = PD$$
$$\angle A = \angle C$$

Definitions

A *rhombus* is a parallelogram with four equal sides. The diagonals of a rhombus are perpendicular to each other.

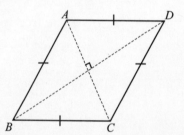

A *rectangle* is a parallelogram with four right angles. The diagonals of a rectangle are equal and can be found using the Pythagorean theorem if the sides of the rectangle are known.

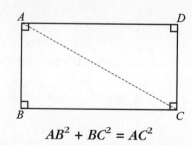

$$AB^2 + BC^2 = AC^2$$

A *square* is a rectangle with four equal sides.

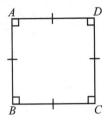

A *trapezoid* is a quadrilateral with only one pair of parallel sides, called *bases*. The nonparallel sides are called *legs*.

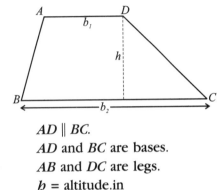

$AD \parallel BC$.
AD and BC are bases.
AB and DC are legs.
h = altitude.in

Finding Areas

The area of any *parallelogram* is the product of the base and the height, where the height is the length of an altitude, a line segment drawn from a vertex perpendicular to the base.

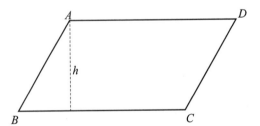

Since rectangles and squares are also parallelograms, their areas follow the same formula. For a *rectangle,* the altitude is one of the sides, and the formula is length times width. Since a *square* is a rectangle for which length and width are the same, the area of a square is the square of its side.

The area of a *trapezoid* is the height times the average of the two bases. The formula is:

$$A = h\frac{b_1 + b_2}{2}$$

The bases are the parallel sides, and the height is the length of an altitude to one of the bases.

Example 1

Find the area of a square whose diagonal is 12 feet. Let s = side of square. By the Pythagorean theorem:

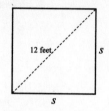

$$s^2 + s^2 = 12^2$$
$$2s^2 = 144$$
$$s^2 = 72$$
$$s = \sqrt{72}$$

Use only the positive value because this is the side of a square.

Since $A = s^2$

$A = 72$ square feet

Example 2

Find the altitude of a rectangle if its area is 320 and its base is 5 times its altitude.

Let altitude = h. Then base = $5h$. Since $A = bh$,

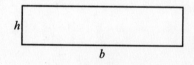

$$A = (5h)(h) = 320$$
$$5h^2 = 320$$
$$h^2 = 64$$
$$h = 8$$

If a quadrilateral is not a parallelogram or trapezoid but is irregularly shaped, its area can be found by dividing it into triangles, attempting to find the area of each, and adding the results.

Example 3

The longer base of a trapezoid is 4 times the shorter base. If the height of the trapezoid is 6 and the area is 75, how long is the longer base?

Recall that the area of a trapezoid is given by the formula

$$A = b\,\frac{b_1 + b_2}{2}.$$

Let b_1 represent the shorter base. Then the longer base is $b_2 = 4b_1$, and we have

$$A = 6\,\frac{b_1 + 4b_1}{2} = 6\,\frac{5b_1}{2} = 15b.$$ Since the area is 72, we get

$$75 = 15b_1$$
$$b_1 = 5.$$

Thus, the short base is 5 and the long base is 20.

Circles

Definitions

Circles are closed plane curves with all points on the curve equally distant from a fixed point called the *center*. The symbol ⊙ indicates a circle. A circle is usually named by its center. A line segment from the center to any point on the circle is called the *radius* (plural, radii). All radii of the same circle are equal.

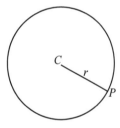

C = center
CP = radius = r

A *chord* is a line segment whose endpoints are on the circle. A *diameter* of a circle is a chord that passes through the center of the circle. A diameter, the longest distance between two points on the circle, is twice the length of the radius. A diameter perpendicular to a chord bisects that chord.

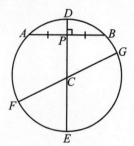

AB is a chord.
C is the center.
DCE is a diameter.
FCG is a diameter.
AB ⊥ *DCE* so *AP* = *PB*.

A *central angle* is an angle whose vertex is the center of a circle and whose sides are radii of the circle. An *inscribed angle* is an angle whose vertex is on the circle and whose sides are chords of the circle.

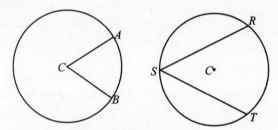

∠*ACB* is a central angle
∠*RST* is an inscribed angle

An *arc* is a portion of a circle. The symbol ⌒ is used to indicate an arc. Arcs are usually measured in degrees. Since the entire circle is 360°, a semicircle (half a circle) is an arc of 180°, and a quarter of a circle is an arc of 90°.

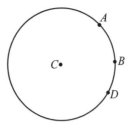

$\overset{\frown}{ABD}$ is an arc.

$\overset{\frown}{AB}$ is an arc.

$\overset{\frown}{BD}$ is an arc.

A central angle is equal in measure to its intercepted arc.

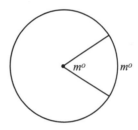

An inscribed angle is equal in measure to one half its intercepted arc. An angle inscribed in a semicircle is a right angle because the semicircle has a measure of 180°, and the measure of the inscribed angle is one half of that.

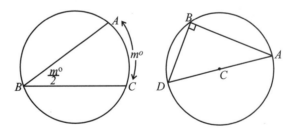

$\overset{\frown}{DA}$ = 180°; therefore,

∠DBA = 90°.

Perimeter and Area

The perimeter of a circle is called the *circumference*. The length of the circumference is πd, where d is the diameter, or $2\pi r$, where r is the radius. The number π is irrational and can be approximated by 3.14159..., but in problems dealing with circles, it is best to leave π in the answer. There is no fraction exactly equal to π.

Example 1

If the circumference of a circle is 8π feet, what is the radius?

Since $C = 2\pi r = 8\pi$, $r = 4$ feet.

The length of an arc of a circle can be found if the central angle and radius are known. Then the length of the arc is $\dfrac{n°}{360°}(2\pi r)$, where the central angle of the arc is $n°$. This is true because of the proportion:

$$\frac{\text{Arc}}{\text{Circumference}} = \frac{\text{central angle}}{360°}$$

Example 2

If a circle of radius 3 feet has a central angle of 60°, find the length of the arc intercepted by this central angle.

$$\text{Arc} = \frac{60°}{360°}(2\pi 3) = \pi \text{ feet}$$

The area A of a circle is πr^2, where r is the radius. If the diameter is given instead of the radius,

$$A = \pi \left(\frac{d}{2}\right)^2 = \frac{\pi d^2}{4}.$$

Example 3

Find the area of a circular ring formed by two concentric circles of radii 6 and 8 inches, respectively. (Concentric circles are circles with the same center.)

The area of the ring will equal the area of the large circle minus the area of the small circle.

Area of ring = $\pi 8^2 - \pi 6^2$

$= \pi(64 - 36)$

$= 28\pi$ square inches

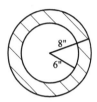

Example 4

A square is inscribed in a circle whose diameter is 10 inches. Find the difference between the area of the circle and that of the square.

If a square is inscribed in a circle, the diagonal of the square is the diameter of the circle. If the diagonal of the square is 10 inches, then, by the Pythagorean theorem,

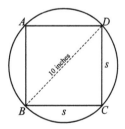

$$2s^2 = 100$$
$$s^2 = 50$$

The side of the square s is $\sqrt{50}$, and the area of the square is 50 square inches. If the diameter of the circle is 10, its radius is 5 and the area of the circle is $\pi 5^2 = 25\pi$ square inches. Then the difference between the area of the circle and the area of the square is:

$25\pi - 50$ square inches
$= 25\ (\pi - 2)$ square inches

Distance Formula

In the arithmetic section, we described the Cartesian coordinate system when explaining how to draw graphs representing linear equations. If two points are plotted in the Cartesian coordinate system, it is useful to know how to find the distance between them. If the two points have coordinates (a, b) and (p, q), the distance between them is:

$$d = \sqrt{(a-p)^2 + (b-q)^2}$$

This formula makes use of the Pythagorean theorem.

Example 1

Find the distance between the two points $(-3, 2)$ and $(1, -1)$.

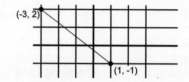

Let $(a, b) = (-3, 2)$ and $(p, q) = (1, -1)$. Then:

$$d = \sqrt{(-3-1)^2 + [2 - (-1)]^2}$$
$$= \sqrt{(-4)^2 + (2+1)^2}$$
$$= \sqrt{(-4)^2 + 3^2}$$
$$= \sqrt{16 + 9} = \sqrt{25} = 5$$

Example 2

What is the area of the circle that passes through the point $(10, 8)$ and has its center at $(2, 2)$?

We can use the distance formula to find the radius of the circle.

$$r = \sqrt{(10-2)^2 + (8-2)^2} = \sqrt{8^2 + 6^2} = \sqrt{100} = 10$$

Thus, the radius of the circle is 10. The area would be $A = \pi r^2 = \pi(10)^2 = 100\pi$.

Volume

Definitions

The volume of any three-dimensional solid figure represents the amount of space contained within it. While area, as we have seen, is measured in square units, the volume of an object is measured in cubic units, such as cubic feet, cubic meters, and cubic centimeters. One cubic foot is defined as the amount of space contained within a cube that is 1 foot on each side.

There are several volume formulas for common solid figures that you should be familiar with.

A rectangular solid is a six-sided figure whose sides are rectangles. The volume of a rectangular solid is its length times its width times its height.

A cube is a rectangular solid whose sides are all the same length. The volume of a cube is the cube of its side.

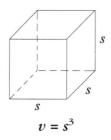

$$v = s^3$$

The volume of a cylinder is equal to the area of its base times its height. Since the base is a circle, the volume is $V = \pi r^2 h$.

A pyramid has a rectangular base and triangular sides. Its area is given by the formula $V = \frac{1}{3}lwh$.

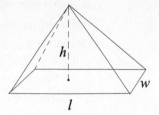

The volume of a cone is given by the formula $V = \frac{1}{3}\pi r^2 h$.

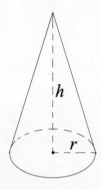

Finally, the formula for the volume of a sphere is given by the formula $V = \frac{4}{3}\pi r^3$.

Example 1

What is the surface area of a cube whose volume is 125 cubic centimeters?

Since the formula for the volume of a cube is $V = s^3$, we have $V = s^3 = 125$. Thus, $s = \sqrt[3]{125} = 5$ centimeters.

If the side of the cube is 5 centimeters, the area of one of its faces is $5^2 = 25$ square centimeters. Since the cube has 6 faces, its surface area is $6 \times 25 = 150$ square centimeters.

Example 2

The volume of a cylinder having a height of 12 is 144π. What is the radius of its base?

The formula for the volume of a cylinder is $V = \pi r^2 h$. Since $V = 144\pi$ and $h = 12$, we have

$$144\pi = \pi r^2 (12).$$

Divide both sides by π.

$$144 = 12r^2$$
$$12 = r^2$$
$$r = \sqrt{12} = 2\sqrt{3}.$$

Thus, the radius of the base is $2\sqrt{3}$.

GEOMETRY PROBLEMS

1. A chair is 5 feet from one wall of a room, and 7 feet from the wall at a right angle to it. How far is the chair from the intersection of the two walls?

2. In triangle XYZ, XZ = YZ. If angle Z has a°, how many degrees are there in angle x?

3. In a trapezoid of area 20, the two bases measure 4 and 6. What is the height of the trapezoid?

4. A circle is inscribed in a square whose side is 8. What is the area of the circle, in terms of π?

5. PQ is the diameter of a circle whose center is R. If the coordinates of P are (8, 4) and the coordinates of Q are (4, 8), what are the coordinates of R?

6. The volume of a cube is 64 cubic inches. What is its surface area?

7. The perimeter of scalene triangle EFG is 95. If FG = 20 and EF = 45, what is the measure of EG?

8. In the diagram below, AB is parallel to CD. Find the measures of x and y.

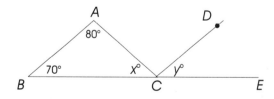

9. In the triangle below, find the measures of the angles.

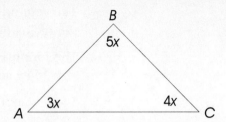

10. If the base of a parallelogram decreases by 20%, and the height increases by 40%, by what percent does the area increase?

11. In the circle below, AB = 9 and BC = 12. If AC is the diameter of the circle, what is the radius?

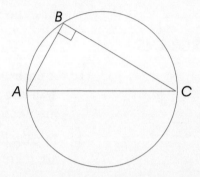

12. In the right triangle below, AB is twice BC. What is the length of BC?

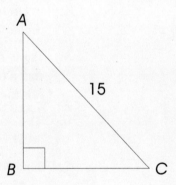

Peterson's Math Review for the GRE, GMAT and MCAT

SOLUTIONS

1. As the drawing below shows, we need to find the length of the hypotenuse of a right triangle with legs of 5 and 7. The formula tells us that $5^2 + 7^2 = x^2$, or $74 = x^2$. Thus, $x = \sqrt{74}$.

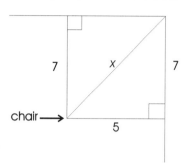

2. The diagram below shows that triangle XYZ is isosceles, and thus angle X and angle Y are the same.

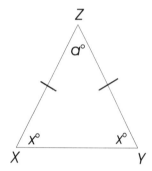

If we call the measure of these angles $x°$, we have $x° + x° + a° = 180°$, or $2x° + a° = 180°$. From this we have $2x° = 180° - a°$ or $x° = \dfrac{(180° - a°)}{2}$.

3. The formula for the area of a trapezoid is $A = \dfrac{1}{2} h (b_1 + b_2)$, where h is the height and b_1 and b_2 are the bases. Substituting, we have $20 = \dfrac{1}{2} h (4 + 6)$ or $40 = 10h$, so $h = 4$.

4. As the picture below shows, the diameter of the circle is 8 and the radius is 4.

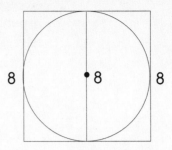

Since $C = \pi r^2$, we have $C = \pi(4^2) = 16\pi$.

5. The center of the circle is the midpoint of the diameter. The formula for the midpoint of a line segment is
$$\left(\frac{(x_1 + x_2)}{2}, \frac{(y_1 + y_2)}{2}\right).$$
Thus, the center is at $\left(\frac{12}{2}, \frac{12}{2}\right) = (6, 6)$.

6. Since the volume of a cube is given by $V = s^3$, where s is the side of the square, it can be seen that s is 4 (since $4^3 = 64$). Then, the surface area of one of the sides is $4 \times 4 = 16$, and, since there are six sides in a cube, the surface area is $16 \times 6 = 96$.

7.
$$20 + 45 + x = 95$$
$$65 + x = 95$$
$$x = 30$$

8. Since AB and CD are parallel, $\angle BAC$ and $\angle ACD$ are alternate interior angles, and are therefore equal. Thus, $x = 80$. Similarly, $\angle ABC$ is a corresponding angle to $\angle DCE$, and so $y = 70$.

9. Since there are 180° in a triangle, we must have
$$3x + 4x + 5x = 180$$
$$12x = 180$$
$$x = 15,$$

and $3x = 45$, $4x = 60$, and $5x = 75$. Thus, the angles in the triangle measure 45°, 60°, and 75°.

10. Let b = the length of the base and h = the height in the original parallelogram. Then, the area of the original parallelogram is A = bh.

    If the base decreases by 20%, it becomes $.8b$. If the height increases by 40%, it becomes $1.4h$. The new area, then, is A = $(.8b)(1.4)h = 1.12bh$, which is 12% bigger than the original area.

11. Note that triangle ABC is a right triangle. Call the diameter d. Then, we have $9^2 + 12^2 = d^2$, or

    $$81 + 144 = d^2$$
    $$225 = d^2$$
    $$d = 15.$$

    If the diameter is 15, the radius is $7\frac{1}{2}$.

12. Let the length of BC be x. Then, the length of AB is $2x$. By the Pythagorean Theorem, we have

    $$x^2 + (2x)^2 = 15^2$$
    $$x^2 + 4x^2 = 225$$
    $$5x^2 = 225$$
    $$x^2 = 45$$
    $$x = \sqrt{45} = \sqrt{9 \times 5}.$$

    The length of BC is $3\sqrt{5}$.

ADDITIONAL MATH TOPICS
FOR THE MCAT

In addition to the math topics already discussed, students taking the MCAT must be familiar with several additional areas of mathematics. These areas are covered in this section. The topics in this section *do not* appear on the GRE or on the GMAT, so students taking those tests do not need to worry about them.

EXPONENTS AND LOGARITHMS

DEFINITIONS AND PROPERTIES

When we discussed exponents in the arithmetic review section, all of the exponents we looked at were positive integers. However, meaning can also be given to negative and fractional exponents.

Negative exponents are defined by the definition

$$a^{-n} = \frac{1}{a^n}.$$

Thus, for example, $5^{-2} = \frac{1}{5^2}$, and $7^{-9} = \frac{1}{7^9}$.

By definition, we say that $a^0 = 1$. In other words, any number raised to the 0 power is defined to equal 1. We have therefore given meaning to all integral exponents.

There are five rules for computing with exponents. In general, if k and m are integers, and a and b are any numbers:

Rule 1: $a^k \times a^m = a^{k+m}$

Rule 2: $\dfrac{a^k}{a^m} = a^{k-m}$

Rule 3: $(a^k)^m = a^{km}$

Rule 4: $(ab)^m = a^m \times b^m$

Rule 5: $\left(\dfrac{a}{b}\right)^m = \dfrac{a^m}{b^m}$

Examples

Rule 1: $2^2 \times 2^3 = 4 \times 8 = 32$ and $2^2 \times 2^3 = 2^5 = 32$.

Rule 2: $\dfrac{3^5}{3^7} = \dfrac{243}{2187} = \dfrac{1}{9} = \dfrac{1}{3^2} = 3^{-2}$ and $\dfrac{3^5}{3^7} = 3^{(5\ -\ 7)} = 3^{-2}$.

Rule 3: $(3^2)^3 = 9^3 = 729$ and $(3^2)^3 = 3^6 = 729$

Rule 4: $(3 \times 4)^2 = 12^2 = 144$,
and $(3 \times 4)^2 = 3^2 \times 4^2 = 9 \times 16 = 144$

Rule 5: $\left(\dfrac{6}{2}\right)^4 = 3^4 = 81$,
and $\left(\dfrac{6}{2}\right)^4 = \dfrac{6^4}{2^4} = \dfrac{1296}{16} = 81$

SCIENTIFIC NOTATION

Any number can be written as the product of a number between 1 and 10 and some power of 10. A number written this way is said to be written in *scientific notation*.

To express a number in scientific notation, begin by repositioning the decimal point, so that the number becomes a number between 1 and 10. In other words, place the decimal point so that there is one digit to its left. Then, the appropriate power of 10 can be determined by counting the number of places that the decimal point has been moved. The examples below will clarify this concept.

Example 1:

Write the following numbers in scientific notation:

(A) 640,000

In writing this number as 6.4, the decimal point is moved 5 places to the left. Thus, $640{,}000 = 6.4 \times 10^5$.

(B) 2,730,000

To change this number to 2.730, the decimal point needs to be moved 6 places to the left. Thus, $2{,}730{,}000 = 2.73 \times 10^6$.

(C) .00085

To change this number to 8.5, the decimal point must be moved 4 places to the right. Thus, $.00085 = 8.5 \times 10^{-4}$.

(D) .000000562

To change this number to 5.62, the decimal point needs to be moved 7 places to the right. Thus, $.000000562 = 5.62 \times 10^{-7}$.

Example 2

Write the following numbers without scientific notation:

(A) 3.69×10^3

Since $10^3 = 1000$,
we see that $3.69 \times 10^3 = 3.69 \times 1000 = 3690$.

(B) 6.7×10^{-4}

Since $10^{-4} = .0001$, $6.7 \times 10^{-4} = 6.7 \times .0001 = .00067$

FRACTIONAL EXPONENTS

The definitions of exponents can be extended to include fractional exponents. In particular, roots of numbers can be indicated by fractions with a numerator of 1. For example, $\sqrt{2}$ can be written as $2^{\frac{1}{2}}$. Similarly, $\sqrt[3]{7} = 7^{\frac{1}{3}}$. Using rules 1-5 above, we can also make sense of any negative fractional exponents.

Examples

(A) $8^{\frac{-1}{2}} = \dfrac{1}{\sqrt{8}}$.

(B) $7^{\frac{-5}{2}} = (7^{-5})^{\frac{1}{2}} = \left(\dfrac{1}{7^5}\right)^{\frac{1}{2}} = \left(\dfrac{1}{16807}\right)^{\frac{1}{2}} = \dfrac{1}{\sqrt{16807}} \approx .0077$

Note that from Rule 4 we can determine that $(a \times b)^{\frac{1}{k}} = a^{\frac{1}{k}} \times b^{\frac{1}{k}}$. Written in radical notation, this expression becomes $\sqrt{a \times b} = \sqrt{a} \times \sqrt{b}$. This statement justifies the technique we have used for the simplification of square roots.

EXPONENTIAL EQUATIONS

An exponential equation is an equation whose variable appears in a exponent. Such equations can be solved by algebraic means if it is possible to express both sides of the equation as powers of the same base.

Example 1

Solve $5^{2x - 1} = 25$

Rewrite the equation as $5^{2x - 1} = 5^2$. Then it must be true that $2x - 1 = 2$. This means that $x = \dfrac{3}{2}$.

Example 2

Solve $9^{x + 3} = 27^{2x}$.

Rewrite the left side of the equation as $(3^2)^{x + 3} = 3^{2x + 6}$. Rewrite the right side of the equation as $(3^3)^{2x} = 3^{6x}$. Then, it must be true that $2x + 6 = 6x$. This means that $x = \dfrac{3}{2}$.

Exponential equations in which the bases cannot both be changed to the same number can be solved by using logarithms.

The Meaning of Logarithms

The logarithm of a number is the power to which a given base must be raised to produce the number. For example, the logarithm of 25 to the base 5 is 2, since 5 must be raised to the second power to produce the number 25. The statement "the logarithm of 25 to the base 5 is 2" is written as $\log_5 25 = 2$.

Note that every time we write a statement about exponents, we can write an equivalent statement about logarithms. For example, $\log_3 27 = 3$ since $3^3 = 27$, and $\log_8 4 = \dfrac{2}{3}$, since $8^{\frac{2}{3}} = 4$.

An important byproduct of the definition of logarithms is that we cannot determine values for $\log_a x$ if x is either zero or a negative number. For example, if $\log_2 0 = b$, then $2^b = 0$, but there is no exponent satisfying this property. Similarly, if $\log_2(-8) = b$, then $2^b = -8$, and there is no exponent satisfying this property.

While logarithms can be written to any base, logarithms to the base 10 are used so frequently that they are called common logarithms, and the symbol "log" is used to stand for "$\log_{10}$".

Examples

1. Write logarithmic equivalents to the following statements about exponents:

    (A) $2^5 = 32$

    The statement $2^5 = 32$ is equivalent to $\log_2 32 = 5$

    (B) $12^0 = 1$

    The statement $12^0 = 1$ is equivalent to $\log_{12} 1 = 0$

2. Use the definition of logarithm to evaluate the following:

    (A) $\log_6 36$

    $\log_6 36 = 2$, since $6^2 = 36$

    (B) $\log_4\left(\dfrac{1}{16}\right) = -2$ since $4^{-2} = \dfrac{1}{16}$.

PROPERTIES OF LOGARITHMS

Since logarithms are exponents, they follow the rules of exponents previously discussed. For example, when exponents to the same base are multiplied, and their exponents are added, we have the rule: $\log_a xy = \log_a x + \log_a y$. The three most frequently used rules of logarithms are:

Rule 1: $\log_a xy = \log_a x + \log_a y$

Rule 2: $\log_a \left(\dfrac{x}{y}\right) = \log_a x - \log_a y$

Rule 3: $\log_a x^b = b\log_a x$

Examples

Rule 1. $\log_3 14 = \log_3(7 \cdot 2) = \log_3 7 + \log_3 2$

Rule 2. $\log \left(\dfrac{13}{4}\right) = \log 13 - \log 4$

Rule 3. $\log_7 \sqrt{5} = \log_7(5^{\frac{1}{2}}) = \left(\dfrac{1}{2}\right)\log_7 5$

By combining these rules, we can see, for example, that $\log \left(\dfrac{5b}{7}\right) = \log 5 + \log b - \log 7$.

SOLVING EXPONENTIAL EQUATIONS BY USING LOGARITHMS

Exponential equations, in which neither side can be written as exponents to the same power, can be solved by using logarithms.

Example

Solve $3^{2x} = 4^{x-1}$

Begin by taking the logarithm of both sides. We could take the logarithm with respect to any base; in this example, to keep things simple, we will take the logarithm to the base 10.

$$\log 3^{2x} = \log 4^{x-1}$$
$$2x\log 3 = (x - 1)\log 4$$
$$2x\log 3 = x\log 4 - \log 4$$
$$2x\log 3 - x\log 4 = -\log 4$$
$$x(2\log 3 - \log 4) = -\log 4$$
$$x = \frac{-\log 4}{(2\log 3 - \log 4)}$$

We now need to obtain values for log 3 and log 4. These can be obtained from either a table of logarithms or a scientific calculator. We obtain log 3 = 0.4771, and log 4 = 0.6021. Thus,

$$x = -\frac{(0.6021)}{((2(0.4771)) - 0.6021)} = \frac{-0.6021}{0.3521} = -1.7100$$

EXPONENTS AND LOGARITHMS PROBLEMS

In exercises 1 and 2, write an equivalent exponential form for each radical expression.

1. $\sqrt{11}$

2. $\sqrt[3]{13}$

In exercises 3 and 4, write an equivalent radical expression for each exponential expression.

3. $8^{\frac{1}{5}}$

4. $(x^2)^{\frac{1}{3}}$

In exercises 5 and 6, evaluate the given expressions.

5. $27^{\frac{1}{3}}$

6. $125^{\frac{2}{3}}$

7. Express the following numbers using scientific notation.
   (A) 1,234.56
   (B) 0.0876

8. Write the following numbers without scientific notation:
   (A) 1.234×10^5
   (B) 5.45×10^{-3}

9. Express the following equations in logarithmic form:
   (A) $3^2 = 9$
   (B) $7^{-2} = \dfrac{1}{49}$

10. Express the following equations in exponential form:
    (A) $\log_6 36 = 2$
    (B) $\log_{10}\left(\dfrac{1}{10}\right) = -1$

11. Find the value of the following logarithms:
    (A) $\log_2 8$
    (B) $\log_{12} 1$

12. Express as the sum or difference of logarithms of simpler quantities:
    (A) $\log 12$
    (B) $\log\left(\dfrac{ab}{c}\right)$

13. Solve the following equation for x: $125 = 5^{2x-1}$.

Solutions

1. $11^{\frac{1}{2}}$

2. $13^{\frac{1}{3}}$

3. $\sqrt[5]{8}$

4. $\sqrt[3]{x^2}$

5. $27^{\frac{1}{3}} = \sqrt[3]{27} = 3$

6. $125^{\frac{2}{3}} = (\sqrt[3]{125})^2 = 5^2 = 25$

7. (A) $1{,}234.56 = 1.23456 \times 10^3$
   (B) $0.0876 = 8.76 \times 10^{-2}$

8. (A) $1.234 \times 10^5 = 123{,}400$
   (B) $5.45 \times 10^{-3} = 0.00545$

9. (A) $3^2 = 9$ is equivalent to $\log_3 9 = 2$.
   (B) $7^{-2} = \dfrac{1}{49}$ is equivalent to $\log_7\left(\dfrac{1}{49}\right) = -2$

10. (A) $\log_6 36 = 2$ is equivalent to $6^2 = 36$
    (B) $\log_{10}\left(\dfrac{1}{10}\right) = -1$ is equivalent to $10^{-1} = \dfrac{1}{10}$

11. (A) $\log_2 8 = 3$ (The power that 2 must be raised to in order to equal 8, is 3.)
    (B) $\log_{12} 1 = 0$ (The power that 12 must be raised to in order to equal 1, is 0.)

12. (A) $\log 12 = \log(2^2 \times 3) = \log(2^2) + \log 3 = 2\log 2 + \log 3$
    (B) $\log\left(\dfrac{ab}{c}\right) = \log(ab) - \log c = \log a + \log b - \log c$

13. $125 = 5^{2x-1}$. Rewrite 125 as 5^3. Then,

    $5^3 = 5^{2x-1}$. Thus, it must be true that

    $3 = 2x - 1$ or

    $2x = 4$, so that

    $x = 2.$

TRIGONOMETRY

Trigonometry enables you to solve problems that involve finding measures of unknown lengths and angles.

THE TRIGONOMETRIC RATIOS

Every right triangle contains two acute angles. With respect to each of these angles, it is possible to define six ratios, called the trigonometric ratios, each involving the lengths of two of the sides of the triangle. For example, consider the following triangle *ABC*.

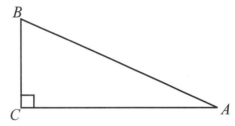

In this triangle, side *AC* is called the side adjacent to angle *A*, and side *BC* is called the side opposite angle *A*. Similarly, side *AC* is called the side opposite angle *B*, and side *BC* is called the side adjacent to angle *B*. Of course, side *AB* is referred to as the hypotenuse with respect to both angles *A* and *B*.

The six trigonometric ratios with respect to angle *A*, along with their standard abbreviations, are given below:

Sine of angle $A = \sin A = \dfrac{\text{opposite}}{\text{hypotenuse}} = \dfrac{BC}{AB}$

Cosine of angle *A*

$$= \cos A = \dfrac{\text{adjacent}}{\text{hypotenuse}} = \dfrac{AC}{AB}$$

Tangent of angle $A = \tan A = \dfrac{\text{opposite}}{\text{adjacent}} = \dfrac{BC}{AC}$

Cotangent of angle *A*

$$= \cot A = \dfrac{\text{adjacent}}{\text{opposite}} = \dfrac{AC}{AB}$$

Secant of angle *A*

$$= \sec A = \dfrac{\text{hypotenuse}}{\text{adjacent}} = \dfrac{AB}{AC}$$

Cosecant of angle *A*

$$= \csc A = \dfrac{\text{hypotenuse}}{\text{opposite}} = \dfrac{AB}{BC}$$

The last three ratios are actually the reciprocals of the first three, in particular:

$$\cot A = \frac{1}{\tan A}$$

$$\sec A = \frac{1}{\cos A}$$

$$\csc A = \frac{1}{\sin A}$$

Also note that:

$$\frac{\sin A}{\cos A} = \tan A, \text{ and } \frac{\cos A}{\sin A} = \cot A.$$

In order to remember which of the trigonometric ratios is which, you can memorize the well-known acronym: **SOH–CAH–TOA**. This stands for: **S**ine is **O**pposite over **H**ypotenuse, **C**osine is **A**djacent over **H**ypotenuse, **T**angent is **O**pposite over **A**djacent.

Example

Consider right triangle *DEF* below, whose sides have the lengths indicated. Find sin *D*, cos *D*, tan *D*, sin *E*, cos *E*, and tan *E*.

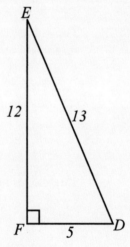

$$\sin D = \frac{EF}{ED} = \frac{12}{13} \qquad\qquad \sin E = \frac{DF}{ED} = \frac{5}{13}$$

$$\cos D = \frac{DF}{ED} = \frac{5}{13} \qquad\qquad \cos E = \frac{EF}{ED} = \frac{12}{13}$$

$$\tan D = \frac{EF}{DF} = \frac{12}{5} \qquad\qquad \tan E = \frac{DF}{EF} = \frac{5}{12}$$

Note that the sine of *D* is equal to the cosine of *E*, and the cosine of *D* is equal to the sine of *E*.

Example

In right triangle ABC, $\sin A = \dfrac{4}{5}$. Find the values of the other 5 trigonometric ratios.

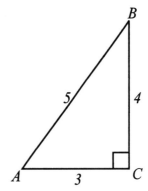

Since the sine of A = opposite over hypotenuse = $\dfrac{4}{5}$, we know that $BC = 4$, and $AB = 5$. We can use the Pythagorean theorem to determine that $AC = 3$. Then:

$$\cos A = \frac{3}{5}, \ \tan A = \frac{4}{3}, \ \cot A = \frac{3}{4}, \ \sec A = \frac{5}{3}, \ \csc A = \frac{5}{4}.$$

TRIGONOMETRIC RATIOS FOR SPECIAL ANGLES

The actual values for the trigonometric ratios for most angles are irrational numbers, whose values can most easily be found by looking in a trig table or using a calculator. On the MCAT, you will not need to find the values for such trig functions; you can simply leave the answer in terms of the ratio. For example, if the answer to a word problem is 35 tan 37°, the correct answer choice will be, in fact, 35 tan 37°. There are, however, a few angles whose ratios can be obtained exactly. The ratios for 30°, 45°, and 60° can be determined from the properties of the 30–60–90 right triangle and the 45–45–90 right triangle. First of all, note that the Pythagorean theorem can be used to determine the following side and angle relationships in 30–60–90 and 45–45–90 triangles:

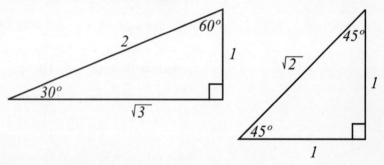

From these diagrams, it is easy to see that:

$$\sin 30° = \frac{1}{2}, \cos 30° = \frac{\sqrt{3}}{2},$$

$$\tan 30° = \frac{1}{\sqrt{3}} = \frac{\sqrt{3}}{3}$$

$$\sin 60° = \frac{\sqrt{3}}{2}, \cos 60° = \frac{1}{2}, \ \tan 60° = \sqrt{3}$$

$$\sin 45° = \cos 45° = \frac{1}{\sqrt{2}} = \frac{\sqrt{2}}{2}, \ \tan 45° = 1$$

Example

From point A, which is directly across from point B on the opposite sides of the banks of a straight river, the measure of angle CAB to point C, 35 meters upstream from B, is 30. How wide is the river?

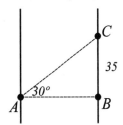

To solve this problem, note that

$$\tan A = \frac{\text{opposite}}{\text{adjacent}} = \frac{BC}{AB} = \frac{35}{AB}.$$

Since the measure of angle A is 30°, we have

$\tan 30° = \dfrac{35}{AB}$. Then:

$$AB = \frac{35}{\tan 30°} = \frac{35}{\sqrt{3}/3} = \frac{105}{\sqrt{3}}.$$

Therefore, the width of the river is $\dfrac{105}{\sqrt{3}}$ meters, or approximately 60 meters wide.

THE PYTHAGOREAN IDENTITIES

There are three fundamental relationships involving the trigonometric ratios that are true for all angles and are helpful when solving problems. They are:

$$\sin^2 A + \cos^2 A = 1$$
$$\tan^2 A + 1 = \sec^2 A$$
$$\cot^2 A + 1 = \csc^2 A$$

These three identifies are called the Pythagorean identities since they can be derived from the Pythagorean theorem. For example, in triangle *ABC* below:

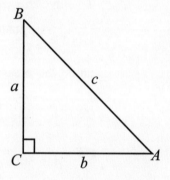

$$a^2 + b^2 = c^2$$

Dividing by c^2, we obtain,

$$\frac{a^2}{c^2} + \frac{b^2}{c^2} = 1, \text{ or}$$

$$\left(\frac{a}{c}\right)^2 + \left(\frac{b}{c}\right)^2 = 1.$$

Now, note that $\frac{a}{c} = \sin A$ and $\frac{b}{c} = \cos A$. Substituting these values in, we obtain $\sin^2 A + \cos^2 A = 1$. The other two identities are similarly obtained.

Example

If, in triangle ABC, $\sin A = \dfrac{7}{9}$, what are the values of $\cos A$ and $\tan A$?

Using the first of the trigonometric identities, we obtain:

$$\left(\frac{7}{9}\right)^2 + \cos^2 A = 1$$

$$= \frac{49}{81} + \cos^2 A = 1$$

$$\cos^2 A = 1 - \frac{49}{81}$$

$$\cos A = \sqrt{\frac{32}{81}}$$

$$= \frac{4\sqrt{2}}{9}$$

Then, since $\tan A = \dfrac{\sin A}{\cos A}$, we have

$$\tan A = \frac{\left(\dfrac{7}{9}\right)}{\left(\dfrac{4\sqrt{2}}{9}\right)} = \frac{7}{4\sqrt{2}} = \frac{7\sqrt{2}}{8}.$$

TRIGONOMETRY PROBLEMS

1. In right triangle PQR, cot $P = \dfrac{5}{12}$. Find the value of tan P, sin P, and sec P.

2. Find the value of cot 45° + cos 30° + sin 150°.

3. If sin $a = \dfrac{3}{7}$, and cos $a < 0$, what is the value of tan a?

4. A wire extends from the top of a 50 foot pole to a stake in the ground. If the wire makes an angle of 55° with the ground, find the length of the wire.

5. A road is inclined at an angle of 10° with the horizontal. If John drives 50 feet up the road, how many feet above the horizontal is he?

6. If sin $\theta = \dfrac{1}{2}$, and cos $\theta = -\dfrac{\sqrt{3}}{2}$, find the values of the other 4 trigonometric functions.

7. Demonstrate that $\dfrac{1}{\sin^2 x}$ is equivalent to $\dfrac{(1 + \tan^2 x)}{\tan^2 x}$.

8. In right triangle DEF, with angle F a right angle, csc $D = \dfrac{13}{12}$. What is the value of tan D?

9. The angle of elevation from an observer at ground level to a vertically ascending rocket measures 55°. If the observer is located 5 miles from the lift-off point of the rocket, what is the altitude of the rocket?

10. What is the value of 3 cos 45° + 3 sin 30°?

SOLUTIONS

1.

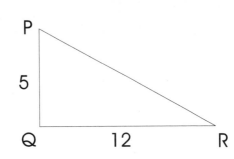

$$\cot P = \frac{5}{12} = \frac{\text{adjacent}}{\text{opposite}}.$$

Thus, $\tan P = \frac{12}{5}$.

From the Pythagorean Theorem, we can compute that the hypotenuse of the triangle is 13.

Thus, $\sin P = \frac{\text{opposite}}{\text{hypotenuse}} = \frac{12}{13}$,

and $\sec P = \frac{\text{hypotenuse}}{\text{adjacent}} = \frac{13}{5}$.

2. Note that $\sin 150° = \sin 30°$. Thus, $\cot 45° + \cos 30° + \sin 150° = 1 + \frac{\sqrt{3}}{2} + \frac{1}{2} = \frac{3 + \sqrt{3}}{2}$.

3. Given $\sin a = \frac{3}{7}$, and $\cos a < 0$, we can find the value of cos a using the Pythagorean Identity $\sin^2 a + \cos^2 a = 1$.

$$\left(\frac{3}{7}\right)^2 + \cos^2 a = 1$$

$$\frac{9}{49} + \cos^2 a = 1$$

$$\cos^2 a = 1 - \frac{9}{49} = \frac{40}{49}$$

$$\cos a = .\sqrt{\frac{40}{49}} = \frac{2\sqrt{10}}{7}$$

Since $\tan a = \sin \frac{a}{\cos a}$, we have

$$\tan a = \frac{\left(\frac{3}{7}\right)}{\frac{2\sqrt{10}}{7}} = \frac{3}{(2\sqrt{10})} = \frac{(3\sqrt{10})}{20}.$$

4. Let L = length of the wire

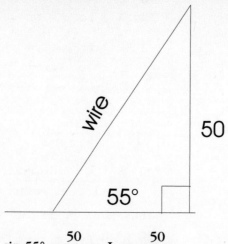

$$\sin 55° = \frac{50}{L}, \text{ so } L = \frac{50}{\sin 55°}.$$

5   Let x = the distance above the horizontal.

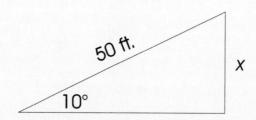

$\sin 10° = \frac{x}{50}$. Therefore, $x = 50 \sin 10°$

6. First of all, we have $\csc \theta = \frac{1}{\sin \theta} = 2$.

Similarly, $\sec \theta = \frac{1}{\cos \theta} = \frac{-2}{\sqrt{3}} = \frac{-2\sqrt{3}}{3}$.

Next, $\tan \theta = \frac{\sin \theta}{\cos \theta} = \frac{\left(\frac{1}{2}\right)}{\left(\frac{-\sqrt{3}}{2}\right)} = \frac{-1}{\sqrt{3}} = -\frac{\sqrt{3}}{3}$.

The value of $\cot \theta$ is the reciprocal of $\tan \theta$, which is $-\sqrt{3}$.

7. Solving this problem simply requires the application of several of the fundamental trigonometric identities. First of all, recall that $1 + \tan^2 x = \sec^2 x$. Therefore,

$$\frac{(1 + \tan^2 x)}{\tan^2 x} = \frac{\sec^2 x}{\tan^2 x}.$$

Now, use the fact that $\sec x = \dfrac{1}{\cos x}$ and $\tan x = \dfrac{\sin x}{\cos x}$ to obtain

$$\frac{\sec^2 x}{\tan^2 x} = \frac{\left(\dfrac{1}{\cos^2 x}\right)}{\left(\dfrac{\sin^2 x}{\cos^2 x}\right)} = \frac{\left(\dfrac{1}{\cos^2 x}\right)}{\left(\dfrac{\cos^2 x}{\sin^2 x}\right)} = \frac{1}{\sin^2 x}.$$

8. In a right triangle, the csc of an angle is equal to the hypotenuse divided by the side opposite the angle. Since we know $\csc D = \dfrac{13}{12}$ we know that the triangle in question has a hypotenuse of 13, and the side opposite angle D is 12.

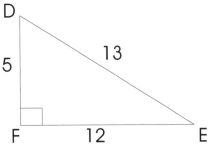

The Pythagorean theorem can be used to determine that the missing (adjacent) side is 5. Now, the tangent of an angle is the ratio of the opposite side to the adjacent side. Therefore

$$\tan D = \frac{\text{opposite}}{\text{adjacent}} = \frac{12}{5}.$$

9.   The best way to begin is with a diagram of the situation:

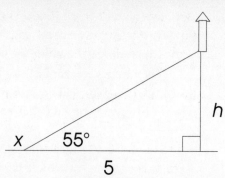

Let h = the altitude of the rocket. Then, since the tangent of an angle is equal to the opposite side divided by the adjacent, we have

$$\tan 55° = \frac{h}{5} \text{ or}$$

$$h = 5 \tan 55°.$$

10.   In this problem, we need to know that $\cos 45° = \frac{\sqrt{2}}{2}$ and $\sin 30° = \frac{1}{2}$.

Then,

$$3 \cos 45° + 3 \sin 30° = 3 \left(\frac{\sqrt{2}}{2} \right) + 3 \left(\frac{1}{2} \right) = (3\sqrt{2}) + \frac{2}{2}.$$

COORDINATE GEOMETRY

We have already seen that a coordinate system is an effective way to picture relationships involving two variables. In this section, we will learn more about the study of geometry using coordinate methods.

Lines

Recall that the general equation of a line has the following form:

$$Ax + By + C = 0$$

where A and B are constants and are not both 0. This means that if you were to find all of the points (x, y) that satisfy the above equation, they would all lie on the same line as graphed on a coordinate axis.

If the value of B is not 0, a little algebra can be used to rewrite the equation in the form

$$y = mx + b$$

where m and b are two constants. Since the two numbers m and b determine this line, let's see what their geometric meaning is. First of all, note that the point $(0, b)$ satisfies the above equation. This means that the point $(0, b)$ is one of the points on the line; in other words, the line crosses the y-axis at the point b. For this reason, the number b is called the *y-intercept* of the line.

To interpret the meaning of m, choose any two points on the line. Let us call these points (x_1, y_1) and (x_2, y_2). Both of these points must satisfy the equation of the line above, and so:

$$y_1 = mx_1 + b \text{ and } y_2 = mx_2 + b.$$

If we subtract the first equation from the second, we obtain

$$y_2 - y_1 = m(x_2 - x_1)$$

and solving for m, we find

$$m = (y_2 - y_1)/(x_2 - x_1).$$

The above equation tells us that the number m in the equation $y = mx + b$ is the ratio of the difference of the y-coordinates to the difference of the x-coordinates. This number is called the *slope* of the line. Therefore, the ratio $m = (y_2 - y_1)/(x_2 - x_1)$ is a measure of the number of units the line rises (or falls) in the y direction for each unit moved in the x direction. Another way to say this is that the slope of a line is a measure of the rate at which the line rises (or falls). Intuitively, a line with a positive slope rises from left to right; one with a negative slope falls from left to right.

Because the equation $y = mx + b$ contains both the slope and the y-intercept, it is called the *slope-intercept* form of the equation of the line.

Example

Write the equation $2x - 3y = 6$ in slope-intercept form.

To write the equation in slope-intercept form, we begin by solving for y.

$$-3y = 6 - 2x$$
$$3y = 2x - 6$$
$$y = \frac{2x}{3} - \frac{6}{3} \text{ or}$$
$$y = \frac{2x}{3} - 2$$

Thus, the slope of the line is $\frac{2}{3}$, and the y-intercept is -2.

This, however, is not the only form in which the equation of the line can be written.

If the line contains the point (x_1, y_1), its equation can also be written as:

$$y - y_1 = m(x - x_1).$$

This form of the equation of a line is called the *point-slope* form of the equation of a line, since it contains the slope and the coordinates of one of the points on the line.

Example

Write the equation of the line that passes through the point $(2, 3)$ with slope 8 in point-slope form.

In this problem, $m = 8$, and $(x_1, y_1) = (2, 3)$. Substituting into the point-slope form of the equation, we obtain

$$y - 3 = 8(x - 2)$$

Two lines are parallel if and only if they have the same slope. Two lines are perpendicular if and only if their slopes are negative inverses of each other. This means that if a line has a slope m, any line perpendicular to this line must have a slope of $-1/m$. Also note that a horizontal line has a slope of 0. For such a line, the slope-intercept form of the equation reduces to $y = b$.

Finally, note that if $B = 0$ in the equation $Ax + By + C = 0$, the equation simplifies to

$$Ax + C = 0$$

and represents a vertical line (a line parallel to the y-axis) that crosses the x-axis at $-C/A$. Such a line is said to have no slope.

Example 1

Find the slope and the *y*-intercept of the following lines.

    a. $y = 5x - 7$

    b. $3x + 4y = 5$

a. $y = 5x - 7$ is already in slope-intercept form. The slope is 5, and the *y*-intercept is −7.

b. Write $3x + 4y = 5$ in slope-intercept form:

$$4y = -3x + 5$$

$$y = \left(-\frac{3}{4}\right)x + \left(\frac{5}{4}\right)$$

The slope is $\frac{-3}{4}$, and the *y*-intercept is $\frac{5}{4}$. This means that the line crosses the *y*-axis at the point $\frac{5}{4}$, and for every 3 units moved in the *x* direction, the line falls 4 units in the *y* direction.

Example 2

Find the equations of the following lines:

    a. the line containing the points (4, 5) and (7,11)

    b. the line containing the point (6, 3) and having slope 2

    c. the line containing the point (5, 2) and parallel to $y = 4x + 7$

    d. the line containing the point (−2, 8) and perpendicular to $y = -2x + 9$

Solutions

a. First, we need to determine the slope of the line.

$$m = \frac{(11-5)}{(7-4)} = \frac{6}{3} = 2.$$

Now, using the point-slope form:

$$y - 5 = 2(x - 4).$$

If desired, you can change this to the slope-intercept form: $y = 2x - 3$.

b. Since we know the slope and a point on the line, we can simply plug into the point-slope form:

$$y - 3 = m(x - 6) \text{ to obtain}$$

$$y - 3 = 2(x - 6).$$

c. The line $y = 4x + 7$ has a slope of 4. Thus, the desired line can be written as $y - 2 = 4(x - 5)$.

d. The line $y = -2x + 9$ has a slope of -2. The line perpendicular to this one has a slope of $\frac{1}{2}$. The desired line can be written as $y - 8 = \left(\frac{1}{2}\right)(x + 2)$.

Circles

From a geometric point of view, a circle is the set of points in a plane, each of whose members is the same distance from a particular point called the center of the circle. We can determine the equation of a circle by manipulating the distance formula.

Suppose that we have a circle whose radius is a given positive number r and whose center lies at the point (h, k). If (x, y) is a point on the circle, then its distance from the center of the circle would be

$$\sqrt{(x - h)^2 + (y - k)^2}$$

and since this distance is r, we can say

$$\sqrt{(x - h)^2 + (y - k)^2} = r.$$

Squaring both sides, we get the following result: the equation of a circle whose center is at (h, k) and whose radius is r is given by:

$$(x - h)^2 + (y - k)^2 = r^2$$

Example 1

Find the equation of the circle with radius 7, and center at $(0, -5)$.

Substituting into the formula above, we obtain $x^2 + (y + 5)^2 = 49$.

Example 2

Describe the set of points (x, y) with the property that $x^2 + y^2 > 25$.

The equation $x^2 + y^2 = 25$ describes a circle, centered at the origin, with radius 5. The given set contains all of the points that are *outside* this circle.

COORDINATE GEOMETRY PROBLEMS

1. Find the slope of the line containing the points $(-2, -4)$ and $(2, 4)$.

2. Find the slope of the line given by the equation $4x + 5y = 7$.

3. Find the equation of the line with y-intercept 4 and x-intercept 7.

4. Find the equation of the line through the point $(7, 2)$ and having the same slope as the line through $(2, 4)$ and $(3, -1)$.

5. Find the equation of the line through $(-2, 3)$ and perpendicular to the line $2x - 3y = 4$.

6. What is the center and the radius of the circle given by the equation $(x - 3)^2 + (y + 7)^2 = 81$?

7. Write the equation $4x - 5y = 12$ in slope-intercept form.

8. Find the equation of the line parallel to $x = 7$ and containing the point $(3, 4)$.

9. Write an inequality which represents all of the points inside the circle centered at $(4, 5)$ with radius 4.

10. Find the equation of the line perpendicular to $x = -3$, containing the point $(-3, -6)$.

11. Find the slope of the line containing the points $(-4, 6)$, and $(2, 6)$.

SOLUTIONS

1. If (x_1, y_1) and (x_2, y_2) are two points on a line, the slope is given by slope $= \dfrac{(y_2 - y_1)}{(x_2 - x_1)}$. For the two given points, $(-2, -4)$ and $(2, 4)$, the slope is:

$$\text{slope} = \frac{(y_2 - y_1)}{(x_2 - x_1)}$$
$$= \frac{(4 - (-4))}{(2 - (-2))}$$
$$= \frac{(4 + 4)}{(2 + 2)}$$
$$= \frac{8}{4} = 2.$$

2. The easiest way to find the slope of the line is to rewrite the equation in the slope-intercept form.

$4x + 5y = 7$ Subtract $4x$

$5y = -4x + 7$ Divide by 5

$$y = \left(\frac{-4}{5}\right)x + \left(\frac{7}{5}\right).$$

The slope of the line is the coefficient of x, that is, $\dfrac{-4}{5}$.

3. The line has y-intercept 4, which means it passes through $(0,4)$; it also has x-intercept 7, which means it passes through $(7,0)$.

By the formula, slope $= \dfrac{(y_2 - y_1)}{(x_2 - x_1)} = \dfrac{(4-0)}{(0-7)} = \dfrac{-4}{7}$. Since we know the slope and the y-intercept, we can simply plug into the slope-intercept form, $y = mx + b$, and get $y = \left(\dfrac{-4}{7}\right)x + 4$.

4. The line through $(2, 4)$ and $(3, -1)$ has slope $\dfrac{(4 - (1))}{(2 - 3)} = \dfrac{5}{(-1)}$ $= -5$. Then, using the point-slope form, the desired line can be written as $y - 2 = -5(x - 7)$.

5. The line $2x - 3y = 4$ can be rewritten as $-3y = -2x + 4$, or $y = \left(\dfrac{2}{3}\right)x - \left(\dfrac{4}{3}\right)$. Therefore, its slope is $\dfrac{2}{3}$, and the line perpendicular to it would have slope $\dfrac{-3}{2}$. Then, using the point-slope form, the requested line can be written as $y - 3 = \left(\dfrac{-3}{2}\right)(x + 2)$

6. The general form for the equation of a circle is $(x - h) +$ $(y - k) = r^2$, where (h,k) is the center, and r is the radius. In this case, the given equation can be written as $(x - 3)^2 +$ $(y - (-7))^2 = 9^2$. Therefore, the center is $(3, -7)$ and the radius is 9.

7. To write the equation in slope-intercept form, we begin by solving for y

$$4x - 5y = 12$$
$$-5y = -4x + 12$$
$$y = \frac{-4x}{-5} + \frac{12}{x} = \frac{4x}{5} - \frac{12}{5}.$$

Thus, the equation in slope-intercept form is

$$y = \frac{4x}{5} - \frac{12}{5}.$$

The slope is $\frac{4}{5}$, and the y-intercept is $\frac{-12}{5}$.

8. Since $x = 7$ is vertical, any line parallel to $x = 7$ will be vertical also. The line parallel to $x = 7$ through $(3, 4)$ is $x = 3$.

9. The equation of the circle with center at $(4, 5)$ with radius 4 is $(x - 4)^2 + (y - 5)^2 = 4^2 = 16$. The points inside this circle are given by the inequality: $(x - 4)^2 + (y - 5)^2 < 16$.

10. The line $x = -3$ is vertical, so any line perpendicular to it is horizontal. The horizontal line through the point $(-3, -6)$ is $y = -6$.

11. The slope of the line containing the points $(-4, 6)$, and $(2, 6)$ is $m = \dfrac{6 - 6}{2 - (x)} = \dfrac{0}{6} = 0$. Thus, the line is horizontal.

PROBABILITY

DEFINITION

Probability is the branch of mathematics that gives you techniques for dealing with uncertainties. Intuitively, probability can be thought of as a numerical measure of the likelihood, or the chance, that an event will occur.

A probability value is always a number between 0 and 1. The nearer a probability value is to 0, the more unlikely the event is to occur; a probability value near 1 indicates that the event is almost certain to occur. Other probability values between 0 and 1 represent varying degrees of likelihood that an event will occur.

In the study of probability, an *experiment* is any process that yields one of a number of well-defined outcomes. By this we mean that on any single performance of an experiment, one and only one of a number of possible outcomes will occur. Thus, tossing a coin is an experiment with two possible outcomes: heads or tails. Rolling a die is an experiment with 6 possible outcomes; playing a game of hockey is an experiment with three possible outcomes (win, lose, tie).

COMPUTING PROBABILITIES

In some experiments, all possible outcomes are equally likely. In such an experiment, with, say, n possible outcomes, we assign a probability of $\frac{1}{n}$ to each outcome. Thus, for example, in the experiment of tossing a fair coin, for which there are two equally likely outcomes, we would say that the probability of each outcome is $\frac{1}{2}$. In the experiment of tossing a fair die, for which there are 6 equally likely outcomes, we would say that the probability of each outcome is $\frac{1}{6}$.

How would you determine the probability of obtaining an even number when tossing a die? Clearly, there are three distinct ways that an even number can be obtained: tossing a 2, a 4, or a 6. The probability of each one of these three outcomes is $\frac{1}{6}$. The probability of obtaining an even number is simply the sum of the probabilities of these three favorable outcomes; that is to say, the probability of tossing an even number is equal to the probability of tossing a 2, plus the probability of tossing a 4, plus the probability of tossing a 6, which is $\frac{1}{6} + \frac{1}{6} + \frac{1}{6} = \frac{3}{6} = \frac{1}{2}$.

This result leads us to the fundamental formula for computing probabilities for events with equally likely outcomes:
The probability of an event occurring =

$$\frac{\text{The number of favorable outcomes}}{\text{The total number of possible outcomes}}$$

In the case of tossing a die and obtaining an even number, as we saw, there are 6 possible outcomes, three of which are favorable, leading to a probability of $\frac{3}{6} = \frac{1}{2}$.

Example 1

What is the probability of drawing one card from a standard deck of 52 cards and having it be a king? When you select a card from a deck, there are 52 possible outcomes, 4 of which are favorable. Thus, the probability of drawing a king is $\frac{4}{52} = \frac{1}{13}$.

Example 2

Human eye color is controlled by a single pair of genes, one of which comes from the mother and one of which comes from the father, called a genotype. Brown eye color, B, is dominant over blue eye color ℓ. Therefore, in the genotype Bℓ, which consists of one brown gene B and one blue gene ℓ, the brown gene dominates. A person with a Bℓ genotype will have brown eyes.

If both parents have genotype Bℓ, what is the probability that their child will have blue eyes? To answer the question, we need to consider every possible eye color genotype for the child. They are given in the table below:

mother \ father	B	ℓ
B	BB	Bℓ
ℓ	ℓB	$\ell\ell$

The four possible genotypes for the child are equally likely, so we can use the formula above to compute the probability. Of the four possible outcomes, blue eyes can occur only with the $\ell\ell$ genotype, so only one of the four possible outcomes is favorable to blue eyes.

Thus, the probability that the child has blue eyes is $\frac{1}{4}$.

Two events are said to be *independent* if the occurrence of one does not affect the probability of the occurrence of the other. For example, if a coin is tossed and a die is thrown, obtaining heads on the coin and obtaining a 5 on the die are independent events. On the other hand, if a coin is tossed three times, the probability of obtaining heads on the first toss and the probability of obtaining tails on all three tosses are not independent. In particular, if heads is obtained on the first toss, the probability of obtaining three tails becomes 0.

When two events are independent, the probability that they both happen is the product of their individual probabilities. For example, the probability of obtaining heads when a coin is tossed is $\frac{1}{2}$, and the probability of obtaining 5 when a die is thrown is 12; thus, the probability of both of these events happening is

$$\left(\frac{1}{2}\right)\left(\frac{1}{6}\right) = \frac{1}{12}.$$

In a situation where two events occur one after the other, be sure to correctly determine the number of favorable outcomes and the total number of possible outcomes.

Example

Consider a standard deck of 52 cards. What is the probability of drawing two kings in a row, if the first card drawn is replaced in the deck before the second card is drawn? What is the probability of drawing two kings in a row if the first card drawn is *not* replaced in the deck?

In the first case, the probability of drawing a king from the deck on the first attempt is $\frac{4}{52} = \frac{1}{13}$. If the selected card is replaced in the deck, the probability of drawing a king on the second draw is also $\frac{1}{13}$, and, thus, the probability of drawing two consecutive kings would be $\left(\frac{1}{13}\right)\left(\frac{1}{13}\right) = \frac{1}{169}$. On the other hand, if the first card drawn is a king and is not replaced, there are now only three kings in a deck of 51 cards, and the probability of drawing the second king becomes $\frac{3}{51} = \frac{1}{17}$. The overall probability, thus, would be $\left(\frac{1}{13}\right)\left(\frac{1}{17}\right) = \frac{1}{221}$.

PROBABILITY PROBLEMS

1. A bag contains 7 blue marbles, three red marbles, and two white marbles. If one marble is chosen at random from the bag, what is the probability that it will be red? What is the probability that it will not be blue?

2. A woman's change purse contains a quarter, two dimes, and two pennies. What is the probability that a coin chosen at random will be worth at least 10 cents?

3. A bag contains four white and three black marbles. One marble is selected, its color is noted, and then it is returned to the bag. Then a second marble is selected. What is the probability that both selected marbles were white?

4. Using the same set up as given in problem 3, what is the probability that both selected marbles will be white if the first marble, is not returned to the bag?

5. A man applying for his driver's license estimates that his chances of passing the written test are $\frac{2}{3}$, and that his chances of passing the driving test are $\frac{1}{4}$. What is the probability that he passes both tests?

6. If two cards are selected at random from a standard deck of 52 cards, what is the probability that they will both be diamonds?

7. A bag contains 9 marbles, 3 of which are red, 3 of which are blue, and three of which are yellow. If three marbles are selected from the bag at random, what is the probability that they are all of different colors?

8. If two standard dice are rolled, what is the probability that the sum of the digits on the two dice is a prime number?

9. What is the probability that, if you roll a standard die three times, you will get three different numbers?

10. If you select three cards from a standard deck of 52 cards and they are all kings, what is the probability that the next card you select will also be a king?

Solutions

1. There are 12 marbles in the bag. Since 3 of them are red, the probability of picking a red marble is $\frac{3}{12} = \frac{1}{4}$. There are 5 marbles in the bag that are not blue, so the probability of picking a marble that is not blue is $\frac{5}{12}$.

2. There are 5 coins in the purse, and 3 of them are worth at least 10 cents. Thus, the probability that a coin chosen at random will be worth at least 10 cents is $\frac{3}{5}$.

3. There are $7 \times 7 = 49$ ways in which two marbles can be selected. Since there are four ways to select a white marble on the first draw, and 4 ways to select a marble on the second draw, there are a total of $4 \times 4 = 16$ ways to select a white marble on two draws. Thus, the probability of selecting white on both draws is $\frac{16}{49}$.

4. The two selections can be made in $7 \times 6 = 42$ ways. Two white marbles can be selected in $4 \times 3 = 12$ ways. Thus, the desired probability is $\frac{12}{42} = \frac{2}{7}$.

5. Since these two events are independent, the probability of passing both is $\left(\frac{2}{3}\right) \times \frac{1}{4} = \frac{1}{6}$.

6. The probability of drawing a diamond from the full deck is $\frac{13}{52} = \frac{1}{4}$. After the first diamond has been removed, there are 51 cards in the deck, 12 of which are diamonds. The probability of selecting a diamond from this reduced deck is $\frac{12}{51}$. The probability, thus, of selecting two diamonds is $\frac{1}{4} \times \frac{12}{51} = \frac{1}{17}$.

7. After the first marble is selected, the bag has 8 marbles left, 6 of which are of a different color than that of the first marble selected. Thus, the probability that the second marble is of a different color is $\frac{6}{8}$. If the second marble is different, there are then 7 marbles in the bag, three of which are of the color not yet selected. The odds of drawing a marble of the third color is $\frac{3}{7}$. Overall, then, the probability of drawing three different colors is $\frac{6}{8} \times \frac{3}{7} = \frac{18}{56} = \frac{9}{28}$.

8. If two dice are rolled, the possible outcomes for the sums of the two dice are 2 through 12. Of these, 2, 3, 5, 7, and 11 are prime. These is one way to get a sum of two, two ways to get a sum of three, four ways to get a sum of five, six ways to get a sum of seven, and two ways to get a sum of 11. Thus, the probability of rolling a prime sum is $\dfrac{15}{36} = \dfrac{5}{12}$.

9. After you roll the die the first time, there is a five out of six chance that the next roll will be different. Then, there is a 3 out of six chance that the third roll will be different. Thus, the probability of rolling three different numbers is $\dfrac{5}{6} \times \dfrac{4}{6} = \dfrac{5}{9}$.

10. After three cards are selected, there are 49 cards left in the deck, of which only one is a king. Thus, the probability of drawing a king on the fourth draw is $\dfrac{1}{49}$.

STATISTICS

Statistics is the study of collecting, organizing, and analyzing data. There are several important numerical measures for data that you should be familiar with prior to taking the MCAT.

MEASURES OF LOCATION

Measures of location describe the "centering" of a set of data; that is, they are used to represent the central value of the data. There are three common measures of central location. The one that is typically the most useful (and certainly the most common) is the *arithmetic mean*, which is computed by adding up all of the individual data values and dividing by the number of values.

Example 1

A researcher wishes to determine the average (arithmetic mean) amount of time a particular prescription drug remains in the bloodstream of users. She examines five people who have taken the drug and determines the amount of time the drug has remained in each of their bloodstreams. In hours, these times are: 24.3, 24.6, 23.8, 24.0, and 24.3. What is the mean number of hours that the drug remains in the bloodstream of these experimental participants?

To find the mean, we begin by adding up all of the measured values. In this case, $24.3 + 24.6 + 23.8 + 24.0 + 24.3 = 121$. We then divide by the number of participants (5), and obtain $\frac{121}{5} = 24.2$ as the mean.

Example 2

Suppose the participant with the 23.8-hour measurement had actually been measured incorrectly, and a measurement of 11.8 hours obtained instead. What would the mean number of hours have been?

In this case, the sum of the data values is only 109, and the mean becomes 21.8.

This example exhibits the fact that the mean can be greatly thrown off by one incorrect measurement. Similarly, one measurement that is unusually large or unusually small can have great impact upon the mean. A measure of location that is not impacted as much by extreme values is called the *median*. The median of a group of numbers is simply the value in the middle when the data values are arranged in numerical order. This numerical measure is sometimes used in the place of the mean when we wish to minimize the impact of extreme values.

Example 3

What is the median value of the data from example 1? What is the median value of the modified data from example 2?

Note that in both cases, the median is 24.3. Clearly, the median was not impacted by the one unusually small observation in example 2.

In the event that there are an even number of data values, we find the median by computing the number halfway between the two values in the middle (that is, we find the mean of the two middle values).

Another measure of location is called the *mode*. The mode is simply the most frequently occurring value in a series of data. In the examples above, the mode is 24.3. The mode is determined in an experiment when we wish to know which outcome has happened the most often.

MEASURES OF VARIABILITY

Measures of location provide only information about the "middle" value. They tell us nothing, however, about the spread, or the variability, of the data. Yet sometimes knowing the variability of a set of data is very important. To see why, examine the example below.

Consider an individual who has the choice of getting to work using either public transportation or her own car. Obviously, one consideration of interest would be the amount of travel time associated with these two different ways of getting to work. Suppose that over the period of several months, the individual uses both modes of transportation the same number of times and computes the mean for both. It turns out that both methods of transportation average 30 minutes. At first glance, it might appear, therefore, that both alternatives offer the same service. However, let's take a look at the actual data, in minutes:

Travel time using a car: 28, 28, 29, 29, 30, 30, 31, 31, 32, 32
Travel time using public transportation: 24, 25, 26, 27, 28, 29, 30, 33, 36, 42

Even though the average travel time is the same (30 minutes), do the alternatives possess the same degree of reliability? For most people, the variability exhibited for public transportation would be of concern. To protect against arriving late, one would have to allow for 42 minutes of travel time using public transportation, but with a car one would only have to allow a maximum of 32 minutes. Also of concern are the wide extremes that must be expected when using public transportation.

Thus, we can see that when we look at a set of data, we may wish to not only consider the average value of the data, but also the variability of the data.

The easiest way to measure the variability of the data is to determine the difference between the largest and the smallest values. This is called the *range*.

Example 4

Determine the range of the data from example 1 and example 2 above.

The range of the data from example 1 is $24.6 - 23.8 = 0.8$. The range of the data in example 2 is $24.6 - 11.8 = 12.8$. Note how the one faulty measurement in example 2 has totally changed the range. For this reason, it is usually desirable to use another, more reliable, measure of variability, called the *standard deviation*.

The standard deviation is an extremely important measure of variability; however, it is rather complicated to compute. On the MCAT, you will never be asked to compute a standard deviation; you simply must know how to interpret one when you see it.

To understand the meaning of the standard deviation, suppose that you have a set of data which has a mean of 120 and a standard deviation of 10. As long as this data is "normally distributed" (most reasonable sets of data are), we can conclude that approximately 68 percent of the data values lie within one standard deviation of the mean. This means, in this case, that 68 percent of the data values lie between $120 - 10 = 110$ and $120 + 10 = 130$. Similarly, about 95 percent of the data values will lie within 2 standard deviations from the mean; that is, in this case, between 100 and 140. Finally, about 99.7 percent (which is to say, virtually all) of the data will lie within three standard deviations from the mean. In this case, this means that almost all of the data values will fall between 90 and 150.

CORRELATION

Very often, researchers need to determine whether any relationship exists between two variables that they are measuring. For example, they may wish to determine whether an increase in one variable implies that a second variable is likely to have increased as well, or whether an increase in one variable implies that another variable is likely to have decreased.

The *correlation coefficient* is a single number that can be used to measure the degree of the relationship between two variables. Again, on the MCAT, you will not be expected to compute the value of a correlation coefficient; however, you must be able to interpret them.

The value of a correlation coefficient can range between −1 and +1. A correlation of +1 indicates a perfect positive correlation; the two variables under consideration increase and decrease together. A correlation of −1 is a perfect negative correlation; when one variable increases, the other decreases, and vice versa. If the correlation is 0, there is no relationship between the behavior of the variables.

Consider a correlation coefficient that is a positive fraction. Such a correlation represents a positive relationship; as one variable increases, the other will tend to increase. The closer that correlation coefficient is to 1, the stronger the relationship will be. Now, consider a correlation coefficient which is a negative fraction. Such a correlation represents a negative relationship; as one variable increases, the other will tend to decrease. The closer the correlation coefficient is to −1, the stronger this inverse relationship will be.

As an example, consider the relationship between height and weight in human beings. Since weight tends to increase as height increases, you might expect that the correlation coefficient for the variables of height and weight would be near +1. On the other hand, consider the relationship between maximum pulse rate and age. In general, maximum pulse rate decreases with age, so you might expect that the correlation coefficient for these two variables would be near −1.

One common mistake in the interpretation of correlation coefficients that you should avoid making is the assumption that a high coefficient indicates a cause and effect relationship. This is not always the case. An example that is frequently given in statistics classes is the fact there is a high correlation between gum chewing and crime in the United States. That is to say, as the number of gum chewers went up, there was a similar increase in the number of crimes committed. Obviously, this does not mean that there is any cause and effect between chewing gum and committing a crime. The fact is, simply, that as the population of the United States increased, both gum chewing and crime increased.

The following graphs are three *scatterplots* depicting the relationships between two variables. In the first, the plotted points almost lie on a straight line going up to the right. This is indicative of a strong positive correlation (a correlation near +1). The second scatterplot depicts a strong negative correlation, and the final scatterplot depicts two variables that are unrelated and probably have a correlation that is close to 0.

STATISTICS PROBLEMS

1. During the twelve months of 1998, an executive charged 4, 1, 5, 6, 3, 5, 1, 0, 5, 6, 4, and 3 business luncheons at the Wardlaw Club. What was the mean monthly number of luncheons charged by the executive?

2. Brian got grades of 92, 89, and 86 on his first three math tests. What grade must he get on his final test to have an overall average of 90?

3. In order to determine the expected mileage for a particular car, an automobile manufacturer conducts a factory test on five of these cars. The results, in miles per gallon, are 25.3, 23.6, 24.8, 23.0, and 24.3. What is the mean mileage? What is the median mileage?

4. In problem 3 above, suppose the car with the 23.6 miles per gallon had a faulty fuel injection system and obtained a mileage of 12.8 miles per gallon instead. What would have been the mean mileage? What would have been the median mileage?

5. In a recent survey, 15 people were asked for their favorite automobile color. The results were: red, blue, white, white, black, red, red, blue, gray, blue, black, green, white, black, red. What was the modal choice?

6. An elevator is designed to carry a maximum weight of 3,000 pounds. Is it overloaded if it carries 17 passengers with a mean weight of 140 pounds?

7. The annual incomes of 5 families living on Larchmont Rd. are $32,000, $35,000, $37,500, $39,000, and $320,000. What is the range of the annual incomes?

8. The average length of time required to complete a jury questionnaire is 40 minutes with a standard deviation of 5 minutes. What is the probability that it will take a prospective juror between 35 and 45 minutes to complete the questionnaire?

9. Using the information in problem 8, what is the probability that it will take a prospective juror between 30 and 50 minutes to complete the questionnaire?

10. The scores on a standardized admissions test are normally distributed with a mean of 500 and a standard deviation of 100. What is the probability that a randomly selected student will score between 400 and 600 on the test?

SOLUTIONS

1. The mean number of luncheons charged was
    $$\frac{(4+1+5+6+3+5+1+0+5+6+4+3)}{12} = \frac{43}{12} = 3.58.$$

2. Let G = the grade on the final test. Then,
    $$\frac{(92+89+86+G)}{4} = 90. \quad \text{Multiply by 4}$$
    $$(92+89+86+G) = 360$$
    $$267 + G = 360$$
    $$G = 93.$$
    Brian must get a 93 on the final test.

3. The mean mileage is $\dfrac{(25.3+23.6+24.8+23.0+24.3)}{5} = \dfrac{121}{5}$ = 24.2 miles per gallon. The median mileage is 24.3 miles per gallon.

4. The mean mileage would have been
    $$\frac{(25.3+12.8+24.8+23.0+24.3)}{5} = \frac{110.2}{5} = 22.04 \text{ miles per}$$
    gallon. The median mileage would have been 24.3 miles per gallon, which is the same as it was in problem 3.

5. The modal choice is red, which was chosen by 4 people.

6. Since the mean is the total of the data divided by the number of pieces of data, that is mean = $\dfrac{\text{total}}{\text{number}}$, we have (mean) (number) = total. Thus, the weight of the people on the elevator totals (17)(140) = 2380. It is therefore not overloaded.

7. The range is $320000 − $32000 = $288,000. It can be seen that the range is not a particularly good measure of variability, since 4 of the 5 values are within $7000 of each other.

8. About 68%

9. About 95%

10. About 68%

SCALARS AND VECTORS

There are two kinds of physical quantities that are dealt with extensively in science and mathematics. One quantity has magnitude only, and the other has magnitude and direction. A quantity that has magnitude only is called a *scalar* quantity. The length of an object expressed in a particular unit of length, mass, time, and density are all examples of scalars. A quantity that has both magnitude and direction is called a *vector*. Forces, velocities, and accelerations are examples of vectors.

It is customary to represent a vector by an arrow. The length of the arrow represents the magnitude of the vector, and the direction in which the arrow is pointing represents the direction. Thus, a force, for example, could be represented graphically by an arrow pointing in the direction in which the force acts and having a length (in some convenient unit of measure) equal to the magnitude of the force. The vector below, for example, represents a force of magnitude three units, acting in a direction 45° above the horizontal.

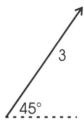

Two vectors are said to be equal if they are parallel, have the same magnitude (length), and point in the same direction. Thus, the two vectors **V** and **U** in the diagram below are equal. If a vector has the same magnitude as **U** but points in the opposite direction, it is denoted as **−U**.

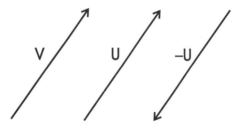

OPERATIONS ON VECTORS

To find the sum of two vectors **A** and **B**, we draw from the head of vector **A** a vector equal to **B**. The sum of **A** and **B** is then defined as the vector drawn from the foot of **A** to the head of **B**.

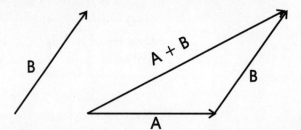

This technique of vector addition can enable us to compute the net effect of two different forces applied simultaneously to the same body.

Example

Two forces, one of magnitude $3\sqrt{3}$ pointing to the east and one of magnitude 3 pointing to the north, act on a body at the same time. Determine the direction in which the body will move and the magnitude of the force with which it will move.

Begin by drawing vectors **OA** and **OB** representing the two forces. Redraw vector **OB** on the tip of **OA**. Then, draw in the vector **OC**, which represents the sum of the two vectors. The body will move in the direction in which this vector is pointing, with a force equal to the magnitude of the vector.

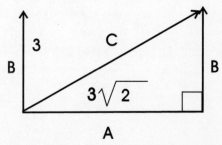

Since **OA** and **OB** operate at right angles to each other, we can use the Pythagorean theorem to determine the magnitude of the *resultant* vector.

$$(3\sqrt{2})^2 + 3^2 = C^2$$
$$27 + 9 = C^2$$
$$36 = C^2$$
$$6 = C$$

Further, by recalling the properties of the 30-60-90 triangle, we can see that the resultant force is 30° to the horizontal. Thus, the body will move with a force of 6 units at an angle of 30° to the horizontal.

To subtract the vector **U** from the vector **V**, we first draw the vectors from a common origin. Then, the vector extending from the tip of **U** to the tip of **V** and pointing to the tip of **V** is defined as the difference **V − U**.

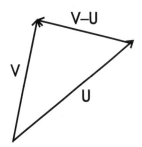

Part IV
Practice Tests

PRACTICE TEST 1

Each of the Questions 1–10 has five answer choices. For each of these questions, select the best of the answer choices given.

1. What is the greatest possible value of integer p if $5^p \leq \dfrac{100,000}{p}$?

    (A) 6
    (B) 7
    (C) 8
    (D) 9
    (E) 10

2. Which of the following is not an even integer if x is prime and y is composite?

    (A) $y - x$
    (B) xy
    (C) $\dfrac{x + y}{x}$
    (D) $\dfrac{2x + y}{y}$
    (E) It cannot be determined from the given information.

3. Red pens cost $1.50 each and blue pens cost $0.80 each. If a total of 18 red and blue pens are purchased for $20.00, how many of each type were bought?

    (A) 9 red, 9 blue
    (B) 12 blue, 6 red
    (C) 10 red, 8 blue
    (D) 8 red, 10 blue
    (E) 6 blue, 12 red

4. How many square tiles with a perimeter of 48 inches must be used to cover a floor that is 10 feet wide by 12 feet long?

    (A) 10
    (B) 12
    (C) 48
    (D) 120
    (E) 480

*Peterson's Math Review for the
GRE, GMAT and MCAT*

5. Which of the following is equivalent to $(2a - 5)(4a + 3)$?

    I. $2(a - 5)(2a + 3)$

    II. $-5(4a + 3) + 2a(4a + 3)$

    III. $8a^2 - 15$

(A) I only

(B) II only

(C) III only

(D) II and III only

(E) I, II, and III

6.

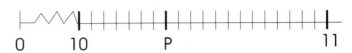

The ruler above is divided into equal increments. What is the length of an item with measure indicated by point P?

(A) 10.25 units

(B) 10.30 units

(C) 10.35 units

(D) 10.40 units

(E) 10.50 units

7. Jaime is 5 years older than Jodie was 10 years ago. In 10 years, Jodie will be twice as old as Jaime is now. How old will Jodie be 5 years from now?

(A) 10

(B) 15

(C) 20

(D) 25

(E) 30

8.

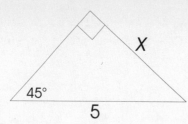

What is the area of the triangle shown above?

(A) $\dfrac{5\sqrt{2}}{2}$

(B) $\dfrac{25}{2}$

(C) $\dfrac{25}{4}$

(D) 25

(E) $\dfrac{25\sqrt{2}}{4}$

9. In a restaurant, there are 3 dinner specials, 2 dessert specials, and 2 drink specials. How many different meals can be ordered taking one dinner, one dessert, and one drink from the specials menu?

(A) 3
(B) 6
(C) 7
(D) 12
(E) 24

10. Which of the following is not a factor of $\dfrac{6}{288}$?

(A) $\dfrac{2}{3}$

(B) $\dfrac{2}{11}$

(C) $\dfrac{1}{4}$

(D) $\dfrac{3}{8}$

(E) $\dfrac{2}{9}$

Each of the Questions 11–20 consists of two quantities, one in Column A and one in Column B. You are to compare the two quantities and choose

(A) if the quantity in Column A is greater;
(B) if the quantity in Column B is greater;
(C) if the two quantities are equal;
(D) if the relationship cannot be determined from the information given.

Note: Since there are only four choices, NEVER MARK (E).

<u>Numbers</u>: All numbers used are real numbers.

<u>Figures</u>: Position of points, angles, regions, etc., can be assumed to be in the order shown; and angle measures can be assumed to be positive.

<u>Lines</u> shown as straight can be assumed to be straight.

<u>Figures</u> can be assumed to lie in a plane unless otherwise indicated.

<u>Figures</u> that accompany questions are intended to provide information that is useful in answering the questions. However, unless a note states that a figure is drawn to scale, you should solve these problems NOT by estimating sizes by sight or by measurement, but by using your knowledge of mathematics.

	Column A	*Column B*
11.	2.22×25	$\dfrac{222}{4}$

12.
$$z < -1$$

	Column A	*Column B*
	-4	$3z - 1$

13. For any non-negative integer p, let $p^{**} = \dfrac{p}{3} - 3$.

	Column A	*Column B*
	$12^{**} + 6^{**}$	$(12 + 6)^{**}$

Column A	*Column B*

14.

4 is 40 percent of *m*

10*n* is 40 percent of 400

m	*n*

15. The average of
2*y* + 6
3*y* − 4, and 5 − 5*y* | The arithmetic mean of
12, 7, 6, −5, −9, and 3

16.

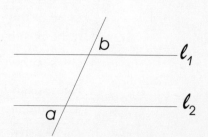

lines l_1 and l_2 are parallel

−(*b* − *a*)	*b* − *a*

17.

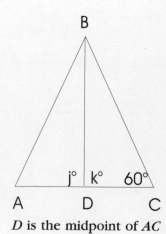

D is the midpoint of *AC*

j	*k*

	Column A	*Column B*

18.

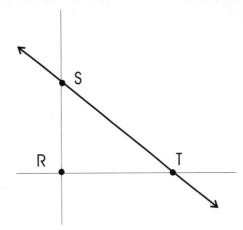

The line $y = -\dfrac{2}{3}x + 4$ is graphed as
ST on the coordinate axis.

	RT	SR

19. $\qquad\qquad\qquad\qquad c = d + 2$

	$c^2 - d^2$	$4d$

20.

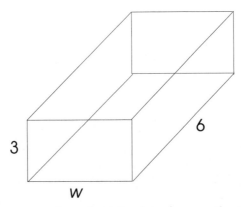

A rectangular box has a volume of 72 cubic feet.

Value of the box's volume if the width is doubled.	Value of double the surface area of the box.

Each of the data questions 21–30 below consists of a question and two statements, labeled (1) and (2), in which certain data are given. Decide whether the data given in the statements are sufficient for answering the question. Using the data provided in the statements and knowledge of mathematics and everyday facts (such as the number of days in October or the meaning of counterclockwise), mark the following:

(A) if statement (1) ALONE is sufficient, but statement (2) alone is not sufficient to answer the question asked;

(B) if statement (2) ALONE is sufficient, but statement (1) alone is not sufficient to answer the question asked;

(C) if BOTH statement (1) and (2) TOGETHER are sufficient to answer the question, but NEITHER statement ALONE is sufficient;

(D) if EACH statement ALONE is sufficient to answer the question asked;

(E) if statements (1) and (2) TOGETHER are NOT sufficient to answer the question asked, and additional data specific to the problem are needed.

21. Jonathan deposited money into a savings account that compounds interest quarterly. How much interest will be made on Jonathan's investment?

   (1) A total of $500.00 was invested.
   (2) The amount of money is in the savings account for one year.

22. Solve for w.

   (1) $w + 6y = 24$
   (2) $w^2 = 45 - 4w$

23. What is the value of km?

   (1) $k - m = k$
   (2) k is a positive integer.

24. If, on a particular night, a movie had an average of 100 attendees, how many viewers went to the movie that night?

   (1) There were exactly 4 viewings of the movie that night.
   (2) The average number of attendees represented 25 percent of the total number of attendees.

25. A fruit punch is created by combining seltzer water with grape juice and cranberry juice. What is the proportion of ingredients contained in the punch?

    (1) The mixture contains 50 percent seltzer water and 50 percent fruit juice.
    (2) Equal amounts of fruit juice are used.

26. Are more than 40 percent of the 250 houses located on Main Street two-level homes?

    (1) 45 percent of the homes contain one level.
    (2) ninety-six houses on Main Street have two levels.

27. A company offers two types of retirement packages, *A* and *B*, for its employees. If each employee chooses only one package, how many choose package *B*?

    (1) Of the 300 employees, 12 perent choose package *A*.

    (2) Package *A* was chosen by 36 employees.

28.

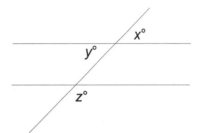

    What is the measurement of $\angle z$?

    (1) $\angle y = 40°$
    (2) $\angle z$ is $3\frac{1}{2}$ times greater than $\angle x$.

29. What is the average number of children at Wee Ones Elementary School who are in the first and second grade classrooms?

    (1) The average number of children in the first grade is 20, and the average number of children in the second grade is 28.
    (2) There are 3 first grade classes and 5 second grade classes.

30.

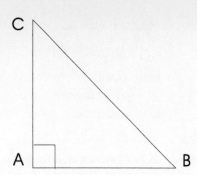

The perimeter of right triangle *ABC* shown above is
$9 + 9\sqrt{3}$.

What is the area of triangle *ABC*?

(1) $AB \neq AC$

(2) $\angle ABC = 60°$

Questions 31–35 are based on the following graph.

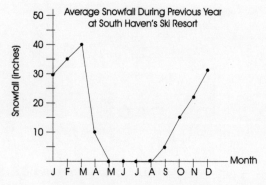

31. Between which two months was there the greatest change in the amount of snowfall?

(A)   February and March
(B)   March and April
(C)   April and May
(D)   September and October
(E)   November and December

32. How many months averaged at least twice the snowfall of October?

(A)   1
(B)   2
(C)   3
(D)   4
(E)   5

33. What month had $\frac{2}{3}$ less snowfall than December?

(A) March
(B) April
(C) September
(D) October
(E) November

34. What percentage drop in snowfall occurred between March and April?

(A) 300%
(B) 30%
(C) 400%
(D) 25%
(E) 75%

35. What was the average amount of snowfall from January through May?

(A) 24 inches
(B) 30 inches
(C) 23 inches
(D) $28\frac{3}{4}$ inches
(E) 15 inches

Questions 36–40 are based on the following pie chart.

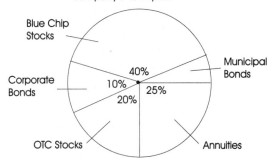

Distribution (%) of earnings into a company's 401K plan

Blue Chip Stocks
Municipal Bonds
Corporate Bonds
OTC Stocks
Annuities
40%
10%
25%
20%

36. What percentage of earnings is invested in bonds?

(A) 5%
(B) 10%
(C) 15%
(D) 25%
(E) 85%

37. What percentage of earning is not invested in stocks?

(A) 20%
(B) 40%
(C) 60%
(D) 80%
(E) 85%

38. If $3,000 was invested last month, what amount went into annuities?

(A) $2,250
(B) $1,500
(C) $1,200
(D) $750
(E) $600

39. How much more money was invested in annuities than in corporate bonds if a total of $10,000 was invested?

(A) $1,500
(B) $2,500
(C) $1,000
(D) $8,500
(E) $3,500

40. Which sector had $800 invested in it from $4,000 earnings?

(A) OTC Stocks
(B) Corporate Bonds
(C) Blue Chip Stocks
(D) Municipal Bonds
(E) Annuities

PRACTICE TEST 2

Each of the Questions 1–10 has five answer choices. For each of these questions, select the best of the answer choices given.

1. $\ln(8) + 3\ln(2) + \ln(125)$ can be simplified to

   (A) $3\ln(135)$
   (B) $\ln(139)$
   (C) $3\ln(20)$
   (D) $\ln(141)$
   (E) none of the above

2. If one leg of a right triangle has length 12, and the other leg has length 5, then the length of the hypotenuse is

   (A) 5
   (B) 12
   (C) 17
   (D) 13
   (E) $\sqrt{17}$

3. What are the roots of the function $f(x) = x^2 + 2x - 35$?

   (A) 0 and 5
   (B) 0 and -7
   (C) 5 and -7
   (D) 2 and -35
   (E) no roots exist

4. The fraction $\dfrac{4x^3 + 16x^2}{2x^3 + 6x^2 - 8x}$ can be simplified to

   (A) $\dfrac{2}{x - 1}$

   (B) $\dfrac{x}{x - 1}$

   (C) $\dfrac{2x}{x - 1}$

   (D) $2x(x - 1)$
   (E) none of the above

5. If $n > 4$, which of the following is equivalent to
$$\frac{n - 4\sqrt{n} + 4}{\sqrt{n} - 2}?$$

   (A) $\sqrt{n}$
   (B) $n + \sqrt{n}$
   (C) $\sqrt{n} - 2$
   (D) $\sqrt{n} + 2$
   (E) none of the above

6. If we eliminate the parameter t from the two equations: $x = \sin(t)$ and $y = \cos(t)$ and graph the resulting equation on the $x - y$ plane, we would obtain

   (A) a line through the origin
   (B) the unit circle
   (C) an ellipse about the origin
   (D) a parabola with the vertex at the origin
   (E) none of the above

7. What is the total angle sum of a pentagon?

   (A) 540°
   (B) 360°
   (C) 720°
   (D) 450°
   (E) none of the above

8. The graph of $f(x) = \dfrac{8}{x^2 - 4}$ has vertical asymptotes at

   (A) $x = 4$
   (B) $x = 16$
   (C) $x = 2$ and $x = -2$
   (D) $x = 16$ and $x = -16$
   (E) there are no vertical asymptotes

9. What is the midpoint of the line segment that has endpoints at $(-6, 8)$ and $(3, -4)$?

   (A) $(-4.5, 6)$
   (B) $(-1.5, 2)$
   (C) $(-2, 2)$
   (D) $(-5, 5.5)$
   (E) none of the above

10. What is an equation of the line that passes through the points $(3, -1)$ and $(9, -5)$?

(A) $y = -2x + 1$

(B) $y = \dfrac{2}{3}x + 1$

(C) $y = -\dfrac{1}{3}x + 1$

(D) $y = 3x - 1$

(E) none of the above

Each of the Questions 11–20 consists of two quantities, one in Column A and one in Column B. You are to compare the two quantities and choose

(A) if the quantity in Column A is greater;
(B) if the quantity in Column B is greater;
(C) if the two quantities are equal;
(D) if the relationship cannot be determined from the information given.

Note: Since there are only four choices, NEVER MARK (E).

<u>Numbers</u>: All numbers used are real numbers.

<u>Figures</u>: Position of points, angles, regions, etc., can be assumed to be in the order shown; and angle measures can be assumed to be positive.

<u>Lines</u> shown as straight can be assumed to be straight.

<u>Figures</u> can be assumed to lie in a plane unless otherwise indicated.

<u>Figures</u> that accompany questions are intended to provide information useful in answering the questions. However, unless a note states that a figure is drawn to scale, you should solve these problems NOT by estimating sizes by sight or by measurement, but by using your knowledge of mathematics.

	<u>Column A</u>	<u>Column B</u>
11.	The perimeter of a triangle with area 13	The circumference of a circle with an area of 13π
12.	$(20)(40)(50)(7)$	$(5)(200)(70)(4)$
13.	$\dfrac{0.09}{0.0003}$	30
14.	$(41)^2 - (21)^2$	400

Column A	**Column B**

15. There are x books in a bookstore. After $\frac{1}{4}$ of them was purchased by customers the bookstore received a shipment of 15 more books, bringing the total number of books on hand to 105.

x 105

16. Two boards with dimensions 4 feet by 8 feet overlap to form the figure below. All angles shown are right angles.

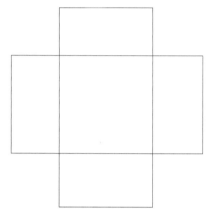

32   The perimeter of the figure in feet

17. Assume that $0 < x < 1$

x^{12} $12x$

18. 25 percent of 59   24 percent of 60

19. Fred is 5 years older than Lisa, but 2 inches shorter.

Fred's weight in pounds   Lisa's weight in pounds

20. $\triangle ABC$ is constructed such that the segment AB has length x, and the segment AC has length y.

The length of segment BC $\sqrt{x^2 + y^2}$

Each of the data questions 21–30 below consists of a question and two statements, labeled (1) and (2), in which certain data are given. Decide whether the data given in the statements are sufficient for answering the question. Using the data provided in the statements and knowledge of mathematics and everyday facts (such as the number of days in October or the meaning of counterclockwise), choose:

(A) if statement (1) ALONE is sufficient, but statement (2) alone is not sufficient to answer the question asked;

(B) if statement (2) ALONE is sufficient, but statement (1) alone is not sufficient to answer the question asked;

(C) if BOTH statement (1) and (2) TOGETHER are sufficient to answer the question, but NEITHER statement ALONE is sufficient;

(D) if EACH statement ALONE is sufficient to answer the question asked;

(E) if statements (1) and (2) TOGETHER are NOT sufficient to answer the question asked, and additional data specific to the problem are needed.

21. What is the selling price of a winter coat after its original price is reduced by 25%?

(1) The original price of the coat was $100.
(2) The price after the reduction is $25 less than the original price.

22. What is the value of x?

(1) $10x = x^2 + 21$
(2) $x^2 = 9$

23. A piece of paper is in the shape of a right triangle and is cut along a line that is parallel to the hypotenuse, leaving a smaller triangle. If the area of the original triangle was 34 square inches before the cut, what is the area of the new triangle?

(1) There was a 35% reduction in the length of the hypotenuse of the triangle.
(2) The cut was made 3.5 inches down from the original hypotenuse.

24. Is quadrilateral *ABCD* a rectangle?

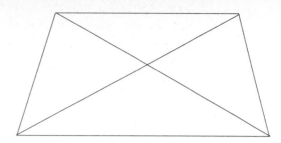

    (1) The area of $\triangle ABC$ is one-half the area of *ABCD*.

    (2) The area of $\triangle$ is one-half the area of *ABCD*.

25. If the ratio of integers *x,y*, and *z* is 1:3:7, what is the value of $2x + 3y - z$?

    (1) $x + y = 12$

    (2) $y - 3z + -54$

26. If *n* is an integer, what is the value of *n*?

    (1) $13 < n < 21$

    (2) $39 < 3n < 45$

27. How many students are taking chemistry?

    (1) There are three times as many students taking chemistry than are taking math.

    (2) There are forty students taking both chemistry and math.

28. Mr. Watson deposits *x* dollars in a savings certificate that earns an APR of *r*%, compounded continuously. How much did he initially deposit?

    (1) During the term of the certificate he earned $250.

    (2) $r = 5.045\%$

29. Is the sum of 3 consecutive positive integers odd?

    (1) The middle integer is odd.

    (2) The first integer is even.

30. A bag holds 13 red checker pieces and 27 black checker pieces. If Jerry picks pieces from the bag at random, does he pick more black pieces than red pieces?

    (1) Jerry picks out 26 pieces.

    (2) Jerry picks 5 pieces and the first piece that he picks is red.

Questions 31–34 refer to Table 1, which gives the average daily weight gain/loss of a pig in kilograms per day as a function of its weight and the air temperature.

Mean Live Weight(kg)	Air Temperature (in degrees Celsius)						
	4.4	10	15.6	21.1	26.7	32.2	37.8
45	0.6	0.62	0.72	0.91	0.89	0.64	0.18
68	0.58	0.67	0.79	0.98	0.83	0.52	-0.09
91	0.55	0.71	0.87	1.01	0.76	0.4	-0.35
113	0.5	0.76	0.94	0.97	0.68	0.28	-0.62
136	0.46	0.8	1.02	0.93	0.62	0.16	-0.88
156	0.44	0.85	1.09	0.9	0.55	0.05	−1.15

31. What is the average daily weight gain/loss for a 91kg pig when the air temperature is 15.6° C?

    (A) 21.1
    (B) 45
    (C) 0.87
    (D) 0.71
    (E) 1.01

32. If the temperature is held constant at 21.1° C, at what weight is a pig gaining weight the fastest?

    (A) 1.01
    (B) 91
    (C) 136
    (D) 156
    (E) 0.85

33. If a pig weighs 136 kg, approximately how much more weight is it gaining per day when kept at 21.1° C compared to being kept at 4.4° C (expressed as a percent)?

    (A) 100%
    (B) 50%
    (C) 200%
    (D) 150%
    (E) 250%

34. If we have a pig that weighs 156 kg and we keep this pig at 37.8° C for one day, how much does the pig weigh at the end of the day?

    (A) 156
    (B) 158.15
    (C) 154.85
    (D) 1.15
    (E) 157.15

Questions 35–37 refer to the following chart that shows the frequency of arrests for different types of traffic violations in two consecutive years.

Arrest for moving violations

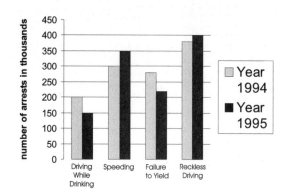

35. How many arrests were made in 1995 for failure to yield?

(A) 220
(B) 220,000
(C) 280,000
(D) 28,000
(E) 2,200

36. In what categories did arrests decrease?

(A) Driving while drinking and speeding
(B) Speeding and failure to yield
(C) Driving while drinking and failure to yield
(D) Speeding and reckless driving
(E) In no categories did arrests decrease

37. In 1994, which violation occurred least often?

(A) Driving while drinking
(B) Speeding
(C) Failure to yield
(D) Reckless driving
(E) Illegal passing

Questions 38–40 refer to the chart below. The chart shows the percentage of airline passengers who choose a particular flight based mainly on one key factor. Various factors are listed along with the percentage of passengers who find a particular factor most important.

How Travelers Choose Airline Flights

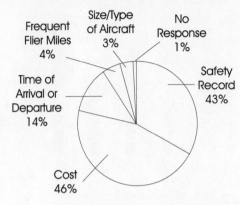

38. What percentage of passengers is most concerned with either Cost or Safety Record?

(A) 78%
(B) 46%
(C) 32%
(D) 22%
(E) 14%

39. What percentage of passengers is not concerned with the Time of Arrival or Departure?

(A) 14%
(B) 54%
(C) 32%
(D) 78%
(E) 86%

40. What percentage of passengers is not concerned with Frequent Flier Miles, Safety Record, or Size/Type of Aircraft?

(A) 39%
(B) 71%
(C) 32%
(D) 61%
(E) 46%

PRACTICE TEST 3

Each of the Questions 1–10 has five answer choices. For each of these questions, select the best of the answer choices given.

1. Simplify $\dfrac{\frac{3}{2}}{\frac{5}{2}}$

   (A) $\dfrac{15}{4}$

   (B) $\dfrac{4}{15}$

   (C) $\dfrac{3}{5}$

   (D) $\dfrac{5}{3}$

   (E) $\dfrac{8}{4}$

2. If $(3x - 2)^2 = 0$, then $x =$

   (A) $\dfrac{2}{3}$

   (B) $\dfrac{3}{2}$

   (C) $\dfrac{4}{9}$

   (D) $\dfrac{-4}{9}$

   (E) 0

3. Which of the following is equivalent to $(6 \times 10^{-3}) + (9 \times 10^{-4})$?

   (A) 96,000
   (B) 0.0000054
   (C) 0.015
   (D) 0.0069
   (E) 0.0015

4. A person can jog 3 miles in 20 minutes. At this rate, about how long will it take to jog 8 miles?

    (A) 75 minutes
    (B) 60 minutes
    (C) 160 minutes
    (D) 53 minutes
    (E) 48 minutes

5.

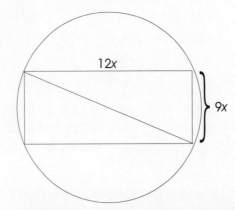

In the figure above, if the area of the inscribed rectangular region is 432 square units, what is the circumference of the circle?

    (A) 240π
    (B) 60π
    (C) 15π
    (D) 108π
    (E) 30π

6. An integer x is a multiple of both 4 and 5. Which of the following must be true?

    I. x is an even integer.
    II. x is a multiple of 10.
    III. x is equal to 20.

    (A) I only.
    (B) III only.
    (C) I and II only.
    (D) II only.
    (E) I, II, and III.

7. What is the remainder when 8^3 is divided by 6?

    (A) 5
    (B) 4
    (C) 3
    (D) 2
    (E) 0

Peterson's Math Review for the GRE, GMAT and MCAT

8. Simplify: $\sqrt{\dfrac{q^2}{4} - \dfrac{q^2}{6}}$

(A) $\dfrac{\sqrt{3}q}{6}$

(B) $\dfrac{\sqrt{3}q}{2}$

(C) $\dfrac{\sqrt{2}q}{3}$

(D) $\dfrac{\sqrt{2}q}{2}$

(E) Cannot be simplified.

9. A shelf holds nine gardening books, six cooking books, nine mysteries, and twelve fiction titles. If a book is chosen at random, what is the probability that the book chosen will be a mystery title?

(A) $\dfrac{1}{9}$

(B) $\dfrac{1}{4}$

(C) $\dfrac{1}{3}$

(D) $\dfrac{1}{2}$

(E) $\dfrac{2}{9}$

10. Simplify: $\dfrac{y + \dfrac{1}{x}}{\dfrac{y}{x}}$

(A) $\dfrac{x + y}{xy}$

(B) $\dfrac{y + 1}{x}$

(C) $\dfrac{xy + 1}{xy}$

(D) $\dfrac{xy^2 + y}{x^2}$

(E) $\dfrac{xy + 1}{y}$

Each of the Questions 11–20 consists of two quantities, one in Column A and one in Column B. You are to compare the two quantities and choose

- (A) if the quantity in Column A is greater;
- (B) if the quantity in Column B is greater;
- (C) if the two quantities are equal;
- (D) if the relationship cannot be determined from the information given.

Note: Since there are only four choices, NEVER MARK (E).

<u>Numbers</u>: All numbers used are real numbers.

<u>Figures</u>: Position of points, angles, regions, etc., can be assumed to be in the order shown; and angle measures can be assumed to be positive.

<u>Lines</u> shown as straight can be assumed to be straight.

<u>Figures</u> can be assumed to lie in a plane unless otherwise indicated.

<u>Figures</u> that accompany questions are intended to provide information useful in answering the questions. However, unless a note states that a figure is drawn to scale, you should solve these problems NOT by estimating sizes by sight or by measurement, but by using your knowledge of mathematics.

	Column A	**Column B**
11.	$5 + 4 \times (-2) \div 2$	$(5 + 4) \times (-2 \div 2)$

12.

x is a negative integer

	Column A	**Column B**
	$\dfrac{3}{x}$	$3x$

	Column A	**Column B**
13.	The number of minutes in z days.	The number of hours in $60z$ days.

	Column A	**Column B**

14.

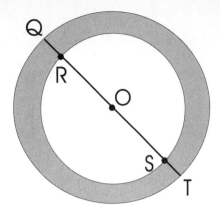

The diameter (d) of the smaller circle is $\frac{2}{3}$ the diameter of the larger circle.

$\dfrac{13\pi d^2}{36}$ Area of shaded region.

15.

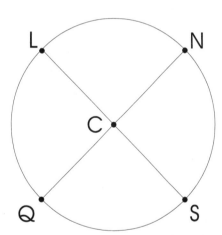

L, N, Q, and *S* are points on the circle shown.
C is the point where *LS* and *QN* intersect.

CN   *CQ*

16.

$$10x = \frac{99}{x} + x$$

x   11

	<u>Column A</u>	<u>Column B</u>

17.

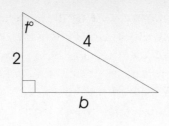

t $2s$

---

18. p is a positive number and $pq = 0$

q $p(q - p)$

19.
$$m^{\bullet} = m^2 - \frac{m}{2}$$

$2^{\bullet} + (3 + 2^{\bullet})^{\bullet}$ $2^{\bullet} + 6^{\bullet}$

---

20. $\dfrac{1}{4}$ of half of $\left(\dfrac{1}{6}\right)^2$ $\left[\dfrac{1}{2}\left(\dfrac{1}{6}\right)\right]^2$

---

*Peterson's Math Review for the
GRE, GMAT and MCAT*

Each of the data questions 21–30 below consists of a question and two statements, labeled (1) and (2), in which certain data are given. Decide whether the data given in the statements are sufficient for answering the question. Using the data provided in the statements and knowledge of mathematics and everyday facts (such as the number of days in October or the meaning of counterclockwise), mark the following:

(A) if statement (1) ALONE is sufficient, but statement (2) alone is not sufficient to answer the question asked;

(B) if statement (2) ALONE is sufficient, but statement (1) alone is not sufficient to answer the question asked;

(C) if BOTH statement (1) and (2) TOGETHER are sufficient to answer the question, but NEITHER statement ALONE is sufficient;

(D) if EACH statement ALONE is sufficient to answer the question asked;

(E) if statements (1) and (2) TOGETHER are NOT sufficient to answer the question asked, and additional data specific to the problem are needed.

21. Lucy must go to the supermarket or the pharmacy to pick up some cold medicine. Which of these is closer to Lucy's home?

   (1) Walking, it takes Lucy an average of 15 minutes to get to the supermarket from her home.

   (2) Walking, it takes Lucy an average of 25 minutes to get from the supermarket to the pharmacy.

22. Is $0 < r < 1$?

   (1) $0 < \sqrt{r} < 1$

   (2) $r^2 = \dfrac{1}{3}$

23.

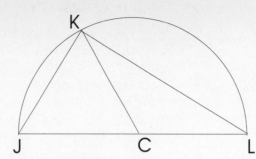

Note: Figure not drawn to scale.

C is the center of semicircle JKL. Points J, K, and L lie on the semicircle. What is the length of KL?

(1) Triangle JKC is equiangular.
(2) The radius of semicircle JKL is 5.

24. What is the area of circular region C?

(1) The circumference of the circle is 10.

(2) The diameter of the circle is $\dfrac{10}{\pi}$.

25. What is the maximum capacity of a measuring cup that contains only water and is filled to half its capacity?

(1) If four ounces of water were added, the measuring cup would be $\dfrac{3}{4}$ full.

(2) If six ounces of water were removed from the measuring cup, it would be $\dfrac{1}{8}$ full.

26. If x and y are negative integers, is $2y - x$ odd?

(1) x is odd.
(2) y is odd.

27. Is the surface area of a rectangular block equal to its volume?

(1) The length of the block equals the product of the height and width of the block.
(2) The volume of the block is 64 ft^3.

28. If S is a set of integers and 5 is in S, is every positive multiple of 5 in S?

(1) For any integer in S, the sum of 5 and that integer is also in S.
(2) For any integer in S, that integer minus 5 is also in S.

29. What is the value of $m + n$ if $m \leq n$?

    (1) $(m + n)(m - n) = 0$

    (2) $m = 3$

30.

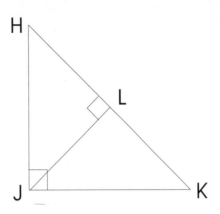

In the figure above, what is the length of *HK* times the length of *JL* ?

    (1) The length of *HK* is 12.

    (2) The length of *HJ* times the length of *JK* is equal to 48.

Questions 31–34 are based on the following bar graph.

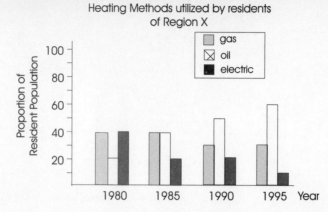

Heating Methods utilized by residents of Region X

31. What year or years had the greatest increase in oil usage by residents from one set of years to the next?

    (A) 1980
    (B) 1985
    (C) 1990
    (D) 1995
    (E) 1990 and 1995

32. If 50,000 residents make up *Region X*, how many more residents chose oil heat over electric heat in 1995?

    (A) 5,000
    (B) 15,000
    (C) 25,000
    (D) 30,000
    (E) 55,000

33. What percentage of gas consumers from 1985 switched to alternative heating methods in 1990?

    (A) 10%
    (B) 25%
    (C) 50%
    (D) 75%
    (E) 100%

34. What is the mean percent of residents who use oil as their main heating source?

(A) $42\frac{1}{2}\%$

(B) 35%

(C) $22\frac{1}{2}\%$

(D) 50%

(E) $37\frac{1}{2}\%$

Questions 35–37 are based on the following chart.

Favorite Ice-Cream Flavors

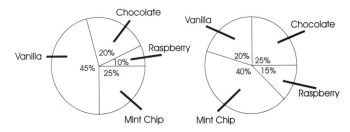

35. If there are 160 girls, how many prefer chocolate ice cream over any other flavor?

(A) 25
(B) 40
(C) 45
(D) 72
(E) 140

36. If there are twice as many girls as there are boys, which flavor ice cream is preferred by most?

(A) Vanilla
(B) Mint Chip
(C) Raspberry
(D) Chocolate
(E) Not enough information is given.

37. Twelve boys like mint chip more than any of the other flavors. How many boys are there in total?

(A) 37
(B) 100
(C) 60
(D) 30
(E) 48

Questions 38–40 are based on the following table.

One Day Summary of Stock Activity			
Stock Symbol	Closing Price ($)	Volume (1,000's)	Change in Price ($)
Arx	53.25	869.45	2¾
Blm	41.4	4110.392	2¹¹⁄₁₆
Csf	27.84	36.411	−1⅛
Mbd	96.33	599.994	−3½
Nys	11.11	546.362	¼
Qug	22.28	8.13	1⁷⁄₁₆
Tvk	81.15	3146.633	⅜

38. Which stock had the greatest price increase for the day?

(A) Arx
(B) Blm
(C) Mbd
(D) Qug
(E) Tvk

39. What was the opening price for Mbd?

(A) $99.70
(B) $96.33
(C) $27.52
(D) $99.83
(E) $92.83

40. How many stocks closed at a higher price than the stock with the greatest amount of activity for the day?

(A) 1
(B) 2
(C) 3
(D) 4
(E) 5

EXPLANATORY ANSWERS FOR PRACTICE TEST 1

1. **The correct answer is (A).** The easiest way to solve this problem is to plug in the possible choices into the equation. The correct choice is the largest integer that produces a true statement. Testing the smallest integer first, 6, results in $5^6 \leq \dfrac{100,000}{6}$, which is equivalent to $15,625 \leq 16,666\dfrac{2}{3}$. This statement is true, so test the next smallest integer, 7. So $5^7 \leq \dfrac{100,000}{7}$ is equivalent to $78,125 \leq 14,285\dfrac{5}{7}$. This statement is false, so the smallest integer that produces a true statement is 6, choice (A).

2. **The correct answer is (E).** A prime number is any number that is divisible only by the number 1 and itself. Examples of prime numbers are: 1, 2, 3, 5, 7, 11, 13, 17, and so on. A composite number is divisible by more numbers than just 1 and itself. Examples of composite numbers are: 4, 6, 8, 9, 10, 12, 14, 15, and so on. Assign an arbitrary prime and composite number for x and y respectively, and test the possible choices to see what produces an even integer. Let $x = 3$ and $y = 4$. For choice (A), $4 - 3 = 1$, which is not an even integer. However, if you let $x = 2$ (still a prime number) and $y = 4$, then $4 - 2 = 2$, which is an even integer. Because you do not know whether the prime number is odd or even (2 being the only even prime number), it is not possible to determine which terms will produce an even integer.

3. **The correct answer is (D).** Let r represent the number of red pens and let b represent the number of blue pens. The cost of the red pens is $1.5r$ and the cost of the blue pens is $0.8b$. The total number of pens purchased is $r + b = 18$, so $18 - b = r$. The total amount spent for the pens is $1.5r + 0.8b = 20$. Substitute $18 - b$ for r in the second equation and solve for b. We see that $1.5(18 - b) + 0.8b = 20$. Therefore $27 - 0.7b = 20$. So $b = 10$ and $r = 8$.

4. **The correct answer is (D).** The perimeter of a square is equivalent to $4s$, or 4 times the length of its side. If the perimeter of a square is 48 inches, then the length of its side is 12 inches, or 1 foot. The area of a square is s^2, or the length of its side squared. A square that is 1 foot by 1 foot has an area of $1\ \text{ft}^2$. A floor that is 10 ft $\times$ 12 ft has a total area of $120\ \text{ft}^2$. Therefore, 120 square tiles with an area of $1\ \text{ft}^2$ must be used to cover the floor. *Note the different units of measure in this problem. Be sure to convert to similar units before performing calculations.*

5. **The correct answer is (B).** $(2a - 5)(4a + 3) = 8a^2 + 6a - 20a - 15 = 8a^2 - 14a - 15.$

   In I: $2(a - 5)(2a + 3) = (2a - 10)(2a + 3)$
   $= 4a^2 + 6a - 20a - 30$
   $= 4a^2 - 14a - 30.$

   In II: $-5(4a + 3) + 2a(4a + 3) = -20a - 15 + 8a^2 + 6a$
   $= 8a^2 - 14a - 15.$

   In III: $8a^2 - 15$

   Only II is equivalent to the original expression.

6. **The correct answer is (C).** The given picture represents a portion of a ruler between the numbers 10 and 11. There are a total of 20 unit marks between these two values, so each unit mark represents $\frac{1}{20}$, or 0.05 of one full unit. Point P falls on the 7th unit marking between 10 and 11. That mark is $\frac{7}{20}$, or 0.35 units greater than 10. Therefore P would measure 10.35.

7. **The correct answer is (D).** Translate the statements in the word problem into math sentences (equations). Let m represent Jaime's age now and d represent Jodie's age now. Since Jaime is 5 years older than Jodie was 10 years ago, $m = (d - 10) + 5 = d - 5$. In 10 years, Jodie will be twice Jaime's current age, so $(d + 10) = 2m$. We know that $m = d - 5$, so substituting that value into the second equation produces $d + 10 = 2(d - 5)$. $d + 10 = 2d - 10$, so $d = 20$. The question asks how old Jodie (d) will be 5 years from now, $20 + 5 = 25$.

8. **The correct answer is (C).** The triangle is a 45°, 45°, 90° right triangle. The sides are in the ratio of x, x, $x\sqrt{2}$, respectively. In the given triangle, the hypotenuse is $x\sqrt{2} = 5$. Solving for x will tell the length of each leg: $x = \frac{5\sqrt{2}}{2}$. The area of the triangle is $\frac{1}{2}x \cdot x = \frac{1}{2} \cdot \frac{5\sqrt{2}}{2} \cdot \frac{5\sqrt{2}}{2} = \frac{25}{4}$.

9. **The correct answer is (D).** This is a combination problem involving three items. To find the total number of possible outcomes, multiply the number of possibilities from each set of items together. With 3 dinner choices, 2 dessert choices, and 2 drink choices, there are $3 \times 2 \times 2 = 12$ possible outcomes.

10. **The correct answer is (B).** The find the factors of $\frac{6}{288}$, find the factors of the numerator and denominator and put them in fraction form: $\frac{6}{288} = \frac{2 \times 3}{2 \times 2 \times 2 \times 2 \times 2 \times 3 \times 3}$. Looking at the possible answer choices, only (B) cannot be formed using a combination of these factors since 11 is not a factor of 288.

11. **The correct answer is (C).** Both columns can be solved by applying simple arithmetic. Start with *Column A*: $2.22 \times 25 = 55.5$. Next, solve *Column B*: $\frac{222}{4} = 55.5$. Since *Column A* and *Column B* are both equal to 55.5.

12. **The correct answer is (A).** This problem requires substitution of a variable, z, into *Column B*. It is given that *Column A* is equal to -4, so no computation is needed there. It is also given that $z < -1$. By replacing z in *Column B* with -1, that result will be the number that *Column B* cannot exceed. Note that the result will not be equivalent to the value *Column B* takes on because z is not equal to -1. So, *Column B* takes on all values less than $3(-1) - 1 = -3 - 1 = -4$. Since *Column B* is less than but not equal to -4, *Column A* is greater.

13. **The correct answer is (B).** Here a function is defined that requires substitution. The function applies to any non-negative integer; that is, any positive integer or 0 (zero is neither positive nor negative). The function, p^{**} is defined as $\dfrac{p}{3} - 3$. In *Column A*, this function must be applied twice—once for the integer 12 and another time for the integer 6. These two values are then added together to get the value for *Column A*. $12^{**} = \dfrac{12}{3} - 3 = 4 - 3 = 1$ and $6^{**} = \dfrac{6}{3} - 3 = 2 - 3$ $= 2 - 3 = -1$. Combining these results is $1 + (-1) = 0$ for *Column A*. In *Column B*, the function is applied only once; 12 and 6 are summed first, and that result is the integer being used in the function's definition. So, $(12 + 6)^{**} = 18^{**} = \dfrac{18}{3} - 3 = 6 - 3 = 3$. The value in *Column B*, 3, is greater than the value in *Column A*, 0.

14. **The correct answer is (B).** This comparison provides you with two statements and two unknown values, both of which are being compared in each of the columns. The best way to solve this is to translate the given statements into mathematical equations and then solve for the unknown values. Keep in mind that the word "is" means equals, and the word "of" refers to multiplication. The first math equation will be $4 = 40\% \cdot m = 0.40m$. The second math equation will be $10n = 40\%$. $400 = 0.40 \cdot 400$. Next solve for m and n. Since $4 = 0.40m$, $m = \dfrac{4}{0.40} = 10$. Since $10n = 0.40 \cdot 400$, $10n = 160$, and $n = \dfrac{160}{10} = 16$. *Column A*'s value is represented by $m = 10$ and *Column B*'s value is $n = 16$. $10 < 16$.

15. **The correct answer is (C).** *Column A* is looking for the average of a set of terms containing one variable, y. *Column B* is looking for the arithmetic mean of a set of integers. The arithmetic mean is the same as an average. Therefore, the values of both columns can be found by solving in the same manner. To find averages, sum each of the given items and divide that result by the total number of items.

For *Column A*,
$$\frac{(2y + 6) + (3y - 4) + (5 - 5y)}{3} = \frac{2y + 3y - 5y + 6 - 4 + 5}{3} = \frac{7}{3}.$$

For *Column B*, $\dfrac{12 + 7 + 6 + (-5) + (-9) + 3}{6} = \dfrac{14}{6} = \dfrac{7}{3}$. Both column values are equivalent.

16. **The correct answer is (C).** The following given diagram shows two parallel lines cut by a transversal. Also shown are two angles, *a* and *b*, which happen to be alternate exterior angles. Alternate exterior angles have the same angle measurement, so $a = b$. In that case, $b - a = 0$. In *Column A*, you are asked for the opposite of $b - a$, and in *Column B* you are asked for the value of $b - a$. Since $a = b$, it does not matter what the exact angle measures of both are, since their difference will always be 0. And since the opposite of 0 is still 0, both columns are equal.

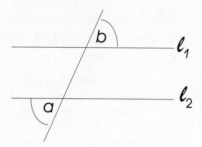

17. **The correct answer is (D).**

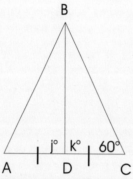

   In the given diagram, you are given triangle *ABC* with one angle equal to 60°. It is also given that *D* is the midpoint of *AC*. This means that $AD = AC$. Point *D* divides triangle *ABC* into two smaller triangles, *ABD* and *BDC*. However, because we know nothing about the measurement of angle *A* or angle *ABC*, and we don't know if *BD* is a perpendicular bisector of *AC*, nothing else can be determined from the diagram. As a result, no conclusions can be drawn about the measurements of angles *j* or *k*.

18. **The correct answer is (A).**

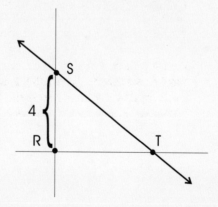

Here you are shown the graph of the line $y = -\frac{2}{3}x + 4$ in a two-dimensional coordinate system. The line is in point-slope form, $y = mx + b$, where $m \left(-\frac{2}{3} \right)$ is the slope and b is the y-intercept (4). Since 4 is the y-intercept, the value of SR in *Column B* is 4. The value of RT as requested in *Column A*, is the value of the x-intercept. To find the x-intercept locate the spot on the coordinate axis where the value of $y = 0$. This can be done by substituting 0 for y in the given point-slope equation and solving for x. So, $0 = -\frac{2}{3}x + 4$; $\frac{2}{3}x = 4$; and $x = 6 = RT$. The value of 6 in *Column A* is greater than the value 4 in *Column B*, so (A) is the correct answer.

19. **The correct answer is (A).** It is given that $c = d + 2$. *Column A* asks for the value of $c^2 - d^2$ while *Column B* asks for the value of $4d$. Solve for the value in *Column A* first, in terms of d, by substituting the given information for c in $c^2 - d^2$. Then, $(d + 2)^2 - d^2 = (d^2 + 2d + 2d + 4) - d^2 = 4d + 4$. Now look again at *Column B*: $4d$. Is $4d + 4$ greater than $4d$? To compare, set up an inequality: $4d + 4 > 4d$. See if this inequality is true by solving for d. $4d + 4 - 4d > 4d - 4d$; so $4 > 0$. Since this is true in every instance, $4d + 4$ must be greater than $4d$ no matter what value d takes on.

20. **The correct answer is (B).** The volume of a rectangular solid is equal to the solid's length (l) $\times$ width (w) $\times$ height (h). Given that the rectangular box has a volume of 72 ft^3, a length of 6, and a height of 3, the value of the width can be determined. By the volume formula, $72 = 6(3)w$, so $w = 4$. *Column A* refers to the value of the box's volume if its width is doubled. In that case, the volume would equal $6(3)(4 \times 2)$ or $6(3)(8) = 144$ ft^3. *Column B* refers to the value of double the surface area of the rectangular box. The surface area must be determined first and then doubled to find the value for *Column B*. The formula for surface area is $2(lw) + 2(lh) + 2(wh)$. Since all values for length, width, and height are known, plug those values into the formula to find the surface area. $2(6 \times 4) + 2(6 \times 3) + 2(4 \times 3) = 2(24) + 2(18) + 2(12) = 108$ ft^2. Twice this number is the value of *Column B*, so *Column B* is equal to 216. 216 which is greater than 144, so the value in *Column B* is larger.

21. **The correct answer is (E).** Interest is calculated by multiplying the amount invested by the rate of interest and multiplying that by the duration of time the money is earning interest. In statement (1), the amount invested is given, but the rate and duration of time are missing, so statement (1) ALONE is not sufficient. In statement (2), only the duration of time is given and not the amount invested or the interest rate, so statement (2) ALONE is not sufficient. Since the interest rate is not supplied in either statement, both statements TOGETHER are NOT sufficient to answer the question asked.

22. **The correct answer is (B).** From statement (1), $w = 24 - 6y$. The value of y is not known, so the value of w cannot be determined from statement (1) ALONE. In statement (2), it follows from $w^2 = 45 - 4w$ that $w^2 + 4w - 45 = 0$. Factoring, $(w + 9)(w - 5) = 0$, so $(w + 9) = 0$ and $(w - 5) = 0$. From statement (2) ALONE, it can be determined what the value of w is, so the correct answer is (B).

23. **The correct answer is (A).** According to statement (1), $k - m = k$, so $m = 0$. Because $m = 0$, the value of km must also be 0, so statement (1) ALONE is sufficient to answer the question. In statement (2), knowing that k is positive tells nothing about the value of m or the value of km. So statement (2) ALONE is not sufficient.

24. **The correct answer is (D).** It is given in statement (1) that there were 4 showings of a particular movie that had an average attendance of 100 viewers per show. The total number of movie goers that night then would be 4×100. Statement (1) is sufficient to answer the question. Statement (2) tells that 100 people represents 25 percent of the total movie viewing population on that particular evening, so represents the total number of attendees. Statement (2), therefore, is also insufficient to answer the question. Since BOTH statements (1) and (2) ALONE supply information to answer the question, the correct choice is (D).

25. **The correct answer is (C).** The initial problem states that three ingredients are in a punch — seltzer, grape juice, and cranberry juice. Statement (1) states that half the punch is made from seltzer and the other half is a combination of the two juices. Because (1) does not state the proportion of each type of juice, it is not sufficient to answer the question by itself. Statement (2) tells the proportion of juices in the punch but says nothing about the amount of seltzer, so statement (2) ALONE is not sufficient. But putting the statements together, the amount of seltzer water is known as well as the proportion of fruit juices. Therefore BOTH statements TOGETHER are sufficient to answer the question, but NEITHER statement ALONE is.

26. **The correct answer is (B).** Statement (1) gives the percentage of one-level homes on Main Street. However, it tells nothing about the amount of homes that have two or more levels on Main Street, so statement (1) ALONE does not give enough information to answer the question asked. Statement (2) gives an exact number of two-level homes on Main Street and since the total number of houses on that street is known, the percentage of two-story homes can be determined by the formula $250x = 96$. Therefore, statement (2) ALONE is sufficient to answer the question asked.

27. **The correct answer is (A).** From statement (1), the total number of employees is given along with the percentage of employees choosing package A. So, the total number of employees choosing package A can be determined by 300×12 percent. Since only two plans are offered, the number of employees choosing package B can be found by subtracting the number choosing A from 300. Statement (1) ALONE is sufficient for solving the problem. Statement (2) tells how many employees chose the alternate package but states nothing about the total number of employees. For that reason, statement (2) ALONE does not give enough information to answer the question asked, so the correct response is (A).

28. **The correct answer is (D).** Based on the given diagram, angle x is congruent to angle y since they are vertical angles. Angle z is a vertical angle to the supplement of angle y, so $\angle y + \angle z = 180°$. Statement (1) gives the angle measure for y, so z can be determined by $40° + \angle z = 180°$. Statement (2) provides the relationship between x and z that $z = 3\frac{1}{2}x$. By substituting for z, $x + 3\frac{1}{2}x = 180$. Once the value of x is found, z can be determined by subtracting x from 180. Since both lines are parallel, statement (2) ALONE is sufficient for answering the problem. Since EACH statement ALONE is sufficient, choice (D) is correct.

29. **The correct answer is (C).** From statement (1), the average number of children in the first grade and the average number of children in the second grade is known. No information is given, though, on the total number of first and second grade classes, so the combined average cannot be figured based on statement (1) ALONE. From statement (2), it is known that there are 3 first grade classes and 5 second grade classes. However, no information on the number of students in each class is provided, so the combined average cannot be found based on statement (2) ALONE. Using both statements together, the average can be calculated by applying the formula. So BOTH statements (1) and (2) TOGETHER are sufficient to answer the question, but NEITHER statement ALONE is.

30. **The correct answer is (B).** All that is known from statement (1) is that all three sides are unequal. This tells nothing about the length of either of the two legs, so the area of the triangle cannot be computed. Statement (2) tells something about the angle measure. Because it is given that triangle ABC is a right triangle, and from (2), angle $B = 60°$, triangle ABC is a special 30°, 60°, 90° right triangle with sides in the relationship $x, x\sqrt{3}, 2x$ as shown here:

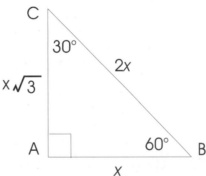

Knowing the relationship among the sides of the triangle and the perimeter of the triangle, you can solve for x using the formula for perimeter. $x + x\sqrt{3} + 2x = 9 + 9\sqrt{3}$. So $3x + x\sqrt{3} = 9 + 9\sqrt{3}$ and $x = 3\sqrt{3}$. Since the value of x is known, the two legs of the triangle are $3\sqrt{3}$ and 9, and therefore the area is equal to $\frac{1}{2} \cdot 3\sqrt{3} \cdot 9$. Statement (2) ALONE is sufficient, then, to answer the question.

31. **The correct answer is (B).** This problem can easily be solved by looking at the steepness, or slope, of the lines connecting the amount of snowfall during each month. The most obvious time frame with the greatest change in snowfall is between March and April. To double check, the change in snowfall can be calculated by finding the difference in snowfall between each set of months given in the choices. From March to April, there was a decrease by about 30 inches, greater than any other set of months.

32. **The correct answer is (D).** The snowfall that accumulated in October was approximately 15 inches. Twice that amount is 30 inches. The months that averaged at least 30 inches, including 30 inches, were January, February, March, and December, for a total of 4 months.

33. **The correct answer is (B).** December had about 30 inches of snow. Two-thirds this amount is $30 \times \frac{2}{3} = 20$ inches. The month that had $\frac{2}{3}$, or 20 inches, less snow than December's 30 inches must have had 10 inches of snow. Find the mark on the graph corresponding to 10 inches. Looking across that point in the horizontal direction, only one month—April—had that amount.

34. **The correct answer is (E).** The amount of snow that fell in March was about 40 inches. The amount of snow that fell in April was about 10 inches. From March to April, the drop in snowfall is $40 - 10 = 30$ inches. The drop in snowfall divided by the original amount of snowfall gives the percentage drop between the two months. So, $\frac{30 \text{ inch drop}}{40 \text{ inches originally}} = \frac{3}{4} = 75$ percent.

35. **The correct answer is (C).** To find the average amount of snowfall, add up the amount of snowfall for each month in the given range, and divide that sum by the total number of months. From January to May, the amount of snowfall, respectively, was $30 + 35 + 40 + 10 + 0 = 115$ inches. Since the range includes a total of 5 months, the average snowfall is $\frac{115}{5} = 23$ inches.

36. **The correct answer is (C).** In the given pie chart, the percentage for distribution in Municipal Bonds is not given. This can be found by summing the remaining percentages and subtracting that amount from 100. The percentage of earnings going into Municipal Bonds, therefore, is $100 - (40 + 10 + 20 + 25) = 5$ percent. The question asks for the percent of earnings put into bonds. From the pie chart, there are two types of bonds—Corporate and Municipal. These, combined, make up $10 + 5 = 15$ percent of the earnings.

37. **The correct answer is (B).** Stocks include Blue Chip and OTC. Together, these make up $40 + 20 = 60$ percent of the distribution. Be careful when answering this question. What is being asked for is the amount *not* being invested in stocks. $100 - 60 = 40$ percent of investments are *not* put into stocks. The correct answer is (B).

38. **The correct answer is (D).** The percentage of earnings going towards Annuities is 25 percent. The dollar amount is $3000 \times 25\% = \$750$, which is choice (D).

39. **The correct answer is (A).** If a total of $10,000 is invested, 25 percent or $2,500 is put into Annuities and 10 percent or $1,000 is put into Corporate Bonds. The difference between these two amounts is $2,500 - $1,000 = $1,500.

40. **The correct answer is (A).** To find the sector with $800 from a $4,000 investment, find the percentage 800 is of 4,000. The correct answer is 0.2 or 20 percent. From the pie chart, only OTC Stocks make up 20 percent of the distribution.

EXPLANATORY ANSWERS FOR PRACTICE TEST 2

1. **The correct answer is (C).** $\ln(8) + 3\ln(2) + \ln(125) + \ln(2^3) + 3\ln(2) + \ln(5^3 = 3\ln(2) + 3\ln(2) + 3\ln(5) = 3\ln(2 \times 2 \times 5) = 3\ln(20)$

2. **The correct answer is (D).** In a right triangle, the length of the hypotenuse is equal to the square root of the sum of the squares of the lengths of the two legs. Hence, $h = \sqrt{12^2 + 5^2} = \sqrt{169} = 13$.

3. **The correct answer is (C).** Using the quadratic formula:
   $x = \dfrac{-2 \pm \sqrt{4 + 4 \times 1 \times 35}}{2}$; after simplification we see that
   $x + -7$ or $x = 5$.

4. **The correct answer is (C).** $\dfrac{4x^3 + 16x^2}{2x^3 + 6x^2 - 8x}$ factors to
   $\dfrac{4x^2(x + 4)}{2x(x + 4)(x - 1)}$, which will simplify to $\dfrac{2x}{x - 1}$.

5. **The correct answer is (C).** $\dfrac{n - 4\sqrt{n} + 4}{\sqrt{n} - 2}$ let $x = \sqrt{n}$.

   Now we have an equivalent expression:
   $\dfrac{x^2 - 4x + 4}{x - 2} = \dfrac{(x - 2)^2}{x - 2} = x - 2 = \sqrt{n} - 2$.

6. **The correct answer is (B).** If we take $x = \sin^2(t)$ and $y = \cos(t)$ and square both sides of both equations we obtain: $x^2 = \sin^2(t)$ and $y^2 = \cos^2(t)$

   Now, because $\sin^2(t) = 1 - \cos^2(t)$ we see that $\sin^2(t) = 1 - y^2$. Hence $x^2 + y^2 = 1$, which is the equation of the unit circle.

7. **The correct answer is (A).** Angle sum of $n - $ gon $= (n - 2) \times 180$ degrees. So for a pentagon, angle sum $= 3 \times 180 = 540$ degrees.

8. **The correct answer is (C).** We have vertical asymptotes when the denominator is zero. We need to solve $x^2 - 4 = 0$. Therefore $x = \pm 2$.

9. **The correct answer is (B).** The midpoint formula tells us that the midpoint is $\left(\dfrac{-6 + 3}{2}, \dfrac{8 - 4}{2} \right) = (-1.5, 2)$.

10. **The correct answer is (E).** To find the equation, we need the slope:
    $m = \dfrac{-1 + 5}{3 - 9} = \dfrac{-2}{3}$. *Note*: None of the choices given has a slope of $\dfrac{-2}{3}$.

11. **The correct answer is (D).** We can draw an equilateral triangle with an area of 13 that has perimeter smaller than a circle with an area of 13π, but if we draw a long skinny triangle with an area of 13, then the perimeter is much larger that that of a circle with an area of 13π, so the correct answer is (D).

12. **The correct answer is (C).** $(20)(40)(50)(7) =$
$(20)(4 \times 10)(5 \times 10)(7) = (20 \times 10)(4)(5)(7 \times 10) = (5)(200)(70)(4)$

13. **The correct answer is (A).** $\dfrac{0.09}{0.0003} = 300 > 30$

14. **The correct answer is (A).**
$(41)^2 - (21)^2 > (41 - 21)^2 = 20^2 = 400$

15. **The correct answer is (A).**

$x - \dfrac{1}{4}x + 15 = 105 \Rightarrow x = 120 > 105$

16. **The correct answer is (C).** If we add up the perimeters starting at the top and moving clock-wise, we see that perimeter $= 4 + 2 + 2 + 4 + 2 + 2 + 4 + 2 + 2 + 4 + 2 + 2 = 32$ ft

17. **The correct answer is (B).** Since $0 < x < 1$, then $x^{12} < x < 12x$.

18. **The correct answer is (A).** $.25 \times 59 = 14.75 < 14.4 = .24 \times 60$.

19. **The correct answer is (D).** We are given no information about their weights.

20. **The correct answer is (D).** We don't know that the triangle is a right triangle or which segments are legs and which would be a hypotenuse.

21. **The correct answer is (D).** If (1) is true, then let $x =$ sale price: $.75 \ast 100 + x \Rightarrow x = \$75$. If (2) is true then $x + 25 = 100 \Rightarrow x = \$75$.

22. **The correct answer is (C).** If (2) is true, then $x = \pm 3$; if (1) is true, then $x = 7$ or $x = 3$; if both (1) and (2) are true, then we have a unique x value where $x = 3$.

23. **The correct answer is (A).** Statement (2) does not tell us the relation between the old triangle and the new one, but (1) tells us that the scale factor is .65, which means that the area factor is $.65 \times .65 = .4225$.

Therefore, the area of the new triangle is $.4225 \times 34 = 14.365$ inches squared.

24. **The correct answer is (E).** An isosceles trapezoid fits both (1) and (2).

25. **The correct answer is (D).** All we need to know is another relationship of any two variables to solve for each one both (1) and (2) give us this.

26. **The correct answer is (B).** If (1) is true, then n is not unique. If (2) is true, then $39 < 3n < 45$.

Dividing by 3 we get $13 < n < 15$, hence $n = 14$.

27. **The correct answer is (E).** Neither (1) nor (2) lets us know how many students are taking chemistry but not math.

28. **The correct answer is (E).** We don't know how long the term lasted.

29. **The correct answer is (D).** Both (1) and (2) say the same thing: even + odd + even = odd

30. **The correct answer is (E).** If (1) is true, he could pick 13 black and 13 red; if (2) is true we know nothing at all.

31. **The correct answer is (C).** Look in row 91 and column 15.6.

32. **The correct answer is (B).** Look in column 21.1 and find the largest value, which is 1.01; find the row 1.01 is in, which is row 91.

33. **The correct answer is (A).** If a pig weighs 136 kg and is kept at 21.1 degrees, then it is gaining .93 kg per day. If it is kept at 4.4 degrees, it is gaining .46 kg per day. We know that .93 is about 100 percent more than .46.

34. **The correct answer is (C).** A pig that weighs 156 kg and is kept at 37.8 degrees will lose 1.15 kg in one day. Hence, the pig weighs 156 − 1.15 = 154.85 kg.

35. **The correct answer is (A).** Look at the black bar above Failure to Yield.

36. **The correct answer is (C).** Look for gray bars that are shorter than their corresponding black bars.

37. **The correct answer is (A).** Look at all the gray bars and choose the shortest.

38. **The correct answer is (A).** The percentage concerned with cost is 46%, with safety record is 32%, when we combine them we have 46 + 32 = 78%

39. **The correct answer is (E).** The percentage of passengers who are concerned with time of arrival or departure is 14%; thus, the percentage of passengers not concerned with time of arrival or departure is 100% − 14% = 86%

40. **The correct answer is (D).** Percentage of passengers who are concerned with frequent flier miles or safety record or size or type of aircraft is 4% + 32% + 3% = 39%. Hence the percentage of passengers not concerned with frequent flier miles or safety record or size or type of aircraft is 100% − 39% = 61%

EXPLANATORY ANSWERS FOR PRACTICE TEST 3

1. **The correct answer is (C).** When dividing by fractions, remember to change the problem to multiplication by inverting the divisor: $\frac{3}{2} \div \frac{5}{2} = \frac{3}{2} \times \frac{2}{5} = \frac{6}{10} = \frac{3}{5}$.

2. **The correct answer is (A).** Simplify this problem by taking the square root of both sides first: $\sqrt{(3x - 2)^2} = \sqrt{0}$. This results in $3x - 2 = 0$. The value of x is $\frac{2}{3}$.

3. **The correct answer is (D).** Change each term written in scientific notation into decimal form, and then add: $(6 \times 10^{-3}) = .006$ and $(9 \times 10^{-4}) = .0009$. So, $.006 + .0009 = .0069$.

4. **The correct answer is (D).** This word problem can be changed into a proportion: $\frac{3 \text{ miles}}{20 \text{ minutes}} = \frac{8 \text{ miles}}{x \text{ minutes}}$. Cross multiply to eliminate the fractions and solve for x: $3x = 8 \cdot 20$; $3x = 160$; $x = \frac{160}{3} \approx 53$ minutes.

5. **The correct answer is (E).**

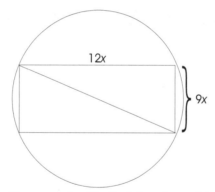

You are asked to find the circumference of the circle. The formula for a circle's circumference is $2\pi \cdot r$ or $\pi \cdot d$, since $2r = d$. Finding the diameter of the circle will help determine its circumference.

In the given diagram, the diameter of the circle is the diagonal of the rectangle. It is also the hypotenuse of the right triangle with legs measuring $12x$ and $9x$ units in length. By the Pythagorean Theorem, the length of the hypotenuse of the right triangle is $d^2 = (12x)^2 + (9x)^2 = 144x^2 + 81x^2 = 225x^2$. Since $d^2 = 225x^2$, $\sqrt{d^2} = \sqrt{225x^2}$ and $d = 15^x$.

Next, you need to figure out the value for x. You are given that the area of the rectangle equals 432, so $12x \cdot 9x = 432$. $108x^2 = 432$, $x^2 = 4$, therefore, $x = 2$. The diameter of the circle is $15 \cdot 2 = 30$, so the circumference is 30π.

6. **The correct answer is (C).** If an integer is a multiple of both 4 and 5, then its factors must include 4 and 5. Integers that have factors of both 4 and 5 include: 20, 40, 60, 80, 100, and so on. The first condition in the problem states that x is an even integer. This is true since each multiple has an even factor of 4 in it and is therefore divisible by 2. The second condition states that x is a multiple of 10. This is also true since the factors of 10 are 2 and 5. If an integer is divisible by the numbers 4 and 5, then it must be divisible by the numbers 2 and 5 as well. The third condition states that x is equal to 20. This is true in only one instance. However, as shown above, x can also take on values that are multiples of 20. Therefore, the third condition is false. Only conditions I and II are true in every instance.

7. **The correct answer is (D).** 8^3 is equivalent to $8 \times 8 \times 8$ or 512. 512 divided by 6 is the same as $\dfrac{512}{6}$ or $85\dfrac{2}{6}$. The remainder is equal to 2.

8. **The correct answer is (A).** When solving a problem dealing with the subtraction of fractions, be sure that a common denominator exists before actually subtracting. In $\sqrt{\dfrac{q^2}{4} - \dfrac{q^2}{6}}$, the common denominator is 12. Placing in the common denominator results in $\sqrt{\dfrac{3q^2}{12} - \dfrac{2q^2}{6}}$ or $\sqrt{\dfrac{q^2}{12}}$. Simplifying this results in $\dfrac{q}{2\sqrt{3}}$. Since none of the possible answer choices contains a radical in the denominator, the solution must be rationalized to eliminate the radical from the denominator. Therefore, $\dfrac{q}{2\sqrt{3}} \cdot \dfrac{\sqrt{3}}{\sqrt{3}} = \dfrac{\sqrt{3}q}{2 \cdot 3} = \dfrac{\sqrt{3}q}{6}$.

9. **The correct answer is (B).** Probability is determined by taking the number of possible outcomes and dividing that by the number of total outcomes. In the case with choosing a mystery title from the bookshelf, since there are 9 mystery titles on the shelf holding a total of 36 books, the probability is $\dfrac{9 \text{ possible outcomes}}{36 \text{ total outcomes}} \cdot \dfrac{9}{36}$ reduces to $\dfrac{1}{4}$.

10. **The correct answer is (E).** Change the fraction problem into a multiplication problem by inverting the denominator:

$$\dfrac{y + \dfrac{1}{x}}{\dfrac{y}{x}} = \left(y + \dfrac{1}{x}\right) \div \dfrac{y}{x} = \left(y + \dfrac{1}{x}\right) \times \dfrac{x}{y}.$$

In order to solve this multiplication problem, the first term, $y + \dfrac{1}{x}$, must be combined. To do this, first find a common denominator. Remember that $y = \dfrac{y}{1}$. The common denominator is x. So $y \cdot \dfrac{x}{x} + \dfrac{1}{x} = \dfrac{xy}{x} + \dfrac{1}{x} = \dfrac{xy + 1}{x}$. Now the first term is ready to be multiplied by the second term:

$$\dfrac{xy + 1}{x} \times \dfrac{x}{y} = \dfrac{xy + 1}{y}.$$

11. **The correct answer is (A).** Both columns can be solved using simple arithmetic. Remember to apply the appropriate order of operations. PEMDAS → parenthesis, exponents, multiplication and division (from left to right), and addition and subtraction (from left to right).

For *Column A*, $5 + 4 \times (-2) \div 2 = 5 + (-8) \div 2$
$$= 5 + (-4) = 1$$

For *Column B*, $(5 + 4) \times (-2 \div 2) = 9 \times (-1) = -9$.

Since $1 > -9$ and *Column A > Column B*, the correct answer is (A).

12. **The correct answer is (D).** Here are two expressions with the same variable, x. It is known that x is a negative integer, so x may be any whole number less than 0. Suppose $x = -1$. Then in *Column A*, the expression $\frac{3}{x}$ would equal $\frac{3}{-1} = -3$. The expression in *Column B*, $3x$ would equal $3(-1) = -3$. Since these two values are equivalent, you might think the answer is (C), but what happens if x is equal to a different negative integer? Suppose $x = -2$. Then *Column A* would be $\frac{3}{x} = \frac{3}{-2} = -1.5$ and *Column B* would be $3x = 3(-2) = -6$. These two values are not equivalent. Further information about the value that x equals is needed to determine which column is greater.

13. **The correct answer is (C).** It is easiest to first calculate the number of minutes and hours for one day and then apply that to the scenario given in each of the columns. The number of minutes in one day is equivalent to $1\text{ day} = \dfrac{24\text{ hours}}{1\text{ day}} \times \dfrac{60\text{ minutes}}{1\text{ hour}} = 24 \times 60 = 1{,}440$ minutes in 1 day *(note that days and hours cancel each other out)*. So there are $1440z$ minutes in z days for *Column A*. Now focusing on *Column B*, there are 24 hours in 1 day, so there are $24 \times 60z$ or $1440z$ hours in $60z$ days. Since $1440z$ equals the value of both columns, the correct answer is (C).

14. **The correct answer is (A).** To answer this problem, find what the area of the shaded region is equal to and compare that value with what is given in *Column A*. To solve for the shaded region, first calculate the area of the larger circle and subtract from that the area of the smaller circle. Remember that the area of a circle is $\pi \cdot r^2$ where r is the length of the radius, or half the length of the diameter. The diameter of the larger circle is QT, so the radius is $\dfrac{QT}{2}$. So the area of the larger circle is $\pi \cdot$ $\left(\dfrac{QT}{2}\right)^2 = \dfrac{QT^2 \cdot \pi}{4}$. It is given that $RS = d = \dfrac{2}{3}QT$. The radius of the smaller circle is $\dfrac{RS}{2} = \dfrac{\frac{2}{3}QT}{2} = \dfrac{QT}{3}$. So the area of the smaller circle is $\pi \cdot \left(\dfrac{QT}{3}\right)^2 = \dfrac{QT^2 \cdot \pi}{9}$. The area of the shaded region, then, is $\dfrac{QT^2 \cdot \pi}{4} - \dfrac{QT^2 \cdot \pi}{9} = \dfrac{9QT^2 \cdot \pi - 4QT^2 \cdot \pi}{36} = \dfrac{5QT^2}{36}$. Putting the shaded region in terms of d ($d = \dfrac{2}{3}QT$ so $\dfrac{3}{2}d = QT$) results in $\dfrac{5\left(\frac{3}{2}d\right)^2 \cdot \pi}{36} = \dfrac{\frac{45}{4}\pi \cdot d^2}{36} =$

$\dfrac{11.25\pi \cdot d^2}{36} < \dfrac{13\pi \cdot d^2}{36}$. Therefore, the value in *Column A* is greater and the correct response is (A).

15. **The correct answer is (D).** From the given circle, we have two chords, *LS* and *QN*, that intersect at point *C*. However, it is not known whether or not *C* is the center of the pictured circle. Therefore, chord *LS* may or may not bisect chord *QN*. If *C* is the center of the circle, *LS* is a diameter that cuts chord *QN* into 2 equal segments, *CN* and *CQ*. But if *C* is not the center of the circle, *LS* would not cut *QN* into two equal segments. In order to determine the length of segments *CN* and *CQ*, further information must be given.

16. **The correct answer is (B).** Solve the algebraic expression for *x* and compare the result with the value in *Column B*.

    $10x = \dfrac{99}{x} + x$. Multiply both sides of the equation by *x* to eliminate the fraction with the *x* in the denominator: $10x^2 = 99 + x^2$. Isolate the *x* by collecting all *x* terms to one side of the equation: $9x^2 = 99$; $x^2 = 11$; $x = \pm\sqrt{11}$. Whether $x = -\sqrt{11}$ or $\sqrt{11}$, 11 in *Column B* will always be greater.

17. **The correct answer is (C).** Use the Pythagorean theorem, $c^2 = a^2 + b^2$, to find the length of the unknown sides in both triangles. In *Column A*, $4^2 = 2^2 + b^2$. $b^2 = 12$, so $b = 2\sqrt{3}$. In *Column B*, $12^2 = a^2 + (6\sqrt{3})^2$, so $a^2 = 36$ and $a = 6$. The triangles in both columns are special 30°, 60°, 90° right triangles with sides in the ratio of x, $x\sqrt{3}$, $2x$ (in *Column A*, $x = 2$, in *Column B*, $x = 6$).

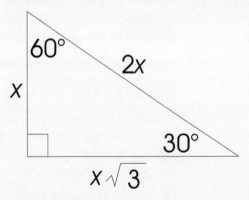

The angle measures in both triangles are therefore equivalent. Since angle *t* in *Column A* is opposite the longer leg, its degree measure is 60°. Since angle *s* in *Column B* is opposite the shorter leg, its degree measure is 30°. When this measure is doubled, it is then equal to angle *t*.

18. **The correct answer is (A).** It is given that *p* is a positive number, so $p > 0$. If $pq = 0$, then $q = 0$. The value of *Column A* is 0. The value in *Column B* is $p(q - p) = pq - p^2$. Since $q = 0$, $pq - p^2 = 0 - p^2 = -p^2$. When any number is squared, its result is always positive. When the negative of a squared number is taken, its result is always negative. Zero is greater than any negative number, so *Column A* is greater than *Column B*.

Peterson's Math Review for the GRE, GMAT and MCAT

19. **The correct answer is (C).** Here a function is defined that requires substitution. The function $m^{\bullet}$ is defined as $m^2 - \dfrac{m}{2}$. In *Column A*, the function must be applied three times: to the first 2, the second 2, and to the sum $(3 + 2^{\bullet})$. This results in the following: $2^{\bullet} = 2^2 - \dfrac{2}{2} = 3$ and $(3 + 2^{\bullet})^{\bullet} = (3 + 3)^{\bullet} = 6^{\bullet} = 6^2 - \dfrac{6}{2} = 33$. So, in *Column A*, $2^{\bullet} + (3 + 2^{\bullet})^{\bullet} = 3 + 33 = 36$. In *Column B*, the function is applied twice; once to the 2 and once to the 6. It is already known that $2^{\bullet} = 3$ and $6^{\bullet} = 33$, so in *Column B*, $2^{\bullet} + 6^{\bullet} = 3 + 33 = 36$. Both columns are equivalent.

20. **The correct answer is (B).**

    In *Column A*, $\dfrac{1}{4}$ of half of $\left(\dfrac{1}{6}\right)^2$ is $\dfrac{1}{4} \cdot \dfrac{1}{2}\left(\dfrac{1}{6}\right)^2 = \dfrac{1}{4} \cdot \dfrac{1}{2} \cdot \dfrac{1}{36} = \dfrac{1}{288}$.

    In *Column B*, $\left[\dfrac{1}{2}\left(\dfrac{1}{6}\right)\right]^2 = \left(\dfrac{1}{2} \cdot \dfrac{1}{6}\right)^2 = \left(\dfrac{1}{12}\right)^2 = \dfrac{1}{144}$.

    Therefore $\dfrac{1}{288} < \dfrac{1}{144}$. So *Column B* has the larger value.

21. **The correct answer is (E).** Statement (1) ALONE is not sufficient because the distance to the pharmacy from Lucy's home is not discussed. Statement (2) ALONE is also not sufficient for the same reason. Since further data are needed to answer the question, statements (1) and (2) TOGETHER are not sufficient.

22. **The correct answer is (A).** Squaring each part of statement (1) results in $0^2 < \sqrt{r^2}^2 < 1^2$ or $0 < r < 1$. Since this is in the same statement as the question being asked, (1) ALONE is sufficient to answer the question. In statement (2), $r^2 = \dfrac{1}{3}$. Solving for r results in $r = \pm\sqrt{\dfrac{1}{3}}$. If r is positive, then the question being asked is true, but if r is negative, the question is false. Since r can be both true and false, statement (2) is not sufficient to answer the question.

23. **The correct answer is (C).** From the given diagram, it is known that triangle *JKL* is a right triangle since the triangle is inscribed inside a semicircle. Angle *JKL* is a right angle and *JL*, the diameter of the circle, is also the hypotenuse of the triangle. According to statement (1), $JK = KC = JC$, so the hypotenuse is twice the length of the shorter leg. *JK* and *KL* is $\sqrt{3}$ times longer than the shorter leg (triangle *JKL* is a special 30°, 60°, 90° right triangle with sides in the ratio $x, x\sqrt{3}, 2x$). Since the length of the shorter leg is unknown, the lengths of the other sides cannot be determined from statement (1) ALONE. Statement (2) tells the length of the radius is 5, so the diameter, *JL*, is equal to 10. From (2), it is not known what the relationships of the legs are to the hypotenuse of the triangle, so (2) ALONE is not sufficient to answer the question. However, BOTH statements TOGETHER supply enough information to find the length of *KL*.

24. **The correct answer is (D).** The area of the circle is equal to πr^2. In order to find the area, the value of the radius must be known. Statement (1) tells us the circumference. The formula for the circumference of a circle is $2\pi r$. If $2\pi \cdot r = 10$, then $r = \dfrac{10}{2\pi}$. Knowing r, the area can be found, so statement (1) ALONE is sufficient to answer the question. Statement (2) tells us the diameter is $\dfrac{10}{\pi}$. Since the diameter is twice the length of the radius, $\dfrac{10}{\pi} = 2r$ and $r = \dfrac{10}{2\pi}$. Since r can be determined, statement (2) ALONE is sufficient. The correct response, then, is (D) because EACH statement ALONE is sufficient.

25. **The correct answer is (D).** It is known that a measuring cup that can hold x ounces is $\dfrac{1}{2}$ full. According to statement (1), $\dfrac{1}{2}x + 4 = \dfrac{3}{4}x$. This equation can be solved for x easily, determining the maximum capacity of the measuring cup, so statement (1) ALONE is sufficient. By statement (2), $\dfrac{1}{2}x - 6 = \dfrac{1}{8}x$. Again, this equation can be solved for x easily, so statement (2) ALONE is sufficient. Since BOTH statements ALONE are sufficient to answer the question asked, the correct answer is (D).

26. **The correct answer is (A).** If x is an odd negative integer, by statement (1), the expression $2y - x$ must be odd. The term $2y$ will always be even, no matter what negative integer y is, since $2y$ is a multiple of 2. And when a negative integer is being subtracted, both negative signs change to positive. Adding an even value ($2y$) to an odd value (x) will always result in an odd value, so statement (1) ALONE is sufficient to answer the question. Statement (2), however, is not sufficient to answer the question because the sign of the result is not dependent on the sign of the y value ($2y$ is always even) but rather on the sign of the x value, about which nothing is known in (2).

27. **The correct answer is (E).** The volume of a rectangular block equals *length*(l) $\times$ *width*(w) $\times$ *height*(h). The surface area of a rectangular block equals $2(lw) + 2(lh) + 2(wh)$. In order to determine if these are equal, the values of each edge must be known. Statement (1) states that $l = hw$. Substituting that value for l, see if the volume and surface area can be found. So $lwh = 2lw + 2lh + 2wh$ becomes $(hw)(wh) = 2w(hw) + 2h(hw) + 2wh$ or $h^2w^2 = 2hw^2 + 2h^2w + 2wh$. Without knowing the values of h or w, however, nothing more can be determined by statement (1), so (1) ALONE is not sufficient to answer the question asked. Statement (2) states that $lwh = 64$. This is not sufficient enough to answer the question asked either. Combining both statements shows $64 = 2hw^2 + 2h^2w + 2wh$. The values of h and w are still unknown, so statement (1) and (2) TOGETHER are not sufficient to answer the question and additional data are needed.

28. **The correct answer is (A).** According to statement (1), since 5 is in S, then $5 + 5 = 10$ is contained in S and $5 + 10 = 15$ is contained in S and $5 + 15 = 20$ is contained in S and so forth—all of which are positive multiples of 5. Statement (1) ALONE is sufficient. According to statement (2), since 5 is in S, then $5 - 5 = 0$ is in S and $0 - 5 = -5$ is in S and $-5 - 5 = -10$ is in S and so forth—values that are negative multiples of 5, including 0. No information is given to determine if the positive multiples of 5 are in S based on statement (2), so (2) is not sufficient. Only (1) ALONE is sufficient.

29. **The correct answer is (C).** From statement (1), $(m + n)(m - n) = m^2 - n^2 = 0$. Therefore, $m^2 = n^2$, so $\sqrt{m^2} = \sqrt{n}$ and $m = n$. This states nothing about the values of m or n, so statement (1) ALONE is not sufficient for solving $m + n$. From statement (2), $m = 3$. This states nothing about the value of n, however, so statement (2) ALONE is not sufficient. Combining both statements show that $m = n = 3$, so the value of $m + n$ can be determined. Because BOTH statements TOGETHER are sufficient for solving the problem, and NEITHER statement ALONE is sufficient, the best answer is (C).

30. **The correct answer is (B).** In the given figure, JL is an altitude of triangle HJK, and HK is its corresponding base. Therefore, half the product of HK and JL will equal the area of the right triangle. $\left(\dfrac{HK \times JL}{2} = A\right)$ and $HK \times JL = 2A$. Statement (1) ALONE is not sufficient to determine the area since only the value of HK is given and no information about the length of JL is provided. Statement (2) tells us that $HJ \times JK = 48$. Since HJ and JK are the two legs of right triangle HJK, $\dfrac{HJ \times JK}{2} = A$ and $HJ \times JK = 2A = HK \times JL$. Both values resulting from $HJ \times JK$ and $HK \times JL$ are equal, so statement (2) ALONE is sufficient to answer the question asked.

31. **The correct answer is (B).** Find the proportion of oil usage by residents for each of the given years. In 1980, 20% used oil; in 1985, 40% used oil; in 1990, 50% used oil; and in 1995, 60% used oil. The greatest increase was from 20% to 40%, which occurred in 1985.

32. **The correct answer is (C).** The proportion of residents who used oil heat in 1995 was 60%. The proportion that used electric heat that year was 10%. The percentage difference between these two types of heating methods is 50%; 50% of 50,000 is 25,000.

33. **The correct answer is (B).** The percentage of gas consumers in 1985 was 40%. In 1990, gas consumers made up 30% of the population. So 10% of the gas users from 1985 changed to alternative heating methods in the following time frame. $\dfrac{10\%}{40\%} = \dfrac{1}{4} = 25\%$.

34. **The correct answer is (A).** Mean refers to the average. To find the average, sum all percentages of oil usage from the given years and divide by the number of given years. The average is $\dfrac{20 + 40 + 50 + 60}{4}$

$= \dfrac{170}{4} = 42.5\%$.

35. **The correct answer is (B).** The percentage of girls who prefers chocolate ice cream is 25%. If there are 160 girls, then $160 \times 25\% = 160 \times .25 = 40$ girls in total who prefer chocolate.

36. **The correct answer is (B).** Since there are twice as many girls as there are boys, the proportions preferred by the girls are counted twice when calculating the combined averages for both boys and girls. The proportions, then, are:

    vanilla, $\dfrac{45 + 20 + 20}{3} = 28\dfrac{1}{3}\%$; chocolate, $\dfrac{20 + 25 + 25}{3} = 23\dfrac{1}{3}\%$;

    raspberry, $\dfrac{10 + 15 + 15}{3} = 13\dfrac{1}{3}\%$; and

    mint chip, $\dfrac{25 + 40 + 40}{3} = 35\%$.

    Since mint chip is preferred by most, (B) is the correct answer.

37. **The correct answer is (E).** 25% of the boys like mint chip and 12 boys make up 25% of the total number of boys. The total number of boys $\times$ the percentage who prefer mint chip = the number of boys who prefers mint chip. Therefore $T \times 5\% = 12$. Solving for T, $\dfrac{12}{25\%} = T$, so $T = 48$.

38. **The correct answer is (A).** The greatest price increase is found in the column labeled Change in Price (\$). The largest dollar amount in that column is $2\dfrac{3}{4} = \$2.75$. This amount reflects the change in Arx stock, so the correct answer is (A).

39. **The correct answer is (D).** The opening price is found by subtracting the change in price from the closing price of stock. The change in price for Mbd stock is $-3\dfrac{1}{2}$ or $-\$3.50$. The closing price for Mbd stock is \$96.33. The opening price, then is $96.33 - (-3.50) = 96.33 + 3.50 = \$99.83$.

40. **The correct answer is (C).** The stock with the greatest amount of activity is the stock with the greatest volume. Blm stock had the greatest amount of activity on this particular day. Its closing price is \$41.40. Three stocks have closing prices greater than \$41.40 (Arx, Mbd, and Tvk).

Peterson's Math Review for the GRE, GMAT and MCAT